THEY DIED CRAWLING

And Other Tales of Cleveland Woe

THEY DIED CRAWLING

And Other Tales of Cleveland Woe

True Stories of the Foulest Crimes and
Worst Disasters in Cleveland History

John Stark Bellamy II

GRAY & COMPANY, PUBLISHERS
CLEVELAND

© 1995 by John Stark Bellamy II

Gray & Company, Publishers
11000 Cedar Ave.
Cleveland, OH 44106
(216) 721-2665

The title chapter of this book originally appeared in a somewhat altered form in the May/June 1995 issue of *Timeline*, published by the Ohio Historical Society.

This book is the first of several planned volumes on the Cleveland of yesteryear. Narrative slide shows chronicling Chapters 2–6 are available for a fee and additional slide shows are under development. For more information or bookings, contact John Stark Bellamy II via e-mail (jbellamyII@aol.com) or by mail via the publisher of this book.

Text design and composition by Drawbridge Studio, Inc.

10 9 8 7 6 5 4 3 2 1

To the memory of my father,
Peter Bellamy

CONTENTS

Preface 9

1 **Cleveland's Saddest Fourth**
   The 1908 S. S. Kresge Fireworks Explosion 15

2 **Horror On The Heights**
   The 1910 Murder of William Lowe Rice 29

3 **"They Died Crawling"**
   The 1916 Waterworks Tunnel Explosion 47

4 **She Got Her Money's Worth**
   Eva Kaber, Lakewood's 1919 Lady Borgia 61

5 **Streets Of Hell**
   The 1944 East Ohio Gas Company Explosion and Fire 79

6 **"God, The Devil, Man or Beast"**
   The Incredible 1923 Saga of John Leonard Whitfield 97

7 **"Five Minutes Out of Nowhere"**
   The 1932 Ellington Apartments Inferno 115

8 **"Cold Lead for Breakfast"**
   The 1870 Galentine-Jones Melodrama 127

9 **"Horror of All Horrors!"**
   The 1895 Central Viaduct Disaster 141

10 **Death Takes a Powder**
   Hazel Gogan's Bizarre 1950 Demise 157

11 **Third Man at Hamilton**
   The Rise and Fall of Judge William H. McGannon, 1920–1921 . . .171

12 **Red Dawn in Cleveland**
   The 1919 May Day Riots 191

13 **High Noon at Bedford**
   The Violent Saga of "Jiggs" Losteiner, Cleveland's Baddest Man . . .205

14 **Breath of Death**
   The 1929 Cleveland Clinic Disaster 221

15 **"We're Going to Burn You . . ."**
   The Enduring Sheppard Tragedy 237

PREFACE

"Why did you decide to write about . . . *that?!*" It was with these blunt words that someone (my mother, actually) questioned me early in my career as a chronicler of some of the more desperate chapters of Cleveland history. And so might you, reader of this melancholy compendium of local horrors and homicides. My short, smart-aleck answer is purloined from the evasive wit of Benjamin Disraeli: when queried as to what kind of book he liked to read, he said, "When I want to read an interesting book, I write one." There's a kernel of truth in that answer.

The chief reason I have recorded these disquieting tales is because I wanted to read about them, and there was little in print to satisfy that sort of literary craving. George Condon, Peter Jedick, Albert Borowitz, and Steve Nickel have all glanced at these kinds of Cleveland subjects in their writings, but nothing comprehensive has ever been attempted. *Cleveland Murders,* a fine collection of reportorial articles covering some vintage killings, appeared in 1947—and there has been nothing like it since. And while the anniversary of some bloody municipal disaster usually generates at least a feature story in *The Plain Dealer* or *Cleveland Magazine,* the only book-length treatments of a Cleveland catastrophe have been minor works on the Collinwood School Fire of 1908.

The real reason I write about this stuff—aside from morbid curiosity—is that I have always been fascinated by the behavior of people under stress, the more severe, the better. Two decades ago I spent some years at the University of Virginia studying the behavior of 19th-century slaves in the southern United States and the oppressed sharecroppers of the 1930s because I believed that you can't really know what human beings are capable of until you subject them to the most awful angers and duress . . . with little or no warning whatsoever. Aspects of human character may lie latent in average human beings until a dreadful day comes . . . and sublime or reprehensible things emerge under circumstances of mortal peril or compulsion. That is why Anna Trefall ran back into the burning S. S. Kresge store on Ontario to rescue her sister in 1908; it is why Eva Kaber tried to ensure her daughter's financial security by feeding her own husband Dan 40 grains of arsenic and having him stabbed 11 times in the scrotum in 1919. It is why, one fine October day in 1920, E. W. Porter leveled a gun out of the window of his Bedford automobile accessories store and brought Cleveland's most vicious, dangerous killer to heel. And it is why Gus Van Duzen, the hero of repeated waterworks tunnel disasters, ended up on an inquest stand attempting to deny his part in the worst tunnel tragedy in Cleveland history.

My debts to many persons are unpayable but appreciated. I never would have thought of doing something like this without the inspiration provided by the writings of George Condon and Peter Jedick. George provided evidence—otherwise lacking—that one can write both inspiringly *and* amusingly about Cleveland topics, while Peter's dual vocations as a Cleveland firefighter and free lance Cleveland historian gave me the guts to try to squeeze this peculiar labor of love into an overcrowded life. This book could not have happened without the encouragement and support, above all, of my mother, Jean Bellamy. It would likewise have been impossible without the technical expertise, cunning advice, and perpetual help of my brother Stephen and his wife, Gail. The former saved me from my technical incompetence when I developed these chapters initially as slide shows, while the latter helped me promote my historical obsessions into print form. Gail also introduced me to the miracle of word processing, and this manuscript benefited greatly from Gail and Steve's mutual intolerance for sloppiness, prolixity, and obscurity.

My institutional researches have been much aided by the knowledge, professionalism, and kindness of these individuals: Anne Sindelar and Barbara Waitkus Billings of the Western Reserve Historical Society; William Becker & Gail Marradeth of the Cleveland Press Collection, Cleveland State University; Joan Clark and the staff of the Cleveland Public Library; Dr. Judith Cetina, Cuyahoga County Archives; Elizabeth Tidwell, Cuyahoga County Coroner's Office; and Therese Spellacy, Cuyahoga County Courthouse. Fred Lautzenheiser and Carol Tomer opened the Cleveland Clinic Archives to me and provided photographs of the 1929 wreckage. Faith Corrigan kindly loaned me her rich archives documenting divers Cleveland scandals and horrors and generously pointed me toward many worthy topics; I must also mention her shrewd insight and ironic humor as aids and encouragements in my doleful researches. Doris O'Donnell, the agelessly fetching and acute doyenne of Cleveland newspaperdom kindly indulged a neophyte's curiosity about the Sheppard case, an episode in which she played a memorable part. Albert Borowitz shared with me the benefit of his knowledge of the William Rice murder; Terry Meehan of the East Ohio Gas Company provided me with material, cooperation, and criticism on the 1944 liquid gas explosion. I am particularly indebted to Mary Strassmeyer of *The Plain Dealer*, who provided needed publicity at a fateful moment in this enterprise. Many thanks are due to *The Plain Dealer*–specifically William Barnard and Robert McAuley for generous permission to reprint material on most of the subjects herein. All errors of fact or emphasis are all my fault. My sole excuse is that of Samuel Johnson: "Ignorance, madam, sheer ignorance!"

My deep regret is that my father, Peter Bellamy, did not live to see me undertake and complete this curious project. I grew up listening from a tender age to his stories about many of these macabre doings and I like to think that he, cigarette and whiskey in hand, is reading these tales over my shoulder in Heaven. He was one of the last of the great, old-style newspapermen—"a gentleman," in his friend Robert Finn's elegant phrase, "in a profession not known for spawning them"—and it is to his colorful and loving memory that this book is dedicated.

John Stark Bellamy II
June 1, 1995

P. S. Okay, I'll tell you the *real* reason why I'm interested in this . . . *intense* stuff. When I was about 10 years old in the late 1950s, my brothers and I used to spend several weeks at CYO Camp Isaac Jogues every summer at Madison-on-the Lake. The counselors there, young Catholic seminarians, competed with each other, I realize now, in seeing how badly they could frighten their youthful charges with midnight tales of vengeful ghosts, hammer murders, and Grand Guignol stories. On the last night of camp in August 1958 they outdid themselves. There had been some sort of disturbance in the cabin where we slept that night, and some boys had momentarily awakened, only to be told to go back to sleep.

The next morning one of our counselors appeared at breakfast with an enormous bandage and sling on his arm. Although seemingly reluctant to talk, he eventually told, in a hushed, tense voice, a bloodcurdling story, which was supported in every detail by his fellow counselors. My memory is that these pious Catholic seminarians actually swore on a Bible that their story was true. It seems that some time the previous day, Ohio's most *dangerous* and *psychopathic* killer, a near-flesh-eating maniac named "Mad Dog Cahill" had escaped from a maximum-security prison, brutally slaying several of his guards in the process. Pursued to the Madison area by police with shoot-to-kill orders, "Mad Dog" had actually broken into *our* cabin *the night before!*—and the convincingly bandaged counselor had been viciously stabbed by the enraged Cahill while defending his sleeping campers from the killer. The police had been summoned and our brave protector had been rushed to the hospital, where his "still-spurting artery" was clamped. "Mad Dog," alas for him, had not been so lucky. The police had somehow picked up his trail near Camp Isaac Jogues and chased him to some nearby railroad tracks. In attempting to escape from them, "Mad Dog" had tried to outrun a speeding train . . . and finally lost the race. "He almost made it, boys," our hero counselor told us, "but the . . . *last car* . . . on the train—the caboose—caught his sleeve and dragged him under the wheels. The police said he didn't stop screaming until the last wheel on the train rolled over him."

I'm not ashamed to admit that I *believed* in the legend of "Mad Dog" Cahill for many, many years after that memorable morning in 1958. And in my heart of hearts–where that 10-year-old boy still dwells—I *still* believe in "Mad Dog" Cahill. This book is written for that child and all like him who still dote on what Charles Dickens called "the romantic side of familiar things."

"Mad Dog" Cahill did not die in vain!

THEY DIED CRAWLING

And Other Tales of Cleveland Woe

Chapter 1

CLEVELAND'S SADDEST FOURTH

The 1908 S. S. Kresge
Fireworks Explosion

You wouldn't know to look at it now. If you drive by 2025
Ontario Street today you might easily miss it: the sign simply says
"Society Corporate Center," an anonymous-looking business
office. But on July 3, 1908, that address became history—terrible
history, indeed—although it is almost completely forgotten today.
You'd never guess, to look at its modern glass-and-trim front, that
it was once the scene of a fiery, exploding holocaust that brought
death to seven, injury to dozens, and a day of terror, tears, heroism,
and shame to the city of Cleveland. For this is the site of the S. S.
Kresge fireworks explosion and fire.

Let us set the stage for the chief actors in this melancholy tale.
For Anna and Freda Trefall, sisters and fellow-clerks at the Ontario
S. S. Kresge store, the fateful day began early. They got up at 6 a.m.
at their 2308 Carnegie Avenue boarding house, lest they be tardy
when the dime store opened at 9 a.m. sharp. Anna and Freda were
orphans from Wisconsin, who had come to Cleveland a year previously to live with their sister-in-law. Everyone noticed how close
they were to each other; the coming day would offer sublime proof
of their sisterly bond.

Mary Hughes, 27, of Whitman Avenue didn't work at the Kresge
store. She was an assistant to a downtown dressmaker. But the
necessities of her job would bring her to the Ontario dime store that
morning to buy some material for her work.

Ed Bolton didn't work for the S. S. Kresge Company either. But
his day as a shipping clerk at the W. P. Southworth store next door
began early, too, and he expected to spend it slaving over the moun-
tain of orders that had to go out before the July 4th holiday. Ed
came from a surprisingly heroic bloodline: his uncle, Captain John

Grady, had bravely lost his life fighting a terrible 1891 Cleveland fire, and three other uncles were members of the Cleveland Fire Department.

The day came early, too, for Jimmy Parker, Four years old, of Hampden Avenue. Jimmy's father, George Parker, had promised Jimmy that this year he could join in the noisy fireworks at the Parker home. But first, Jimmy Parker had to go shopping downtown with his mother, Minnie . . .

Up early also that fine July morning was Luther Roberts, the janitor of the Kresge store. Luther was short, quiet and self-effacing—but his incredible courage would resound throughout the city before the day was done.

Winifred Duncan was excited that morning. Only 18, one of the many teenaged clerks at Kresge's, she usually sold postcards on the first floor. But today she was going to do something unusual . . . and thereby step unwittingly into history.

The S. S. Kresge store occupied the first two floors of a four-story structure, with a restaurant in the basement and offices on the third and fourth floors. Toward the center and rear of the ground floor, a stairway rose upward, dividing at a landing into left and right flights to the second floor. From the right side of the landing, a balcony stretched out over the right rear of the store, forming a mezzanine level that contained the manager's office. The second floor was generally unobstructed, with windows both at the front on Ontario Street and the back, facing an alley, where there was also a fire escape. The only dangerously obscure aspect of the building was this: although there was a rear exit to the building on the left side of the first-floor staircase, there was no exit whatsoever in the identical-looking area to the right of the staircase. There, instead of an exit, were three windows, blocked with temporary shelves and further secured with steel bars, wire netting, and sheet-iron doors to prevent break-ins from the rear alley. Under normal circumstances this layout presented no problem. But if someone were in a hurry to get out the back of the store and turned to the right of the staircase instead of the left . . . it might make all the difference between life and death.

Owing to the ensuing deaths and the confusion of the tragedy, we cannot know the exact sequence of events that day. We do know, however, that at about 10:50 that Friday morning, Mrs. Minnie Parker and her four-year-old son Jimmy entered the Kresge store.

Cleveland Public Library Photograph Collection.

S. S. Kresge store with fire department ladders raised, July 3, 1908.

Jimmy had been lured there by the sight of clerk Winifred Duncan, demonstrating a sizzling sparkler near the store's front window. D. E. Greene, the store manager, had just ordered her to do so and had assured her that the sparklers were "harmless." Winifred stood in the aisle, three feet wide, separating the postcard department from the ample counters of firecrackers, Roman candles, rockets, and sparklers that were stacked all over the first floor in that era of virtually unregulated Fourth of July mayhem.

This was the scene in Kresge's as 10:50 a.m. arrived: Minnie and Jimmy Parker were watching Winifred demonstrate a sparkler. Manager Greene was in his mezzanine office with Cashier Celia Zak, scanning the day's mail. Mrs. Fannie Frank, 50, a Collinwood Village matron, was shopping on the second floor with her four-year-old granddaughter, Grace. Mary Hughes, the dressmaker's assistant, was probably in the sewing section on the second floor. Ed Bolton was next door at the Southworth Company, busily getting out the day's orders. Miss Carrie Bubel, a clerk, was selling goods at her counter on the second floor. Erma Schumacher, 18,

Cleveland Public Library Photograph Collection.
Water Tower in Action at S. S. Kresge Fire, July 3, 1908.

was pacing the floor, keeping a vigilant eye on the 50 or so female clerks who worked the floor. Although only 18, Erma had just been promoted to floorwalker, and it was well known that she aspired to even higher rank. Muriel Mayes, a Kresge clerk, was at her second floor counter. So, too, was Freda Trefall, while her older sister Anna worked downstairs. Mary Podowski, a charwoman, was awaiting change from the $20 bill she had handed a clerk. Andrew Lempke, a Kresge employee, was trimming lamps as he worked atop a ladder on the first floor. And staff pianist Hazel Thompson, one of the several Kresge pianists who demonstrated the store's sheet music for curious customers, had just launched into a rendition of "I Don't Want To Go Home in the Dark" . . . when all hell broke loose on the first floor.

This is probably what happened. After remarking to Minnie and Jimmy Parker that her sparkler was "perfectly harmless," Winifred turned sideways toward a fireworks display that included an American flag. Sparks from the sparkler in her hand suddenly ignited the fabric of the flag, which in turn set fire to Mrs. Parker's voluminous, flammable dress. As the two terrified women attempted to beat out the flames, sparks from the dress fell on adjacent fireworks counters and the fire and explosions began their deadly race through the store.

It was about as close to instantaneous combustion as you can get. The store contained about $30,000 worth of fireworks, and within seconds of the initial spark, the entire stock ignited in an inferno of blazing colors, dense smoke, and terrifying, deafening explosions. In a minute or less the entire first floor of Kresge's was a fiery nightmare, with up to 200 panic-stricken shoppers and clerks trying to flee the sudden conflagration. Max Zucker, a customer on the ground floor, had a typical experience. One moment he was staring at the sizzling electric sparkler, and the next: "I heard a sputtering noise—a skyrocket whizzed past my face and darted over the heads of the crowd and set fire to combustible material on the counters. People around me stood aghast for a few seconds. A giant cracker exploded with a roar that set all into a mad dash for the front and rear exits."

The fire spread with shocking speed, setting merchandise and people alike on fire as it raced from counter to counter, aisle to aisle through the store. The next morning's *Plain Dealer* well conveyed the horror of the next few minutes:

> Big piles of fireworks exploded and added to the noise and confusion. Giant crackers pounded and boomed, skyrockets whizzed through the crowded room, roman candles sputtered and flashed. It was a mimic battle, magnificent if it had not been so full of terror and death.

Several patterns of movement developed during the fire's first minutes. On the blazing first floor, customers tried to escape in three directions. Those near the front headed for the Ontario exit. For those toward the rear, the aisles to the left and right of the rear center staircase beckoned toward seeming safety. This was true of the aisle to the left, a corridor that led to an unlocked door on the back alley. The corridor to the right of the staircase, however, led only to the rear wall of the store, blocked there by shelving and barred windows.

Things were better on the second floor. When it became apparent there that the first floor was afire, movement surged toward the front and rear windows, the elevator, and the staircase. The elevator was not working, and it was immediately abandoned after one attempt to use it. Most of the shoppers and clerks fled to the front and back windows and most of them survived, albeit injured and traumatized. Some, however, tried to escape down the stairs, and the vast crush and hysterical panic there quickly precipitated a pile-up of screaming, suffocating women, girls and children on the stairs and the landing on the ground floor. All of them were pulled out or managed to wriggle free and stagger into the inferno waiting below.

The evidence is that the Fire Department arrived soon after the fire started, but by the time the engines got there, Kresge's was already a fiery pyre, with smoke pouring out of every door and window. Customers and employees were still streaming out of the exits and frightened women were leaping out the second floor windows. Firemen quickly deployed ladders and nets. The nets saved many lives but could not prevent some terrible injuries. Owing to the smoke, many could not even see the nets and fell beyond them to the pavement below. And quite a number of people jumped into the same nets simultaneously, injuring each other and bringing the nets crashing to the ground.

Let us see how our cast of characters fared. Poor little Jimmy Parker disappeared into the interior of the store during the first few panicky moments of the fire. His mother, although badly burned, frantically searched the burning store for Jimmy. Told, however, that a little boy had been rescued from the store, she was persuaded to leave and return home. By the time she got there her husband George had already identified Jimmy's corpse at the County Morgue.

D. E. Greene, the Kresge store manager, did his best. As he was in the middle of sorting his mail, an exploding firecracker alerted him to the danger. He immediately seized cashier Celia Zak and rushed her to safety outside on Ontario Street. He then returned and tried to save others until flames and smoke drove him back out into the street for good.

The chief hero of the Kresge tragedy was Luther Roberts, the Kresge janitor. Realizing that the elevator was useless, he began to smash open the windows on the second floor. He then went to the fatal staircase, clogged with screaming, writhing, piled-up bodies and began to drag and throw them out the back windows of the second floor onto the fire escape. Time after time, Roberts returned to the staircase, until the flames and smoke drove him back, "blinded and dizzy." But he had cleared everybody from the staircase.

Roberts's courage, if not his fate, was matched by that of Anna

Cleveland Press Collection, Cleveland State University.

Trefall. When the fire started, 24-year-old Anna was working with several clerks on the first floor. Her companions immediately seized her and tried to drag her out the Ontario exit. She resisted, saying, "I must find my sister!" She broke free and ran toward the staircase to get to Freda on the second floor. Her first attempt failed; the hysterical sea of bodies surging down the staircase soon forced her back toward the Ontario exit and safety. But she again freed herself from the crowd and resumed the search for her 17-year-old sister. We don't know the exact sequence of events after that, except that Freda was one of the last to make it down the staircase during the fire. Upon reaching the ground floor, she was immediately overwhelmed in the pile-up of terrified women there. An eyewitness saw Anna try to pull Freda toward the Ontario exit, and then saw both sisters stumble and fall to the floor. Freda and Anna Trefall died with the rest of those trapped by the three barred windows, their arms around each other's necks. Freda's dead face was so crazed with fear that her fellow employees could not identify her corpse.

Ed Bolton, too, proved himself a hero that July day. Becoming aware of the fire, he ran into the burning building. He dragged several persons out of the building onto Ontario and then reentered the store on his hands and knees to search for others, until the fire drove him out again. He then held nets for those leaping from the second floor.

This almost proved Bolton's undoing. As a girl prepared to leap from the second floor, she opened her umbrella like a parachute to aid in breaking her fall. By the time Bolton shouted, "Never mind your umbrella," it was already too late. As the young lady landed in the net, her umbrella smashed Bolton's arm, breaking it and sending him out of the fray. Staying in character, Bolton merely had his broken arm set, returned home to change out of his wet clothing, and resumed shipping out the holiday orders for Southworth Company, Grocers Wholesale and Retail.

Mary Hughes was just in the wrong place at the wrong time. The dressmaker's assistant survived the crushing pile-up at the staircase—only to die with the rest of the victims by the three back barred windows.

Mrs. Fannie Frank of Collinwood was a heroine, too, that July day. On the second floor with her four-year-old granddaughter, Grace, Mrs. Frank quickly led the child to a window and out onto a projecting ledge. From there she jumped, holding Grace so as to shield her from the impact of the fall. Fannie hit the ground, injuring herself but saving Grace from injury. As Fannie put it, "I could not bear to think of what my daughter would say if the child was hurt."

Erma Schumacher, the newly promoted floorwalker, died in character. When the fire started, she tried to stem the panic of her employees at the flashpoint—the staircase—and it was near there and by the three barred back windows that firemen found her body later in the afternoon.

Muriel Mayes, a second-floor clerk, was one of the first to escape from the second floor. At first she thought the explosions were the work of mischievous boys blowing off fireworks in the rear alley, but she eventually made her way to a front window and was the first person to jump into the nets below. She survived the jump, but was badly injured by the force of collision with the bodies that jumped into the net after her.

Miss Emma Schaef, 17, was something of a heroine, too, after a fashion. She had fled to the second-floor windows looking out on Ontario. There was a woman with a child there, afraid to jump through the suffocating smoke toward the nets below. So Emma pushed them out toward the net below. The woman missed it, hit-

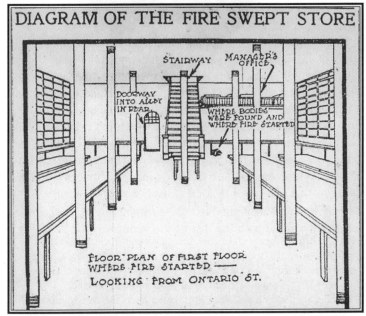

DIAGRAM OF THE FIRE SWEPT STORE

STAIRWAY   MANAGER'S OFFICE

DOORWAY INTO ALLEY IN REAR

WHERE BODIES WERE FOUND AND WHERE FIRE STARTED

FLOOR PLAN OF FIRST FLOOR WHERE FIRE STARTED —
LOOKING FROM ONTARIO ST.

The Plain Dealer.

Simplified diagram of the S. S. Kresge 1st Floor.

ting the sidewalk. Then Emma jumped—and missed it, too. The child was unhurt.

Miss Carrie Bubel, 18, had one of the fire's typical injuries. Selling goods on the second floor when the fire started, she was paralyzed by terror for some minutes. By the time she got to the windows, everyone else had already jumped. She jumped, missing the net, breaking her left leg and spraining her right.

Let us not forget charwoman Mary Podowski. Just as she handed her $20 bill to a clerk, the fire exploded around her. Initially disoriented by the blaze, Mary recovered her nerve and began searching through the burning, smoky store for the clerk who had taken her money. After fighting her way into the store through the frightened crowd surging out, Mary finally spotted the clerk who had taken her $20 bill: "I want my money! Give it to me!" she shrieked. The clerk, who must have marvelled at Mary's single-mindedness, muttered, "Haven't got it!," as the surging, terrified mob swept the clerk by Mary and toward the Ontario exit. After the fire was extinguished, Mary could be seen, still in front of the smoldering store, weeping and sobbing over and over again, "My money! I want my twenty-dollar bill!"

The fire was over in about an hour. It had quickly gutted both floors of the dime store and outside the smoldering ruin milled multitudes of firemen, policemen, and spectators—the latter doing their usual best to impede the work of safety forces. The initial belief was that everyone had been rescued from the burning building. It wasn't until about 12:30 p.m. that Fire Chief George A. Wallace and a crew of searchers entered the sizzling building and found seven bodies in the rear right alcove by the three barred windows. Captain James Granger of Cleveland Fire Company #1 (later Chief of the Cleveland Fire Department) described the gruesome scene to a reporter from the *Cleveland Leader*:

> "I heard what sounded like the mewing of a cat," he said. "I had heard that sound before, however, and I shuddered. . . . [There] was a mass of humanity, it seemed, intertwined. There were [six] women. It seemed all had huddled together in the belief they would get air at that particular point, and when the fumes of the powder and paper became too strong all had given up at the same time. The arms of [most] of them were free, but their legs were intertwined so that it would have been impossible for any one to have dragged herself out. At the farther end of the bunch was a little lad. He was living . . ."

The lad was Jimmy Parker, who died soon after his removal from the store. The fact that he was still living when found may have led to the false report that convinced his mother he had survived.

By now, it had begun to rain, and the bodies were removed and laid in the muddy back alley behind the Kresge store. It soon became apparent, however, that two of the victims were still breathing. Two female trained nurses forced themselves through the police line and tried to revive the two survivors. Their efforts were in vain: Erma Schumacher was dead on arrival at Lakeside Hospital later that afternoon. The other survivor, S. S. Kresge clerk Elizabeth Reis, recovered consciousness at Huron Road Hospital before dying at 6:30 that evening.

The awful afternoon was not yet finished. While police and firemen searched the smoking ruins of the store and questioned sur-

STAYS TO SAVE SISTER AND BOTH DIE

Anna Trefall.
Heroine and martyr was Anna Trefall at the Kresge store fire yesterday. She died while trying to save her little sister Freda. The two were found by the firemen with arms locked around each other's neck.
The two girls were working in different parts of the store. Freda un-

The Plain Dealer.

Anna and Freda Trefall.

vivors, heartbreaking scenes unfolded at the County Morgue, where most of the seven bodies had been taken. Through it streamed a mournful procession of relatives, survivors, and a goodly proportion of the morbidly curious to see and identify the dead. Catching sight of his dead four-year-old son, George Parker collapsed, sobbing, "My son, my son! My poor little Jimmy!" Two sisters of Mary Hughes identified her corpse—by her teeth—but then became hysterical and had to be led away. Throughout that ghastly July afternoon crawled a sad procession of stunned men and women through that house of death, all with the same, simple, sad question on their lips, "Is my girl here?"

The rest of the S. S. Kresge fire saga—except for the ultimate legal result—is the stuff of sour anti-climax. The inquest, managed by Coroner Burke, began on July 9 and featured a parade of witnesses, rigorous cross-examination, and a lot of contradictory testimony. Winifred Duncan testified about her sparkler demonstration—but firmly denied that it caused the blaze. All witnesses corroborated her belief and that of the store management that the sparklers were "harmless." Testimony disclosed that no one in the store knew that the right rear windows were barred—or even that there were windows there at all. Testimony also revealed that there had never been a fire drill in the Kresge store—and that it was not legally required. As to the display and storage of fireworks, all officials and witnesses agreed that it was in full compliance with all Cleveland fire and safety laws. Or as Coroner Burke lamely summarized the inquest: "I am satisfied that the law was violated in spirit, while it seemed no one was legally culpable. It was morally wrong for that condition to be permitted to exist." The inquest concluded with the finding that while the fire was due to "carelessness in handling fireworks," no one was legally at fault because everyone involved acted under the belief that the sparkler was "harmless."

That wasn't quite the end of the matter. Cleveland newspapers cultivated public outrage over the fire for several weeks afterwards. And the enduring outcome of the Kresge tragedy was a public demand for an end to the homicidal mayhem that had become the norm for Fourth of July celebrations. On July 6, 1908, Cleveland Councilman Daniel Pfahl introduced the following ordinance in Council:

> That no person, firm or corporation, shall, within the city, sell, offer for sale or have in his or its possession or custody any toy pistol, squib, rocket crackers or roman candles or other combustible fireworks, or any article for making of a pyrotechnic display.

The Pfahl ordinance passed Cleveland Council by a vote of 21 to 11 on the night of Monday, July 13, 1908, and was soon signed into law by Mayor Tom Johnson. This landmark legislation and the tragedy that precipitated it were important milestones in the movement, ultimately nationwide, to end the annual toll of deaths and injuries due to fireworks. Other cities and states copied the Cleveland fireworks law and the Pfahl ordinance is remembered now as a pioneer triumph in the crusade for a "safe and sane" Fourth of July. So the Kresge Seven did not die entirely in vain—something to think about the next time you are stalled in traffic opposite 2025 Ontario Street.

Chapter 2

HORROR ON THE HEIGHTS

The 1910 Murder of William Lowe Rice

August 1910 was a good time to be rich. It was an especially good time to be rich in Cleveland, Ohio. Inflation was unknown and there was no income tax. You could buy a 26-piece case of silverware for five dollars from the George Bowman Co., a Hart, Schaffner & Marx suit from S. Baum Co. on Superior for $17.50, and a round trip by boat to Cedar Point for a mere dollar.

Sure, there were problems for most people. Most Clevelanders, especially those living in its teeming, overcrowded immigrant slums, had incomes so small that the items mentioned were rare or even impossible luxuries. And the world outside was harsher still: cholera was killing thousands in Russia; a Congressional investigation was exposing peonage in the company coal towns of Pennsylvania; and a mob of 300 white men had just butchered 20 black men in the streets of Palestine, Texas, over a dispute about a $10 debt.

But if you were rich it could be a comfortable, pleasant, and smiling world. And if you were William Lowe Rice, prominent Cleveland attorney, clubman, horseman, and socialite—rich, male, white, and powerful—it must have been very nice indeed. This is the story of how 47-year-old William Lowe Rice went from the pinnacle of a powerful, envied life to a sudden, scandalous excruciating death in just a few seconds of violence on Euclid Heights Boulevard in Cleveland Heights, one warm summer August night in 1910.

Until that fateful evening, William Lowe Rice's life was one of the most amazing success stories of early-20th-century Cleveland. Born the son of a respectable Pennsylvania lawyer in 1863, Rice was educated as a civil engineer before deciding on a law career. Passing the bar in 1883, Rice journeyed to Cleveland to seek his fortune.

It was not long in coming. Rice was a man on the make, and bustling, growing Cleveland offered much to reward a young man of talent and ambition. Starting at a six-dollar-a-week clerking job in the law firm of Adams & Russell, Rice rose to become L. A. Russell's law partner in only four years. When that firm was dissolved in the early 1890s, Rice joined in creating a new firm, the legal powerhouse of Blandin and Rice, with former Common Pleas Judge E. J. Blandin. (Over the next century, the partnership would evolve into the modern law firm of Jones, Day, Reavis & Pogue.)

Just what kind of lawyer was William Lowe Rice? His public-relations copy bragged that he was "recognized as a lawyer of ability and by his clients is considered a safe and reliable advisor. His clientage is of a most substantial and remunerative character." His obituaries made it clear, however, that his success did not come in the courtroom and that Rice had from an early point in his career eschewed trial work to concentrate on "business and financial matters." What were those matters?

Well, William Lowe Rice was a legal pioneer in the art of "adjusting" the affairs of businesses that were in financial trouble, usually very desperate trouble indeed. When Captain Levi Schofield's new building at East 9th and Euclid developed financing problems in the early 1900s, Rice was able to "readjust" its finances and return it to its owner—for a substantial fee, of course. During his legal salad days Rice became a local legal legend for his almost uncanny ability to save such foundering enterprises. Perhaps the last operation of this type was Rice's attempt to refinance the architecturally innovative but financially insolvent John Hartness Brown Building in 1910. Only this time, Rice somehow wound up with a controlling interest in the building. This maneuver may have cost him his life—but more of that later.

By the early 1900s, Rice was one of the most successful lawyer-entrepreneur-developers in Cleveland. In partnership with Patrick Calhoun and John Hartness Brown, Rice had developed Cleveland Heights itself into a housing development for the wealthy, known mainly as "Euclid Heights." But by 1910, both Calhoun and Brown

Cleveland Public Library Photograph Collection.

William Lowe Rice.

were in financial trouble—and Rice apparently controlled most of their assets in the Euclid Heights Realty Company. In addition, Rice was involved in Shaker Heights development, participated in coal mining and distribution operations worth millions, and was a director of 13 corporations. He was 5 feet 8 inches tall and an athletic 140 pounds, with blue eyes, brown hair, a brown mustache, good teeth, and a reputed net worth of anywhere from half a million to four million dollars. Professionally and financially, he was sitting on top of the world.

As it happened, he literally *was* sitting on top of the world of Cleveland. Rice had lived in relatively modest homes during his early career but by the mid-1890s his financial success allowed him to realize his lofty residential aspirations by building a spectacular, 11-pillared colonial brick mansion—"Lowe Ridge"—at the center and summit of Overlook Road, perched high atop Cleveland's Little Italy. The house and grounds were reputed to be worth at least $200,000—in 1910 dollars, mind you—at the time of his death.

His nearest neighbor on the east was John Hartness Brown, the owner of a sandstone mansion, and virtually everyone within shouting or shooting distance was a millionaire.

By 1910 William Rice had climbed financially and socially about as high as a former six-dollar-a-week clerk could ever have dared dream. He had an estate 700 feet deep by 300 to 400 feet wide, with formal gardens that were the envy of gardeners throughout the United States. He had seven servants, a stable full of magnificent horses, a beautiful wife, four daughters, membership in the Union Club, University Club, Cleveland Yacht Club, and the Euclid Golf Club, and a well-deserved and -cultivated reputation as a high-powered lawyer, clubman, horseman, and man-about-town. Not a little of his equine and social prestige came from his activity in the Four-in-Hand and Tandem Club, an elite group that included only Cleveland's most socially prominent horsemen.

Of William Rice's personal life we know tantalizingly little. We know that he had an aggressive personality and was known as a man who was used to getting his own way. In the aftermath of his murder, his family, of course, uttered nothing but the expected, inflated pieties about his character. But, as the saying goes, no man is a hero to his valet, and a number of stories have survived that suggest that William Rice was a very hard man with a dollar, especially when it came to servants or anybody else who had to deal with him as an inferior. John Grimes, Rice's coachman, testified at Rice's inquest that one of Rice's former servants had complained Rice cheated him out of several days' pay. Grimes also testified that another employee had argued with Rice over a $3 fine Rice had imposed on him. Perhaps the last word on Rice's manner with the help belongs to Albert Stanley, who was briefly employed by Rice as a coachman at the turn of the century. Fifty years after Rice's death, Stanley recalled an argument in which Rice had ended a dispute over an eight-dollar debt by shouting that Stanley would be "gray! gray! gray!" before he ever got the disputed sum out of William Lowe Rice.

Before proceeding to the bloodletting, all that remains is to convey the tone of life as it was graciously lived in the palatial Rice mansion during his golden years. That tone is admirably evoked by a clipping from Cleveland *Town Topics*, the fawning outlet for turn-of-the-century Cleveland society news:

On Wednesday Mrs. William Lowe Rice was the hostess at a very fashionable luncheon of twenty-four covers given in honor of Mrs. Albert Johnson of New York. The three tables were set in the handsome dining room of the Rice residence on Euclid Heights, and each held a large white hat tied with white satin ribbons and filled to over-flowing with cornflowers and maiden hair ferns. Corsage bouquets of the flowers were given to each guest. The house throughout was decorated in spring blossoms and there was harp and violin music.

[*Cleveland* Town Topics, *June 8, 1901, p. 13*]

And now it is time for William Lowe Rice to die.

On Friday morning, August 4, Rice rose at 8:10 and was driven downtown to his law office in the Scofield Building. Rice was relatively alone at Lowe Ridge, as his family had departed in early July for their regular summer vacation at Weona, Massachusetts, where Rice planned to join them soon. After a day of business, Rice left work for the Euclid Golf Club and was out on the links with club pro Harry Reece by 4:30 p.m. The Euclid Golf Club and its links are only words now, but they once occupied a great deal of the western part of the Euclid Heights allotment of Cleveland Heights Village. There were nine holes north of Cedar and nine holes south, with a magnificent, Frank Meade-designed Tudor clubhouse located near the current southeast corner of Norfolk and Derbyshire Roads. A path led from the clubhouse across the greens to Euclid Heights Boulevard, where club members could catch frequent streetcars east or westbound. Rice, an avid golfer, was a frequent visitor at the Euclid Golf Club. He usually had himself driven to the club, but he sometimes walked home from there late in the evening to the back entrance of his property, only 500 yards away on Euclid Heights.

Rice played golf that evening until sunset. He was happy with his game, and he bragged moderately about it to his fellow club members. He then took a shower, followed by dinner with friends who would later testify that that Rice talked "cheerfully" and was in "the best of spirits." Legend has it that the conversation touched on the prevalence of chicken thieves in the neighborhood and that Rice averred he would defend himself vigorously against such miscreants.

For all its repute as a sleepy hamlet inhabited chiefly by millionaires, it would seem that the western end of Cleveland Heights

Cleveland Press Collection, Cleveland State University.

Lowe Ridge.

was seething with strange characters and phenomena that warm summer night. At around 10:25 to 10:35 p.m. there was a power blackout on the Heights. Although officials of the power company later claimed that the western area of Cleveland Heights was not affected, the conductor of the Euclid Heights streetcar testified that the streetlight was out when he passed the top of Cedar Hill at 10:09 p.m. At about 10:30, just before Rice went out the Club's front door, John C. Chandler, who lived at the Club, saw two men, "small of stature" and "roughly dressed," walking up Euclid Heights Boulevard. Several minutes later, attorney Rufus Ranney, alighting from a streetcar at the top of Cedar Hill, saw two "suspicious"-looking men sitting on a bulldozer parked by the boulevard, who subsequently matched the description of the two men that Chandler saw. About the same time, a man alighted from the same or another streetcar at the Overlook-Euclid Heights intersection and met another man on the corner whom he engaged in conversation. Meanwhile, M. A. Wood, a motorist driving down Harcourt towards the top of Cedar Hill, noticed an odd couple on the street. The man, solidly built, had a mustache, and the woman wore a shawl over her head. Wood, whose headlight had gone out, asked the man for a match but the man merely muttered "Me got no match" and continued on with his female companion. And Thomas Capstock, Rice's gardener, would later testify that he thought there might have been a man and a woman trespassing on the Rice estate sometime that same evening but he was rather vague as to the details and the exact time. Another witness also added that he had seen two "foreigners" on the north side of Euclid Heights at that time of night and that they had "smooth, dirty faces."

At 10:30 p.m. William Lowe Rice said good night to Grover Higgins, a Club member, at the door and walked out into the night. He took the path that led south towards Euclid Heights Boulevard. On that path he met John C. Chandler; they exchanged greetings, and Rice continued on his way. It was the last time he was seen alive.

No one knows whether Rice stayed on the path all the way to Euclid Heights Boulevard or cut diagonally southwest across the slope of the golf course toward the intersection of Derbyshire and Euclid Heights.

We know that Rice got at least as far as the corner of Derbyshire and Euclid Heights, to a point in the street just in front of the red door of the English Lutheran Church that stands there today. It was only several hundred feet from the back entrance to his estate, but the empty corner lot was covered with trees and shrubbery. And it seems an inescapable fact that one or more persons came out of that thicketed field towards William Lowe Rice, just as he reached the corner at about 10:40 p.m.

Around 10:43 p.m. a number of people heard strange things going on in the neighborhood of Derbyshire and Euclid Heights. William Webb, a gardener at the Eels estate at the northeast corner of Overlook and Cedar Hill, heard, he thought, at least two, perhaps three gunshots and a cry of distress. Across the road from Webb, William McKenzie, a chauffeur for George N. Chandler, was awakened by the shots but went back to sleep. Charles Stanley, former city golf champion, who lived with his wife in the vicinity, heard two gunshots so loud that he thought someone was shooting on his property. "That means business," he told his wife. Rebecca Hogsett of Kenilworth Road, also heard shots and then the footsteps of unknown persons running away. Michael Brown, who slept in a coach house adjacent to the lane near the murder scene also heard shots and later testified that he saw a "neatly attired" man "wearing a straw hat" running by the servants' quarters where Brown slept. Police would later report that almost everyone living within a quarter mile of the killing told them they heard shots. One of those who heard shots was Clarence Jones, the conductor of a streetcar westbound on the Heights line that left Lee Road at 10:36 p.m. Seven minutes later he thought he heard several shots to the south. At about the same time, Patrolman C. L. Wahl of Cleveland Heights Village was in the Mornington-Edgehill area checking on some residences when he heard shots coming from the west. Wahl immediately ran down to the Boulevard and hopped on Jones's streetcar, discussed the gunfire with the conductor, and jumped off by the path that led to the Euclid Golf Club. He ran toward the Club to see what was the matter.

Things were unsettled at the Club. Earl Davis, a student earning money there as a bellboy, was out on the porch when he heard two shots, followed, he thought, by two more reports, possibly echoes. As he turned to go into the Club he suddenly heard the sound of footsteps running on the west side of the Club toward the boulevard. Catching sight of Patrolman Wahl, he alerted him to the running man, and Wahl took off in pursuit of the apparent fugitive. He caught up with his quarry, a short, stocky black man, just before they reached the Club streetcar stop at the boulevard. The man, apparently unconcerned, said "You're a pretty good runner, Officer." Wahl scrutinized the man to see if he seemed frightened or out of breath. He was apparently neither, and since Wahl had no evidence yet of any crime committed, he merely boarded another streetcar with the man and took it west to the Derbyshire stop. What he found when he got off there wasn't pretty.

The streetcar Wahl had previously taken to the Euclid Golf stop had gone on its way and it was only minutes later that Conductor Jones thought he saw a body lying in the street on the north side of the road. He mentioned it to his motorman, who dismissed the idea as a shadow and Jones's streetcar continued on down to Cedar Hill. Several more minutes went by.

Sometime after 10:50 but before 11 p.m., Dr. W. H. Phillips, an ophthalmologist, left his home on Cadwell Avenue, just east of Coventry. Phillips and his wife had been entertaining another couple, Dr. and Mrs. T. H. George, at home, and the four of them piled into the Phillips's car so that Dr. Phillips could return the Georges to their home in the city.

It was probably Dr. George who saw the body first, and Phillips brought the auto to a sudden stop only 50 feet or so beyond it. Both

The Cleveland Press

HOME EDITION

CLEVELAND, SATURDAY, AUGUST 6, 1910.

ONE CENT

BATTLING FOR LIFE, RICE MET DEATH, SMALL KNIFE IN HAND

Police Baffled, but Clews Furnished by Chauffeur and Friend May Throw Light.

Diagram Showing Route Rice Took from the Euclid Club to Home, Scene of Murder and Latest Photos of Victim and His Residence

MARKS ON RICE'S BODY INDICATE LAWYER WAS FIRST ATTACKED WITH KNIVES, THEN SHOT, SAYS CORONER

4 Daughters of Lawyer.

Cleveland Press Collection, Cleveland State University.

doctors got out and ran back to find the bloody body of William Lowe Rice. When they found him he was bleeding from the nose and mouth, and from an apparent wound above the right eye. His clothes were slashed at both sleeves and the ground around him was "saturated" with his blood. Phillips and George initially assumed that this unknown stranger was the victim of an automobile collision. At this point Patrolman Wahl got off the streetcar and approached the group. As he was talking to them, a neighborhood resident, William Royce, drove up and asked if he could help. As it was clear that Rice was in critical condition, the doctors decided to take him to the hospital and have Royce drive the doctors' wives home. It was now about 11:20 p.m. and just as Phillips and George were hoisting Rice's body into the back of Phillips's touring car, who should get off an eastbound streetcar and join the group? Why, none other than John Hartness Brown, Rice's nearby neighbor and a man with a reputed business grievance against him. Inquest testimony would reveal that while Brown asked the doctors what had happened and whether he could be of assistance, he did not ask who the injured man was or indicate that he had any idea it was Rice in the back of the car.

Dr. Phillips and Dr. George sped to St. Luke's Hospital. But by the time they got there, Rice was dead, and so they took him to Koebler's Morgue on East 55th, where examination of the corpse soon revealed that Rice had been shot twice in the face with a .32-caliber weapon. One bullet had glanced off his head, leaving a superficial wound, but the other smashed into his skull, just over his right eye, crushing the orbital chamber, collapsing the eyeball, shattering the bones at the base of the skull and burying itself in the right occipital brain lobe. Rice's left palm had been slashed to the bone, probably with a knife or razor, which had also slashed his right sleeve several times without inflicting injury. Hemorrhaging in the brain indicated that he had also been bludgeoned with something like a blackjack, an injury that may have knocked him unconscious before he was shot. The wounds suggested to everyone who knew Rice that the athletic lawyer, who was a trained boxer, had put up a hell of a fight before he went down in the street. Found near his body was an open, bloody, two-inch penknife with which he had apparently waged his last, desperate fight.

As you might guess, all hell broke loose in the Euclid Heights neighborhood during the next several weeks. Before the excitement was over, $10,000 in reward money was offered and several dozen suspects were hounded by competing factions of local police and private detectives. Theories by the score were put forward and gossip nurtured a thousand and one lurid and inconsistent theories as to how and why William Lowe Rice had been bludgeoned, shot, and stabbed to death within several hundred feet of his home. Almost everyone involved in the investigation pretended to know the answer—with what results we shall see.

Rice was quickly mourned and buried. His wife, Elise, vacationing at Weona, Massachusetts, fainted when informed of the tragedy but rallied quickly and returned to Cleveland with her daughters on Sunday. Interestingly, the Rices were accompanied back to Cleveland by a certain William Nelson Cromwell. Cromwell had been much involved in Rice's business affairs and most particularly in the takeover of the John Hartness Brown Building. In many ways, in fact, Cromwell was an even more successful version of William Lowe Rice, and Rice had probably learned much from the cunning, secretive Cromwell. Cromwell was the true pioneering specialist in restoring sick business concerns to health for handsome fees, and we can only guess at what combination of personal and professional motives brought Cromwell back to Cleveland to comfort Rice's family and probate his late partner's estate. That estate, based on Rice's 1894 will, left the entirety of his assets, of unspecified character or value, to Elise Gautier Rice, who managed to delay the completion of probate until 1922. Elise's own estate after her death in 1938 is reputed to have been only about $500,000. Rice's funeral, by the way, was a popular event. Hundreds crowded the Rice home for the obsequies, many of them policemen who thronged the Rice house in the quaint belief that the murderer would return, as it were, to the scene of the crime.

For all of the blustering noise they made at the time, it is apparent now that the police had no idea how to solve the crime. The only law officer who spoke candidly about the crime was Chief Fred Kohler of the Cleveland Police. Although he promised Cleveland Heights authorities assistance, Kohler summarized the problem neatly in his comment to a *Cleveland Leader* reporter: "Unless there is a tip-off, there is small chance that the crime will ever be traced home." Kohler subsequently removed Cleveland forces from the investigation, feeling that his men had been snubbed by Cuyahoga County detectives and the Pinkerton sleuths hired by the Rice family

Not knowing what to do, the authorities did what they always do in such situations: they rounded up the usual suspects. After grilling one of Rice's Italian servants, they picked up poor Pasquale Guliano, his former caddy at the Euclid Golf Club, but he provided an alibi. Early Sunday morning, Cleveland Heights Marshall Lorenzo Brockway and other officers raided some rooming houses of Spence Brothers on Mayfield Road and interrogated six black laborers, to no avail.

Most of the motive behind such police procedures was sheer racial and ethnic prejudice. As one of the newspapers commented guilelessly, Rice's murder had included the use of a knife, a weapon not normally used by "an average white American." Or as the *Cleveland Leader* more bluntly put it, justifying the third-degree methods used on the Italian and black employees of the Euclid Golf Club: "The cleanness of the cut in Mr. Rice's coat

WE earnestly request in the interest of justice and the protection of the community that all persons who at about half past 10 o'clock Friday night, August 5th, were in the vicinity of the place where *William L. Rice was killed on Euclid Boulevard, Euclid Heights,* or who may know any one who was in that vicinity about that time, or also that knows of any fact or circumstance whatever which may by any possibility aid in the capture of the criminal, communicate such fact or circumstance to us.

Information communicated will, if desired, be treated as confidential.

Please communicate with us by telephone—Bell Main 286 or Cuy. Cent. 5311 or otherwise as most convenient.

BLANDIN, RICE & GINN,
1300 Schofield Bldg.,
Cleveland, Ohio.

The Plain Dealer.

Advertisement in the *Plain Dealer* asking for
information about the Rice Murder.

sleeve suggested a razor rather than the stiletto of an Italian."

By the middle of the following week, hysteria over the Rice killing had spread throughout northeastern Ohio. A clerk at Lane's Drugstore on East 55th called police on Tuesday, August 9, after her suspicions were aroused by a "clean cut" young man's purchase and immediate use of a bottle of peroxide to remove unidentified stains. Store clerk Alice Puma was treated as a heroine by the local media. An excited report that some murder evidence had been burned in Little Italy proved only to be fiery entertainment at the annual Feast of the Assumption festival. *The Cleveland Press* reported on August 15 that authorities had launched a dragnet in the Geneva-Madison area to apprehend a wounded man who had shown unseemly interest in the Rice case. Another two men were sought who had shown a rubbernecking curiosity in the Rice murder so unseemly that they had demanded that a Euclid Heights streetcar conductor slow down so they could gawk at the back of the Rice estate.

On August 16, *The Plain Dealer* reported that the police were seeking an unidentified "Italian and Negro," who subsequently disappeared from the columns of the morning newspaper—and history. Illusory fugitives were sought in a boat docked on the lakefront, and a fruitless search for phantom suspects sent Cleveland detectives to Detroit and back.

Police investigations and newspaper speculations were dominated by several competing theories. The initial hypothesis, fostered by Patrolman Wahl and eagerly embraced—if only temporarily—by Rice's family, was that Rice had been the victim of a crude, brutal robbery by "footpads" (as highwaymen were then called), and that he had been killed when he resisted. That seemed unlikely. Rice was killed practically in front of his home and other occupied dwellings nearby, within mere feet of a regular streetcar line on which cars ran every 12 minutes per track side. Rice was killed practically directly under an arc street light, surely not a preferred spot for furtive footpads. Moreover, the footpads apparently robbed Rice of *nothing*. Still intact on his body were three gold rings, a diamond collar button, gold cuff links, his impressive bank book, an opal stick pin, and $132.64 in cash.

Other inconsistencies undermined the robbery paradigm. Although the initial party line of Rice's friends and family was that he didn't have an enemy in the world, contrary evidence soon surfaced. Club members claimed that Rice had been warned that "travelling over the lonely roads at night" might be dangerous. And Cleveland newspapers reported hearsay that Rice had received death threats in the weeks before his murder. Such hearsay was amplified by the revelation at the inquest that Rice had been sleeping for some time with two loaded revolvers beneath his mattress. The affair wore itself out in a succession of hysterical, inconsistent newspaper headlines. One day it was reported that Rice had traded angry words with an Italian from Little Italy; another day headlines blared that one of Rice's business clients had held Rice responsible for his business failure and had screamed, "I'll get you for this. I won't say when, but I'll get you!" More recently, crime writer Albert Borowitz has suggested the possibility that Rice was assassinated by the relatives of a girl from Little Italy whose honor the vigorous, masculine clubman had wronged—or at least trifled with.

A bizarre wrinkle entered the investigation the morning after the murder, when a neighborhood boy discovered a bag of dead chickens near the death scene. County Detective Doran theorized that Rice had surprised several chicken thieves, who had then murdered him to prevent exposure. The chickens were subsequently traced to the chicken coop of Rice's neighbor William Palmer, but it seems improbable that robbers would resort to murder to cover up chicken-stealing. In the end, Rice's family and Cleveland Heights authorities leaned toward the theory that Rice had been murdered by a personal enemy or his hirelings, while county officials clung to the footpad/chicken-thieves explanation.

Two officials who did not apparently believe in either footpads or chicken thieves were County Prosecutor John Cline and Assistant Prosecutor Charles Olds, who conducted the inquest during the week after Rice's death. The 100-plus-page transcript of their inquiries makes chilling reading even after fourscore and some years. From the beginning they had only one suspect, and their inquest focused on trying to place that man at the murder scene. That man was Rice's neighbor, former client, and business adversary, John Hartness Brown.

About half the inquest testimony, consisting of the interrogation of numerous streetcar conductors, was spent in trying to disprove Brown's alibi for the evening of August 5. Brown claimed he had spent the evening visiting some people down near East 102nd Street and had not arrived on the Heights until he stepped off the streetcar at Derbyshire and Euclid Heights at about 11:20 p.m. Hours of cross-examination failed to produce a single conductor on the Heights line who could recall Brown from that Friday night. But there were *two* rail employees who remembered him vividly from his ride at about 11 p.m. Friday on the East 105th car line that connected to the Euclid Heights car. The weekend after the murder, Brown had realized that he was the prime suspect. He had spent the days before the inquest frantically interviewing streetcar conductors to see if they could remember him from that fateful Friday night. In the end, prosecutors Olds and Cline could not break his alibi, and no theory of how Brown could have perpetrated such a bloody crime without physical evidence showing on his person so soon afterwards was offered. After 150 pages of testimony, the inquest ended in a muttering of inconclusive uncertainty. It *is* curious, however, that the attendant at Koebler's morgue testified under oath that John Hartness Brown had called there about an hour after

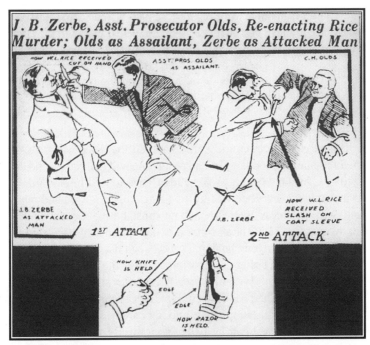

J. B. Zerbe, Asst. Prosecutor Olds, Re-enacting Rice Murder; Olds as Assailant, Zerbe as Attacked Man

Cleveland Press Collection, Cleveland State University.
Re-enactment sketch of Rice murder.

the body arrived and asked if *Mr. Rice's* body had been brought in. The attendant swore that he had not identified the body to Brown, and that it was Brown who had volunteered the fact that the dead man was Rice. This testimony did not jibe, to say the least, with Brown's claim that he did not know who the victim was in the back of Dr. Phillips's car. A decade ago, the late Eric Johannesen toyed with the theory that Brown was the guilty party, driven to homicidal rage by the loss of his building to William Rice that same year. The title of his 1985 article said it all: "A Building Worth Killing For?" But Johannesen had no more success than Cline and Olds in breaking Brown's alibi, and Brown remains only an intriguing figure in this unsolved murder.

But someone *did* kill William Rice, and the knowledge we have of his personality and activities suggests a well-thought-out hit. Several remarks by his peers in the wake of his murder suggest shrewd persons suspected that—sooner or later—bad things would happen to William Lowe Rice. Mrs. Rice sobbed to reporters that she couldn't imagine who "would do such a thing" to a husband who "did not have any enemies"—but does this jibe with the comment of Judge W. A. Babcock the day after the murder?

> The cry of the newsboys that a prominent attorney of Cleveland Heights had been shot led me to say before reading the paper that it was probably Rice.

Business partner Jerome Zerbe warbled that Rice was a "good businessman, a good lawyer, and as anyone will tell you a good citizen of Cleveland Heights." But Judge Theodore Strimple said, "It is my opinion that Rice was killed for revenge. . . Rice had many and wide business interests and he must have inevitably made many enemies." L. Q. Rawson, an ex-law partner of Rice said, "I cannot imagine anyone having a grudge against William L. Rice." But cagey Martin Foran spoke volumes about the unseemly rumors that swirled around William Lowe Rice. After scoffing at the idea that it was a botched robbery attempt, he concluded, "I have very definite ideas on the subject but I do not care to say more."

The various investigations petered out fitfully, replete with braying bravado on the part of bewildered authorities. In 1911, Pinkerton detective F. Dimaio noisily brandished the confession of a certain Vincenzo Pelato, who claimed that he and two other criminals had been the lethal chicken thieves confronted by the luckless Rice. The police did not believe Pelato, nor did they credit the confession of one Wood Finley Brown, who confessed to New Jersey authorities in 1916 that he had once "stuck up" a certain Mr. Rice in Cleveland. Five years later in 1921, County Prosecutor Edward Stanton expressed hope that he could tie the killers involved in the Lakewood Dan Kaber murder-for-hire case to Rice's killing. His hope was in vain.

In the 1950s, lawyers cleaning out the files at the Jones, Day law firm made a grisly discovery when they opened a box containing the bloodstained clothing worn by William Rice on that fatal August evening. Albert Borowitz recounts in his article on the Rice killing that the attorney who found the bloody clothing took it to a couple of senior partners in the firm who had known Rice, and asked them what they thought. They both said, "Yes, everyone knew who did it." Both attorneys then named a different person as the prime suspect. And it is further said that Rice's bloody suit was rent by an incredible number of apparent knife slashes; although the autopsy report doesn't support this, such wounds would back up Borowitz's theory of the murder as a *crime passionel* provoked by lurid aspects of Rice's personal life.

The world that made and unmade William Lowe Rice is long gone and faded away. The Euclid Golf Club was torn down several years after Rice's death, and its golf course carved up into residential lots. Where William Rice played his last nine holes on August 5, 1910, the Alcazar Hotel stands today. Lowe Ridge was sold by his widow in 1919 to Fred and Miriam White, who lived in it until the 1940s. It was subsequently razed, although the ruined sunken garden and the remains of the abandoned outbuildings survived for some years more. In the late 1950s the property was developed, and where Lowe Ridge stood towering over the city now sits the Waldorf Towers apartment building. And to the south, the back part of Rice's property wither he was bound when he was killed, is the Margaret Wagner nursing home. Most of the Overlook mansions have gone the way of Euclid Avenue's "Millionaire's Row" but you can still find a few magnificent houses, occupied chiefly by institutions. Ironically, many of the outbuildings and servants' quarters have survived and are yet admirable residential housing.

Elise Rice spent the years after she left Cleveland in 1919 living on Park Avenue and keeping up with society. She died in 1938 and sleeps by the side of her husband in Lake View Cemetery, next to their daughter Elise, who joined them there in 1968. Mrs. Rice's obituary in *The Plain Dealer* included this unattributed but tantalizing quote:

> "A fellow who had a grudge against Rice got some of these professionals to kill him," a prisoner in County Jail told authorities shortly after the Rice slaying. "This is only a tip for you to try and get the dope on some other way. If I am confronted with the fellows I will deny everything. I would rather lie in jail all my life than let them know that I said a word, for I would be a dead one in no time."

John Hartness Brown lost his investment in Cleveland Heights and even his own stately home several years after the Rice killing. Brown left afterwards for England and supposedly became a respected city planner in his new homeland. He is reputed to have remarked when asked in later years about Cleveland Heights, "I don't think I ever want to come back."

The murder of William L. Rice remains unsolved to this day.

Chapter 3

"THEY DIED CRAWLING"

The 1916 Waterworks Tunnel Explosion

Water. If there is anything that Clevelanders take for granted, it is water. If we think of it at all, the image of Lake Erie's limitless gallons presents itself—and we leave it at that. Yes, we know that the water has to be pumped from the lake, treated with potent chemicals to make it safe, and then sent forth to gush out of our faucets. The historical truth about Cleveland's water supply, however, is a tale of disaster and death, terror and pain, and the seemingly expendable lives of the city's once enormous working-class population. Above all, it is the terrible story of Crib #5 and the events of July 24 and 25, 1916.

Water was no problem for Cleveland's pioneer residents. They took what they needed from Lake Erie and the Cuyahoga River and fretted far more about malarial fevers than water quality, barring the occasional outbreak of cholera. By 1856, however, Cleveland's lakeside water was visibly filthy, and so Cleveland's waterworks was begun with the laying of a 300-foot-long cast-iron pipe, 4 feet in diameter, extending out from the Old River Bed to a depth of 12 feet. The water was pumped to the city's first reservoir at Kentucky and Franklin streets; the elevated promenade atop the Kentucky Reservoir was long considered one of Cleveland's finest views.

By the 1870s, however, more clean water was needed to supply Cleveland's exploding population and thirsty industries and so a tunnel was dug from an intake crib 9,000 feet from shore to the pumping station on Division Avenue. Foreshadowing the unhappy future of the Cleveland waterworks, it cost the lives of 19 men; the first two died while investigating a gas smell by lighting a match. A second, parallel tunnel, however, was completed in May of 1890 without loss of life. Up until almost the turn of the century, most

Cleveland Press Collection, Cleveland State University.
Garrett Morgan and rescued victim, July 25, 1916.

tunnel construction fatalities resulted either from cave-ins or "the bends," that awful complication particular to those who work underground in pressurized conditions.

The modern era of Cleveland water began on May 11, 1898, when tunnelers digging 6,300 feet offshore toward the Kirtland pumping station at East 49th hit a natural gas pocket. It exploded, burning eight of the tunnelers (or "sandhogs," as they called themselves). The eight burned men somehow managed to crawl 2,000 feet back up the tunnel towards shore, where fellow workers dragged them to safety. All eight men, however, subsequently died of their burns.

Exactly two months later, on July 11, 1898, the tragedy repeated itself when 11 sandhogs died as the same tunnel exploded again. After this disaster the tunnel was sealed off with a bulkhead, and workers began to burrow toward shore from two new cribs. On the night of August 14, 1901, one of the cribs caught fire, burning five men to death and drowning another five who jumped into the lake to escape the flames. Almost a week went by. Six days after the fire, Gustaf Van Duzen, a veteran sandhog, was repairing the burned crib when he heard tapping noises coming from the wrecked crib shaft. He and another man went down the shaft and found the exhausted and nearly starved miners Adam Kent and John Eugine. They had miraculously survived the fire but had been too weak and woozy from gas to climb out of the tunnel. This episode was but one chapter in the legend of heroism that grew up around Gus Van Duzen. We shall meet him again in this story.

The day after Van Duzen rescued the two miners, another gas explosion in the other new tunnel at Crib #3 destroyed the shaft, killing six men and flooding the works. Several survivors managed to cling to the crib ruins until they were rescued the next day. And yet another gas explosion the following year in the same tunnel killed four more sandhogs on December 14, 1902.

In all, probably 70 men lost their lives in tunnel operations before the fatal night of July 24, 1916. It was not a proud record, but it was typical of the dangerous mining conditions of the age. Immigrant laborers, mainly Irish and German, were paid little, worked under dangerous and squalid conditions, and could look forward to little more than death, injury, or a premature old age. Perhaps not surprisingly, camaraderie was high among the sandhogs. Most of them were first- or second-generation immigrants, and they were bonded to each other by the constant and terrible risks they faced together. Nothing, however, could have steeled them for what was about to happen at Crib #5 on the night of July 24, 1916.

Crib #5 was begun on August 3, 1914. The two existing parallel tunnels connecting the Division Avenue pumping station with Crib #4 would be extended by a single tunnel to a point five miles north of the Cuyahoga River mouth. Crib #5 was towed out and sunk at the five-mile point, and workers from Cribs #4 and #5 began tunneling towards each other. As with previous tunnels, the project was initially put out for bid to private construction companies. Owing, however, to second thoughts about the unhappy history of previous tunnels, the bids were withdrawn and the Cleveland Waterworks Department itself took over the project.

City officials and sandhogs were feeling self-congratulatory about the #5 tunnel as the scorching summer of 1916 passed by. Unlike most previous tunnels, no lives had been lost during two years of work on #5, and the expected link-up with #4 was only a few months away. And Crib #5 and its shaft and tunnel were absolutely state-of-the-art projects. The crib itself was a 100-by-100-foot steel square. In the middle was the shaft, going 128 feet down from the surface of the lake to a point 40 to 50 feet below the lakebed. The shaft contained an elevator for transporting the sandhogs and removing the excavated dirt. At the bottom of the shaft, the new tunnel ran south to a point 1,500 feet from Crib #5 and about 1,200 feet north from the tunnel being pushed toward it from Crib #4. Not far from the crib shaft was a 30-foot airlock with doors on both ends of it, which, together with powerful air compressors at the crib, kept pressure in the tunnel at about 22 pounds per square inch, sometimes more.

The tunnel itself was a pipe, 10 feet in diameter, made out of interlocking concrete blocks, four to a section. A small railway stretched from the bottom of the shaft up to the tunnel face. There, working behind an ingeniously designed hydraulic shield that was progressively forced forward to hold up the ceiling as the miners advanced, a tunneling machine gouged 30-foot arcs out of the sand, gravel, and clay that lay in its path. Workers behind the shelf quickly seized the flying chunks of dirt and threw them into small railroad cars. Taken to the elevator, the cars were hoisted up and emptied over the side of the crib, adding to its sturdy foundation.

Crib #5 was more, however, than just a work site. About 85 men *lived* at the crib, many of them for months at a time. Working in three eight-hour shifts, sandhogs were scheduled for eight hours work, eight hours sleep, and eight hours for whatever recreation one could find on a 100-foot steel platform five miles out in the middle of Lake Erie. During the winter, sandhogs at #5 were virtually marooned, their only link with the shore being infrequent supply boats. There was no radio, no telegraph, and no telephone; a telephone had been tried with previous cribs but the cables were repeatedly severed by ship anchors. All in all, however, Cleveland officials and mine workers took great pride in Crib #5. Technically, it was a sweet achievement and the boast of a department with a bloody history . . . now thought safely put behind it. In reality, Crib #5 was just a terrible accident waiting to happen.

In hindsight, it seems incredible that the disaster was allowed to occur. It was well known to sandhogs and utility officials that natural gas was a danger in both the #4 and #5 tunnels. There had been minor gas explosions in both tunnels during the year previous to July 1916, and workers in #4 complained that the gas made them too sick to work.

The danger became more immediate on Saturday, July 22. That

Gus Van Duzen in the Crib #5 Tunnel.

night, William Moore, a shield driver working at the #5 face, saw a sudden, foot-wide rupture in the tunnel floor, and gas rushed out with a roar. Nearly overcome, Moore immediately informed his superiors. That same Saturday, Patrick Delaney, an experienced tunneler, quit his job at #5. He told the boatman who taxied him to shore that "there was enough gas in the tunnel to light the city of Cleveland."

Signs of danger increased on Sunday. Gas forced the midnight shift to quit at 4 a.m., and crew foreman Harry Vokes was ordered to build a bulkhead at the tunnel face. Twenty-four hours later, the Monday morning work crew unanimously refused to even enter the gas-filled tunnel. By then, Gus Van Duzen, the #5 tunnel chief, was aware of the gas problem. On Monday morning he met with Water Commissioner Charles Jaeger and Utilities Director Thomas Farrell and was unequivocally ordered to keep workers out of the tunnel until it tested safe for gas and a broken air compressor was repaired. Van Duzen also had air samples sent to the office of City Chemist Wilbur S. White for analysis and ordered a ventilator installed at the shaft to help draw gas out of the tunnel.

But at some point Monday evening, July 24, the decision was made to send workers back into the tunnel. How this happened is still not clear: Van Duzen had strict orders not to let workers back into the tunnel until the air had tested safe and the compressor was fixed. Van Duzen also apparently failed to communicate these orders to John Johnston, the Crib #5 superintendent. The tunnel crew chief that evening, Harry Vokes, should have known better, too—but shortly after 8 p.m. he requested permission to take his work crew into the tunnel and John Johnston told him to go ahead, "conditions permitting." In Vokes's work crew were hoisting engineer Thomas Clark; muckers Jack Welsh, John Mackey, and Frank Captain; and miners Stephen Hayes, William Lahnstein, Fred Caplan, and Nickola Samptr. It was a good cross-section of the Cleveland sandhog community. Harry Vokes was a long-time tunnel veteran; he had spent Monday afternoon shopping for baby clothes with his expectant wife, Hazel. Thomas Clark had lived with his wife and nine-year-old daughter for a year in Cleveland; his family eagerly awaited the arrival of paper-hangers in their new home on Tuesday morning. Perhaps the luckiest man in Cleveland that week, however, was J. A. Flynn, a miner who quit on the spot when Johnston asked him to go into the tunnel with his work crew about 8 p.m. Monday.

Only the doomed members of Vokes's work crew, perhaps, heard the fatal gas explosion that occurred at the tunnel face at 9:22 p.m. It was so powerful that it smashed and hurled the heavy concrete tunnel sections around, killing and burying the Vokes crew in a fiery holocaust of flame and dirt.

The first hints that something had gone wrong below came to Engineer H. H. Rinehald at the compressor turbine gauges and to crib elevator operator George Ellis. At 9:22 p.m. they noticed their air gauges fluctuating wildly, shooting up from the normal level of 22 pounds per square inch (psi) to over 30 psi, and then back down to only 5 psi in the tunnel. In addition, Ellis later testified, he could distinctly smell gas. Crib Superintendent Johnston was immediately notified that something had gone wrong.

Johnston reacted instantly. He tried to telephone Vokes at the tunnel face, but received no answer. Johnston then went down the shaft elevator alone and returned some minutes later to tell the anxious sandhogs topside that the tunnel was filled with gas and that the Vokes crew was trapped somewhere inside. He went down the elevator again, accompanied by a pipe fitter. The two men soon returned, gasping for breath. "Come on boys, we've got to go down for them," shouted Johnston, and he asked for volunteers. Seven men stepped forward, and the rescue party descended the shaft to the airlock below. In the group were Johnston, Peter McKenna, shield driver Archie Turnbull, pipeman Frank Reep, mucker Louis Zappisolli, track finisher Mike Gallagher, William Yeoman, and pipeman James Woods. Armed only with "bugs," as the sandhogs called flashlights, the eight men went through the airlock—and were almost immediately felled by the gas on the other side.

Peter McKenna saw John Johnston fall to the ground ahead of him. They were only about 100 feet past the airlock, and the staggering McKenna dragged Johnston's unconscious body back toward the airlock. Minutes later, Engineer J. W. Dolan heard a faint tapping coming from the bottom of the crib shaft. He and Foreman H. C. Parson, accompanied by miner Mike Kilbane, descended the shaft. At the bottom they met the heroic McKenna; he, Johnston, and Mike Gallagher would be the only survivors of the initial rescue effort.

The crib platform was now ruled by pandemonium and terror. Communication with Cleveland's safety forces over the next 12 hours would be haphazard at best. But the men at Crib #5 did what they could. By 10 p.m. Rinehald had already sounded the Crib's small steam whistle, sending off the standard distress signal: five short blasts, repeated at intervals. Rockets were fired into the night sky, to explode hundreds of feet above the crib. Owing to smoke and fog on the lakefront, however, the rockets were not seen even by lookouts at the downtown United States Lifesaving Station. Nor was the crib's whistle heard. Minutes ticked away, and there was still no sign that anyone on shore had been alerted.

Two residents of Lakewood may have been the first to notice something was wrong. C. G. Prescott of Lake Avenue saw a rocket explode over the lake sometime after 9 p.m. He ran outside, where he could hear the sound of the crib whistle, and he immediately called the U. S. Lifesaving Station. Another alarm was called in by Glen Fuller, also of Lake Avenue. He later testified that he heard the crib whistle about 10 p.m. and later saw some rockets.

As 11 p.m. came, about 90 minutes had elapsed since the explosion, and the men at #5 were frantic. Their greatest need was for pulmotors (mechanical devices used to revive victims of suffocation) and gas masks. Without masks, they couldn't go into the tunnel, and without pulmotors they couldn't revive the rescued sandhogs.

The first response to the Crib #5 distress signals came about 11

Two Probes in Horror to Begin

EXTRA THE NEWS HOME EDITION

TUNNEL DEATH LIST 21, 10 RESCUERS ARE KILLED

BRINGING IN DEAD; REVIVING TUNNEL VICTIMS **HEROES GIVE UP THEIR LIVES, BUT SAVE ONLY FEW**

03.3: Cleveland News headline.

p.m., when two boats from the freighter *Star of Jupiter* pulled alongside the crib. The freighter had neither gas masks nor pulmotors, so its only aid was to take McKenna and Johnston to shore for medical treatment.

Minutes after the *Star of Jupiter's* boats departed, about midnight, Captain Hans Hansen of the U. S. Lifesaving Station arrived in a motor launch, greeted by desperate pleas that screaming, frightened men would repeat again and again over the next four hours: "Helmets! Pulmotors! Is there anyone at all who knows anything about air? Oh God! My God! Is there anyone on this boat who knows anything?!"

Shortly after midnight someone contacted Gus Van Duzen at his West-59th-Street home. He immediately departed for Whiskey Island, gathered volunteers, and took a tugboat to #5. Jumping aboard the crib, he shouted, "Who'll volunteer? I'm going down!" Twelve men instantly stepped forward, followed by another five who formed a backup party. Down the shaft went Van Duzen's group and toward the airlock. Almost immediately they were in trouble.

Martin Nelson went down with Van Duzen. The air was tainted with gas and a man next to Nelson stumbled and fell. Nelson felt "funny" but he went forward, spurred by Van Duzen saying, "Keep up, Nelson! Ahead, man, ahead! They're waiting for us out there." Nelson tried to keep going, but he could not. He soon found himself crawling on his hands and knees. Numbness settled over his body. It seemed as though there were a tremendous weight pressing down on his head . . . and the last thing he would remember was trying to lift his face up out of a mud puddle.

Michael Kehoe, another member of the Van Duzen rescue party, also had terrible memories of the experience. He could see the unconscious bodies of the would-be rescuers who had gone ahead. "It was awful to see those men at whose side you had worked in there and yet be unable to save them," he recalled later. "They lay gasping for air on the floor." And the rescue party that followed Van Duzen's band was immediately driven back by gas.

It was now almost 2 a.m. and no effective help had yet arrived at Crib #5. But about an hour after Van Duzen went down the shaft, someone called his wife and told her he was lying dead in the #5 tunnel. "Mrs. Van," as she was affectionately known to the sandhogs, was not one to submit to fate easily. She called her son, Thomas Clancy, at his Public Square taxi stand and told him to go get his stepfather out of the #5 tunnel. Clancy picked up his friend, Thomas Keating, and the two men sped to the waterfront. Commandeering a boat at the West 11th Street Custom House, they arrived at the crib about 3 a.m.—just as the firetug *George A. Wallace* got there, without bringing any gas masks or pulmotors.

Keating and Clancy did not wait for permission from the authorities. Wrapping wet towels around their heads, they descended the shaft. Minutes later they returned, dragging the bodies of Patrick Sullivan, John McCormick, and Harry Hatcher.

It was now almost 4 a.m., seven hours after the tunnel explosion. Precious minutes were slipping away and Water Commissioner Jaeger faced a terrible dilemma. He could have the air pressure taken off in the tunnel, which would make it easier for the rescuers to work. But it would also increase the risk of the tunnel walls collapsing. Jaeger had the pressure taken off.

At about 4:45 a.m. the *George A. Wallace* returned, this time with smoke helmets, oxygen tanks, and a pulmotor. Richard Kistenmaker, of the Fire Department, and Keating donned helmets and together with Clancy, who was completely unprotected, descended the shaft. Minutes later came the expected tapping sig-

Cleveland Press Collection, Cleveland State University.
Survivors of the Crib disaster: Mike Gallagher, Lawrence Dunn
and Mike Keough, July 25, 1916.

nal and up came the elevator carrying Kistenmaker, Keating, and
the unconscious body of Clancy.

About dawn, more help began to arrive. Most crucial was the
arrival of Garrett A. Morgan of the National Safety Device Company of Cleveland. Years earlier, Morgan had invented a gas mask,
which he frequently demonstrated to fire departments around the
country. John Chafin, a Cleveland policeman, had witnessed one of
these demonstrations, and he persuaded Cleveland authorities to
get in touch with Morgan in the wee hours of July 25. Within an
hour, Morgan arrived at #5 with several of his helmets and accompanied by his brother Frank. The moment had come for the ultimate test of the Morgan gas mask.

Morgan asked for volunteers, but only the ever-heroic Tom
Clancy and a man named Thomas Castelbery stepped forward. As
the Morgan brothers and the two volunteers prepared to descend,
Mayor Harry Davis stepped forward and said, "Goodbye," to Morgan, so doubtful was he of the helmet's effectiveness. The four men
disappeared down the shaft.

On his first trip into the tunnel, Garrett Morgan soon stumbled
over a body. While the other rescuers removed it, Morgan contin-

ued on down the tunnel. Within minutes, he found a man under-neath one of the dirt cars, his face in the slime. It was Gus Van Duzen. "It's Dad, and he's alive!" cried Clancy, as they brought the stupefied Van Duzen to the top.

In all, Garrett Morgan made four trips into the tunnel. With help from his companions, he removed, either dead or alive, Van Duzen, Clarence Welch, and other miners, including Yeoman, Schwind, Woods, Turnbull, Reep, Zappisolli, and Banks.

The living and the dead that could be found were removed from the crib by boat, and the injured were taken to hospitals. Now would come the really difficult part: when everyone sat down and decided who was to blame for the deaths of 19 men and the injury of at least 9 others.

First, however, a grisly task had to be performed. Elmer Kisner, the union business agent, went through the clothes of the dead. No one could actually identify what must have been the corpse of George Banks. In his pocket was the newspaper clipping of a poem entitled "Your Little Wife," probably tucked into his wallet by Mrs. Banks that morning. It read:

Who plans to make your future bright?
Your little wife.
Who cooks to tempt your appetite?
Who tells her women friends that you
Are one grand husband thru and thru,
Who's the best girl you ever knew?
Your little wife.

On Archie Turnbull's body was a letter from his mother that read:

Dear boy. I would like to go and see you. How are you getting on? I hope your cough is better. Don't you need your suit case and clothes? Now Goodbye, and God bless you and keep you safe is the prayer of your mother.

The official city inquest into the disaster opened at 10 a.m. on Thursday, July 27. By this time, the Ohio State Industrial Commission, the U. S. Bureau of Mines, and the U. S. Department of Labor were also promising investigations of the catastrophe. The heat was on Mayor Harry Davis's administration to find someone to blame. Newspaper editorials and the comments of potential witnesses articulated a number of puzzling and explosive questions:

• Why were no physicians on call at #5, as required in the bid specifications demanded of private tunnel contractors offered two years previously?

• Why were there no boats at the crib for communication with the shore—as called for in the private bidding?

• Why were workers allowed to work in the tunnel when the gas level exceeded three percent—a condition prohibited to private contractors?

• Why did a work crew enter the tunnel on Monday evening, contrary to the explicit orders of the Water Commissioner?

• Why were no gas helmets or pulmotors present at Crib #5?

• Why were there no telephone, telegraph, or wireless connections, so that Crib #5 could communicate with the shore?

• Why—perhaps the most important question of all—did at least *seven* hours elapse before effective aid reached the distressed crib?

Despite this intense publicity, the Crib #5 inquest proved anticlimactic. Given the undeniable heroism of many of those involved, the inquest lurched toward an inevitable, indeed predictable verdict. Testimony revealed that the Waterworks Department, city safety officials and the managers of Crib #5 were completely unprepared for the disaster, despite the ample experience of earlier tragedies at other cribs and water tunnels. Gus Van Duzen, John Johnston, and other supervisors admitted that there were no pulmotors or gas masks at #5—and they probably also told the truth when they insisted that there were no such safety frills at comparable mining projects throughout the United States.

The controversy over who was responsible for sending men into the tunnel on Monday night was relatively acrid. Under cross-examination, Van Duzen modified his initial claim that he had explicitly forbidden Harry Vokes to enter the tunnel, finally admitting, after a sensational appearance at the inquest by Vokes's angry widow, Hazel, that he had merely cautioned Vokes that the tunnel wouldn't be in working condition until midnight. Crib Superintendent John Johnston injected a thrill of dramatic tension when he refused to answer two direct questions about what he told Harry Vokes on Monday night. Indeed, on July 23, Assistant County Prosecutor Fred Green told city police to put Johnston under arrest

The Plain Dealer.

Diagram of Crib #5 and where explosion occurred.

at Lakeside Hospital, where he was recovering from his injuries. But the drama passed quickly. For many reasons those guilty of criminal negligence could not be punished. Both Van Duzen and Johnston were guilty of negligence but they had—thanks to sensationalistic newspaper coverage—become the "heroes" of the disaster. City officials, too, were guilty of gross negligence—but Mayor Harry Davis absolved everyone involved only hours after the inquest had begun with his comment: "I believe every man did what he thought was best. It is easy to criticize, but how does anyone know he wouldn't have done the same under similar circumstances?" The formal inquest verdict held no one responsible for the disaster at all.

Shockingly, Garrett Morgan was not even called as an inquest witness. Worse, his heroism went almost unrecorded in white-owned and -staffed Cleveland newspapers. The Davis Administration subsequently even refused to support a drive to have Morgan awarded the Carnegie Hero Fund Commission Medal, a slight that embittered Morgan for the rest of his life. Worse still, the city refused to recognize Morgan's claim for compensation for injuries sustained in his rescue work that terrible morning. So much for the hero to whom Mayor Davis had allegedly said on that same morning, "The city will take care of you for the rest of your days."

The Crib #5 inquest petered out in mutterings of recrimination. Meanwhile, work crews had already returned to #5 to dig out the dead. This unspeakable labor went on for almost a month, the discovery of the mutilated, burned, and often dismembered corpses usually preceded by a "disgusting odor" wafting from the ruined tunnel face.

And the legacies of the Crib #5 disaster? The City of Cleveland quickly implemented the safety measures it had previously ignored. The #5 tunnel was eventually finished and became operational in 1918. The State Industrial Commission paid about $3,800 to each of the bereaved families. And Garrett Morgan was eventually recognized as the hero of the Crib #5 tragedy and the genius who invented the automatic traffic light and other useful devices.

A comic footnote to the tragedy was the appearance of Patrick Kearns at Crib #5 on Wednesday, July 26. Thought to be a member of the Vokes crew, Kearns had initially been listed in the tallies of the dead. The truth was somewhat less dramatic. It seems Kearns drew his pay on Monday afternoon and did not show up for work, as scheduled, that evening. He ended up sleeping that night in Edgewater Park, where he was mugged. "I thought you might be glad to know them papers lied," was his insouciant comment on the whole affair.

But perhaps the last word belongs to "Scotty" Jamieson, a miner in the Cleveland Waterworks Department. Jamieson was a relatively unsung hero of the disaster; his name went unmentioned in early press accounts, despite the fact that he helped carry six tunnel victims out himself. His bitter comment to a *Plain Dealer* reporter is the best epitaph for a disaster that never should have happened. When asked what it was like that terrible night, he simply said, "They died crawling in the slime."

Chapter 4

SHE GOT HER MONEY'S WORTH

Eva Kaber, Lakewood's 1919 Lady Borgia

"Happy families are all alike," runs Tolstoy's best one-liner. "Each unhappy family is unhappy in its own peculiar way." And if you don't believe it, consider the Kaber family.

The time was July 15, 1919. The place was the Dan Kaber house, a posh, neo-Colonial showplace on fashionable Lake Avenue, several blocks west of the city of Cleveland. And the persons were the sharply disparate members of the Dan Kaber family—each desperately and uniquely unhappy.

Dan Kaber, certainly, had the most objective reasons for being unhappy. Forty-six years old and formerly a healthy, active well-to-do printer, Dan had within the past six months become a helpless, bedridden, pain-wracked invalid. Confined most of the time to his second-floor bedroom, Dan had lost the use of all his limbs, with the pitiful exception of the index and middle finger of his left hand. His decline had begun with an apparent influenza attack during the previous November, but despite lengthy hospital stays and futile surgery for suspected cancer of the stomach and appendicitis, Dan had steadily deteriorated. His doctors muttered vaguely about "rheumatism," then "cancer" and "neuritis" but it was plain they did not have a clue as to Dan Kaber's malady. Dan Kaber was increasingly feeble, querulous, and seemingly fearful; he was apparently most fearful of his wife, Eva Kaber. Ever attentive, she insisted on personally feeding him—and quite often the soups, strawberries, and chocolates she proffered made him violently sick. Dan tried to complain to anyone who would listen that there seemed to be an awful lot of paprika in his food of late . . . . but whenever he tried to tell his brother or father about his suspicions Eva would appear in the room.

Eva Kaber wasn't very happy in July of 1919. Thirty-nine years old, she had struggled and schemed her way up from nothing to status as a respected Lakewood matron and the spouse of a wealthy printer's son. Born mere Catherine Brickel to parents of modest origin, she was a trial and trouble to everyone in her life from an early age. Indeed, at the age of seven "Kitty" Brickel already had a reputation as a demonic child, subject to apparently unprovoked rages in which she would assault her playmates, kicking, screaming, and sometimes even tearing both their hair and her own. A chronic juvenile runaway and thief, frequently expelled from school, she spent part of her adolescence at the Home of the Good Shepherd, her sole alternative at age 16 to a prison term for stealing $85 from an acquaintance. After working as a chambermaid at a posh East Side mansion—where she acquired a taste for expensive things—Eva was married at 17 to a barkeep, Thomas McArdle. The marriage lasted two months, and Eva subsequently disappeared—after dumping the fruit of her brief nuptials, her daughter Marion, on her long-suffering parents. Before Dan, Eva was married again, briefly, to a barber named David Frinkle—but it is probable that Dan Kaber knew little about his wife's previous marriages. What Dan Kaber did know was that Eva was quarrelsome, spiteful, financially demanding, and increasingly impatient with his physical deterioration. Eva was particularly upset that July because Dan was reluctant to finance another year at Smith College for her daughter, Marion McCardle. And Eva was beginning to suspect that Dan was thinking about changing his will.

Also at the Kaber home that July was Eva's mother, Mary Brickel. Sixty-seven years old, she had had a hard life; four of her eight children were already dead, and her favorite child, Charles, had frequent trouble with the law, including a short prison term for theft. Mrs. Brickel had decidedly mixed feelings toward Eva—whom she always referred to as "Mrs. Kaber"—but she nevertheless deferred to her daughter in all things. Surely not the ideal mother-in-law for poor, sick Dan Kaber.

Also there that summer of 1919 was Marion McCardle, Eva's daughter by her first marriage. Nineteen years old, Marion was mainly interested in good times, popular music, and her dream of a career as a chorus girl. And like her mother and grandmother, Marion made no secret of her hatred for her stepfather, once screaming at him during a formal dinner party: "What do you mean? I don't have to take any orders from you!" Clearly, the

House of Kaber was beginning to resemble the House of Atreus more than it did your average happy family.

* * * * *

The Kaber case remains the greatest murder story in the history of Cleveland. Its contrivance was worthy of the Borgias and its telling deserves the style of Edgar Allan Poe and the macabre humor of William Roughead, the greatest true-crime writer of all time. It remains the only homicide in the history of the world in which a grandmother, mother, and granddaughter were indicted for the same first-degree murder. Let us set the scene for this most satisfying slaughter.

Sometime in mid-July 1919, Eva Kaber told her family that she was going away to visit her sister, Mrs. H. J. McGinnis, at Cedar Point. On the afternoon of Wednesday, July 16, she drove away, accompanied by her four-year-old adopted daughter, Patricia. Forty-eight hours went by.

On the evening of Friday, July 18, the residents of the Kaber house at 12537 Lake Avenue retired fairly early. Dan Kaber dozed fitfully in his spacious northeast bedroom on the second floor. Next to his room, separated by a locked door, were the sleeping quarters of stepdaughter Marion McArdle, on this night shared by Miss Anna Baehr, Marion's neighborhood school chum, who had just returned from a picture-show with Marion. Up on the third floor slept F. W. Utterback, Kaber's sixtyish male nurse. There is no reason to doubt that everyone retired to their rooms about 10 or 10:15 p.m., with the exception of grandmother Mary Brickel, who later testified at the inquest that she carefully locked the first-floor doors and windows before retiring.

Sometime about 10:30 p.m. all hell broke loose in the Kaber household. Although Marion McArdle and Anna Baehr initially claimed that they heard nothing unusual they eventually allowed that, well, yes, they had heard some screaming. Well, yes, actually a lot of screaming. In fact, Marion finally said, "There was not one call for help but many screams. It will be a long time before we forget those screams!"

The screams that Marion and Anna heard were probably exactly what Kaber's male nurse heard as he was abruptly aroused from a sound sleep: "Utterback! Utterback! Murder! Come quick!"

Come quick Utterback did. Running down the stairs in his bare

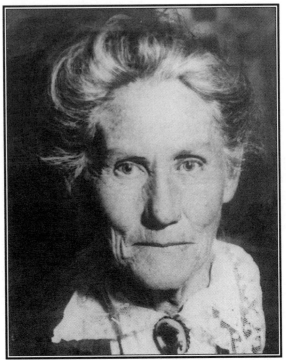

Cleveland Press Collection, Cleveland State University.
The Grandmother: Mary Brickel.

feet and union suit to Kaber's second-floor bedroom, he burst
through the open door to discover a ghastly scene. There was a
bloody knife on the floor and Dan Kaber was lying there in a pool
of his own blood. Kaber was conscious and when Utterback asked
him what had happened, he replied, "A man with a cap. Look for a
man with a finger almost bitten off; I bit his finger. I think there
were two of them. My wife had this done!"

Pandemonium ensued. Marion, Miss Baehr, and grandmother
Brickel appeared soon in the second-floor hallway and contributed
loud hysterics. Doctors were summoned, the police arrived, and
Dan Kaber was rushed to Lakewood Hospital, where doctors
labored to save his life. It could not have been an easy task. He had
been stabbed 24 times: five abdominal wounds on the left side of
the navel, three wounds on the left buttock, three wounds on the
right buttock and—the unkindest cuts of all—11 stab wounds to

the scrotum. Not to mention numerous scratches on the face and throat, clearly indicating that someone had held the invalid down while another wielded a very cruel knife.

Dan Kaber died hard, shortly after 1 p.m. the following day. To his last breath he repeated only that his slayer had been "a man with a cap" and that his "wife had this done."

Meanwhile, where was the dead man's wife? Well, Eva returned to her home at 5:30 p.m. the following day. She expressed appropriate surprise, especially when she found silverware strewn on her dining room floor, the apparent residue of an interrupted burglary. "Robbers have taken my silver!" is probably the most accurate estimate of what she said on this occasion. She quickly posted a reward for her husband's killers, arranged for Dan's funeral, and filed his will for probate.

Eva Kaber was always good at short-term goals, and in the short term, all she had to do was get through the inquest, which was opened by Cuyahoga County Coroner P. J. Byrne on July 23 at 10 a.m. Which she did, in stubborn, crude, typically brazen form. Repeatedly accused of lying by County Prosecutor Samuel Doerfler, Eva responded with a combination of calm denial and strategic outbursts of feminine tears. Suggestions that her relations with Dan had been less than amicable were stoutly denied and, after all, no one could prove that Eva had been anywhere near the murder scene on the fatal night. So Eva simply "wavered and wept" until the prosecutor gave up, and it was clear even before the end of the inquest that the verdict was going to be "willful murder by unknown." That verdict was duly delivered, despite the fact that a second autopsy disclosed up to *40 grains* of arsenic in Dan's emaciated and perforated corpse. Despite heroic efforts, the source of the arsenic could not be traced, nor could it be proven just how or by whom it had been administered to Dan Kaber. And it could have been worse: one of the initial theories given attention by the police was that Dan Kaber had *committed suicide.*

And that, seemingly, was the end of it, despite the suspicions of the police. Eva Kaber cashed in her husband's insurance policies, sold the big Lake Avenue residence, and left town. It appeared at the time that she would have the last word on the subject, which was: "I can't imagine who could be guilty of such a deed. I never heard that my husband had enemies."

No one except Eva was completely satisfied with the inquest

verdict, but the police and other interested parties now dropped the case for lack of evidence. Well, almost all the interested parties. One who didn't was Moses Kaber, Dan's 71-year-old father. He swore a mighty oath in July 1919 that he would spend the rest of his life and all of his considerable fortune to bring his son's murderers to justice.

There had been bad blood between the Kaber family and Eva ever since her abrupt marriage to Dan in September 1907. The Kabers were Jewish, and they apparently took a dim view of the worldly, temperamental gentile who had captivated their Dan. Nothing since the marriage had changed their stance; they knew that Eva had led Dan a dog's life and they never doubted from the beginning that it was she who had arranged his death. So while Eva left Cleveland to enjoy her newfound widow's wealth, Moses Kaber went to talk to the Pinkerton National Detective Agency.

Moses had little choice in the matter. The police had dropped the case and the Pinkertons were the best-known private investigative agency in the world. And there is no question that they gave Moses Kaber his money's worth during the two years that followed. Within weeks, an as-yet-unsuspicious Eva Kaber was eating, sleeping, and breathing undercover Pinkerton detectives wherever she went. She hired a milliner shortly after leaving Cleveland—the milliner was a Pinkerton. She hired a maid, too—also a Pinkerton. When she dined in restaurants, she unknowingly dined with Pinkertons. And when she went to the movies, Pinkertons sat right behind her.

The most important break for Moses Kaber and the Pinkertons was the recruitment of Mrs. Ethel Berman as an operative. Eva's former Lakewood friend had originally met Eva during her honeymoon with Dan in 1908, and Ethel had maintained her ties to Eva after the murder for old times' sake, although Ethel disapproved of much in Eva's character. Ethel had been particularly shocked to find Eva laughing on the day after Dan's funeral, when she dropped in to comfort the grieving widow. "To think that I laid him out in a dirty shirt," Eva cackled uproariously. "Dan wasn't worth a clean shirt!" Given her suspicions, it didn't take long for the Pinkertons to convince Mrs. Berman that she, and only she, could help them get the evidence to convict her friend of first-degree murder.

Next to Eva Kaber, Ethel Berman, unquestionably, is the most fascinating character in the whole Kaber story. A perfectly pleas-

Cleveland Press Collection, Cleveland State University.
The Daughter: Eva Kaber.

ant, respectable, handsome Lakewood matron, happily married wife and mother of an eight-year-old son, Ethel willingly left her conventional life for some months to pose as an unhappy, restless goodtime party girl to her confidante Eva Kaber. After the Pinkertons picked up Eva's trail in New York City, Ethel got in touch with her, painting herself as an aggrieved, bitter spouse of the Eva Kaber type. This was music to Eva's ears and she blandly promised to help Ethel get rid of *her* husband when called upon. Before long the two were travelling around the country, sharing hotel rooms and going to movies and restaurants together. Mrs. Berman would later claim that she did the whole thing merely for the sake of justice, but there is little doubt that it must have been a great adventure for the otherwise staid Lakewood housewife. As to the morality of betraying her former friend, Ethel characterized it this way: "It was not a pleasant thing to have to betray the confidences of one who had been my friend. But if I have helped to serve the ends of justice, I am glad."

It was soon apparent to Mrs. Berman that Eva Kaber was a very troubled individual. A woman of violent temper and increasingly paranoid—or maybe not so paranoid—that she was being tailed by detectives, she would often ask Ethel if she thought someone nearby was a "D.T.S.," Eva's term for a Pinkerton. Paradoxically, however, she could not stop talking obsessively about her late husband's death. Eventually, she became suspicious of Ethel, particularly after Ethel questioned Eva about some words Eva had cried out in her sleep one night: "I did it! I did it! I did it!" At that time Eva confronted Mrs. Berman and demanded to know if she, too, were a "D.T.S." but Ethel convincingly swore this mighty oath at Eva's behest: "I swear to God that I hope to go home and see my son blind before I am in with the Pinkerton people."

Shortly after this, Eva dropped Mrs. Berman as a travelling companion but Ethel's work was not yet done. She returned to Cleveland, where she immediately ingratiated herself in similar fashion with Mary Brickel, Eva's mother. Mrs. Berman had always felt sorry for the weak-willed Mary; she had been aware for years that Eva bullied her mother to do the Kaber laundry for free—while Eva regularly took four dollars per week from her husband to pay the "laundress." Their budding friendship soon yielded the following confidence from Mrs. Brickel, conveniently uttered to Mrs. Berman at the B. F. Keith Theatre in the presence of two movie patrons behind them—who just happened to be Pinkerton detectives. "She did it and she did it for money," said Mrs. Brickel, going on to say, "If they try to put it on Charlie [Eva's brother], I'll tell all I know!"

It was now the spring of 1921. Eva had by now largely exhausted her inheritance and was running a failing millinery shop in New York City. Her daughter Marion was travelling around the United States as a member of the chorus line in "Pretty Baby." And the Pinkertons knew, from information provided by Mrs. Berman and others, that Eva Kaber spent much of her money and a lot of her time with very strange people: fortune-tellers, clairvoyants, spirit-mediums, and petty criminals. They began to shadow these persons, too, sensing that they might have some connection to the two-year-old murder. Finally, Moses Kaber met with County Prosecutor Edward Stanton and Lakewood Police and they set a trap for the end of May 1921.

It sprang perfectly on Eva's mother, Mary Brickel. Called without warning on Sunday afternoon, May 31, to the Lakewood Police

Station with her son Charles, Mary was sent to sit in a room with an open door. Minutes later, she heard Prosecutor Stanton shout at Charles, "Lock this man up and charge him with the murder of Dan Kaber! He's the one who did it!" A split-second later, she heard the clang of a jail cell door.

The trick worked like magic on the 69-year-old grandmother. Within minutes Mary was singing like a canary, just as she had threatened she would "if they try to put it on Charlie." On June 1, 1919, Assistant County Prosecutor John T. Cassidy announced first degree murder indictments against Eva Kaber, Mary Brickel, and Marion McArdle.

Eva tried to flee prosecution but was eventually arrested at the apartment of a New York City friend on the night of Saturday, June 4. Two days later, Marion was picked up and both were arraigned. Both stayed in character; while being led off to the Tombs, Marion whimpered to detectives: "For God's sake, don't make me testify against my mother!" Eva, never at a loss for insouciant denial, said: "Really, if the situation were not so serious it would be laughable! I have nothing to fear." Her bravado was followed within hours by two suicide attempts in her cell.

Waiving extradition, Eva and Marion were brought back to Cleveland in mid-June. William J. Corrigan, a brilliant young defense attorney, was appointed by the court to assist Francis Poulson in Eva's defense and her trial date was set for June 28.

From beginning to end, the arrest, arraignment, and trial of Eva Kaber provided the greatest carnival of publicity and sensationalism Cleveland had ever endured or enjoyed. The Kaber case was front-page news in all three Cleveland daily newspapers from June 1 until late July and no fact, rumor, or speculation was left unpublished. One of the magistrates even allowed a female *Press* reporter, Lewette B. Pollock, to spend a night in jail with Mrs. Kaber and Marion as a feigned prisoner. Hardly a day went by without damning headlines about Mrs. Kaber, and the flavor of unequivocal editorial condemnation was perfectly epitomized by a small headline from the *News-Leader* during the last week of the trial: *"Laughing Time is Over, Paying Time Comes Now!"*

Meanwhile, the police were busy hauling in suspects from the vast subculture of mediums, fortune tellers, and outright criminals Eva Kaber had cultivated in her salad days. Within days, Cleveland police arrested several women suspects, most significantly a Mrs.

Cleveland Press Collection, Cleveland State University.
The Father-in-law: Moses Kaber.

Erminia Colavito, a midwife/fortune-teller/potion vendor, who was apprehended by a flying squad of police sent to Sandusky, Ohio. In mid-June Salvatore Cala, one of the alleged Kaber killers, was picked up by Cleveland detectives at his uncle's farm in New York state. By the beginning of the trial on June 28, the county prosecutor had all the threads of the story in his hands—and what a story it was.

It went something like this, allowing for all the numberless and conflicting lies that the participants in the crime told and retold. Eva Kaber had always been a superstitious soul and from a tender age had consulted fortune-tellers, mediums, and the like. When she was 17, one medium told her something she never forgot through all her years of scheming, mayhem, and treachery: *"You'll always get what you want!"* (Eva apparently was unaware of the medium's handwritten notes, which included these added insights: *"Bold and confident, but not very smart."*) During the decade of her marriage to Dan Kaber, Eva continued to frequent practitioners of the black arts, often spending large sums of money on fortune-telling and lucky charms.

Sometime in the spring of 1918, Eva went to a Mrs. Mary Wade, a medium living on East 82nd Street. Eva painted herself as an unhappy wife and asked Mrs. Wade's spiritual intercession to persuade her first ex-husband, Thomas McArdle, to pay for daughter Marion's tuition at Smith College. Mrs. Wade agreed to do this, but astutely suggested that Mrs. Kaber also make the request directly to McArdle in a letter. One can imagine Eva's jubilation when a handsome check from McArdle forthwith arrived, due no doubt to Mrs. Wade's supernatural intervention. But Eva had a bigger challenge for Mrs. Wade. She now asked the medium to use her powers to kill her husband.

Mrs. Wade, or so she later testified, immediately and piously refused her client's request, righteously telling Eva that her powers could not be used for evil purposes. But Eva Kaber was not one to give up easily. She soon got in touch with a rather hard fellow from Little Italy, Urbano Di Corpo. Like most of her acquaintances, Eva met him through a medium, a certain Mrs. Sauers who lived on East 89th Street. Sometime in late 1918, just before Dan took sick, Eva saw Di Corpo while waiting in line for tickets at the Stillman Theater on Euclid Avenue. Drawing him aside, she pointed out her husband and offered Di Corpo $5,000 to run Dan over with an automobile. Why this plot wasn't pursued is unknown, but around that same time Eva deliberately set the Kaber home on fire with gasoline, although she would later attempt to blame the arson on her pliable mother. Eva also began supplementing Dan's food with match heads and other unwholesome substances.

It was Di Corpo who introduced Eva to Erminia Colavito, mother of five, midwife, neighborhood abortionist, and general all-around hand at the black arts. In good time, Eva journeyed to Mrs. C.'s Mayfield Road home, spoke feelingly to the spiritual practitioner of Dan's supposed "objectionable practices" and begged for a "potion" to set him straight. Potions were soon forthcoming and Dan Kaber began to suffer the mysterious decline that would climax with his violent death in July 1919. Mrs. Colavito would later claim that her potion was composed only of olive oil and ginger ale. It is worth noting that another of her potions—composed mainly of chloral hydrate—sold about the same time to a man named Pasquale Julian to cure his brother John, put the latter in the State Hospital for the Insane in Newburg.

Sometime in late June or early July 1919, Eva became impatient with the progress of Mrs. C's fluids. So Eva decided to have Dan murdered more quickly and went to the accommodating Mrs. Colavito with her problem: "Oh that devil I could kill him! I am looking for someone to kill him! I would pay anything to have him killed!" Mrs. Colativo liked this kind of talk and soon recruited Salvatore Cala and Vittorio Pisselli, young toughs from Little Italy who could neither read nor write. Mrs. Kaber got right to the point with them: "I want my husband killed. I have tried but not succeeded." By mid-July Eva had struck a bargain with them, an arrangement, Cala later recalled, that made Eva just "tickled pink." While she was safely away at Cedar Point, they would enter the house at night—admitted by Mrs. Brickel—and stab Dan Kaber in his bed. Cala was given a penciled map of the house and he and Pisselli were promised that the house would be prepared so that the caper would look like a burglary gone awry. Cala and Pisselli were also promised somewhere between $3,000 and $5,000 for their night's work. And about July 10, Eva took her mother Mary aside and said, "I want you to do some dirty work for me . . . I'm going to have Dan killed."

On July 16, Eva drove away to Cedar Point to establish her alibi. The night before, while Marion generously played the piano on the first floor to mask any noise (her performance included "I'm Always Chasing Rainbows," "Dardanella," and "Hindustan"), Eva brought the two hired killers into the house for a dry run. Marion had already jimmied the dining room bureau at Eva's command, and Eva had shrewdly taken the "stolen" silver to the house of one of her many medium friends. All was in readiness for the murder on Thursday night.

Thursday night came and went. Mary Brickel, who was supposed to be on the porch in her rocking chair after dark to let the killers in, got cold feet and kept to her room. The next morning, the killers contacted Marion and told her if Mary didn't cooperate they would kill her, too. Or as Cala poetically put it: "Tell the old lady we'll blow her brains out!"

The actual killing went off quite smoothly. Marion reportedly gave the signal to the murderers, either by emptying a pitcher of

Cleveland Press Collection, Cleveland State University.

Kaber house on Lake Avenue.

water out the window or flushing the toilet adjacent to her bed-room. Entering through a door left conveniently unlocked by Mary Brickel, the killers stealthily made their way up the stairs and into Dan Kaber's bedroom. There, in the dark, Cala held down the par-alyzed invalid while Pisselli, wearing heavy canvas gloves, stabbed him 24 times. Cala later testified that the helpless cripple cried out, "Mercy! Mercy! What have I done to you?!" Cala, for his pains, got badly bitten on the thumb by the gutsy invalid, and Pisselli appar-ently dropped both his gloves and an unused razor on the way out. Minutes later they boarded an eastbound streetcar and took it to safety and the East Side.

Even before they were caught, the aftermath of the killing was not a happy time for any of the plotters involved. Eva was haunted by the murder, and rightly fearful that her accomplices would either implicate or blackmail her. The only payment anyone ever received for the murder was a $500 bill, some of the "stolen silver" and Dan's Masonic ring, taken from his finger by Eva in the days before his death. The $500 bill and the ring were forwarded to Mrs. Colavito through yet another medium friend of Eva's, Maria Matthews, who insisted on keeping the silver as her own commission in the affair. The rest of the promised $3,000 or $5,000 was never forthcoming, despite threats by Cala and Pisselli to murder everyone connected with the plot if they were not paid.

Eva's trial, a carnival of sensationalism, opened on June 28. The proceedings, held in the old County Courthouse, were packed to suffocation, with rubberneckers fighting for spaces at office windows in adjacent buildings. Most of the spectators in and out of the Courthouse, it is recorded, were female. By this time, both Cala and Colavito had turned state's evidence, and both Marion and Mrs. Brickel had signed confessions implicating Eva for the murder. It was going to be almost impossible to get her off—and yet the actual trial proved to be both a well-matched legal competition and an exciting juridical struggle that made legal history.

Much of the excitement was due to the forensic talents of William J. Corrigan, Eva's court-appointed lawyer. Then a young man, Corrigan was at the beginning of a career that would make him Cleveland's premier defense attorney. (His best-known case would come near the end of his long career, when he acted as the defense attorney at Sam Sheppard's infamous first trial).

Corrigan knew that Eva was guilty, and, worse than that, that she had already confessed to most of the facts of the conspiracy murder plot against her husband. Corrigan therefore concentrated on two procedural aspects of the case in a desperate effort to save his client from the electric chair. His first concern was to keep women off the jury. Sexist or not, he—and virtually everyone involved in the trial—believed that women were inclined to be more merciless in judging a member of their own sex, being less inclined to sentimentality than men when sending females to the hot seat. Although his legal arguments in this regard were overruled, Corrigan managed to keep women off the jury with peremptory challenges.

Corrigan's other, more important, and ultimately successful fight was to persuade the jury that Eva Kaber was insane. The state was demanding that she die in the electric chair, but Corrigan hoped to get her off with either a plea of temporary insanity or simply insanity from birth.

Ultimately, he chose the total insanity plea, and his witnesses provided much support. The state paraded a succession of "alienists" (as psychiatrists were then termed) who solemnly testified that Eva Kaber was sane. The defense responded with several alienists who said she wasn't. But far more convincing, doubtless, was the testimony of Eva's brother, father, and sister, who re-counted many family anecdotes illustrating Eva's crazed behavior from an early age.

Eva herself eventually give dramatic support to the insanity argument. Although she managed to remain hidden behind a hand-kerchief, mute and pale during the early part of the trial, she became progressively and visibly upset as her father, brother, and sister appeared as witnesses to testify to her lifelong dementia. The climax came on Wednesday, July 13, the day her brother Charlie angrily denied Eva's assertion that Mrs. Brickel had been the one who had set the Kaber house on fire in October 1918. Charlie got to his feet, shouting, "That's a lie! I can prove it! She was sick at the time!" Eva went into a fit, screaming, flailing, foaming, and finally collapsing into a moaning heap. She was removed from the court and did not return until the next day. Prosecutor Stanton argued in his summation that her behavior then and afterwards was feigned to support her insanity defense but one suspects the jury believed otherwise. The best comment made about Mrs. Kaber's breakdown was to Marjorie Wilson, a *News* feature writer who covered the trial and later married William J. Corrigan, whom she met for the first time there. A fellow spectator remarked to Wilson as she walked from the courtroom that day, "If that is acting, what an Ophelia she would make!"

Hard-core sensation-mongers may have been disappointed by the Kaber trial. Some expectations raised by pretrial revelations and hints were not fulfilled. Despite a *frisson* of curiosity about what "objectionable practices" Dan Kaber had allegedly practiced to drive his wife to murder, the defense never produced any evi-dence that he mistreated her; no one seems to have believed—or perhaps cared—about Marion McArdle's assertion that Dan Kaber had once hit her mother. To the great disappointment of press and public, Eva herself never took the stand.

On July 15, 1921 the prosecution rested and the jury went into seclusion in the early evening. Early the next morning they returned a verdict of "Guilty of Murder in the First Degree—With a Recommendation of Mercy." Their verdict made Eva the first woman in Cuyahoga County ever convicted of first degree murder, but the "mercy" part meant that she would be facing life in prison rather than death in the electric chair. The reading of the verdict was delayed for two hours, as Eva had suffered yet another fit on

Cleveland Press Collection, Cleveland State University.

being told by her attorneys that the jury had reached a verdict. When she was carried limp into the courtroom by two deputies, the grinding of her teeth was distinctly audible and there was blood on her lips. There, at two minutes past 11 a.m., Eva Kaber was sentenced to the Marysville Reformatory for life and the jury was dismissed. The verdict came just two days shy of the second anniversary of Dan Kaber's murder.

Eva's remaining years were not happy ones. "I'll be out in a year. I'll be free. Eighteen months at the least!" she bragged to reporters as she departed for Marysville Reformatory. Once incarcerated there, she was shocked to discover that she would have to give up her silk stockings and tailored suits for the regular drab prison garb. She eventually settled down to prison routine, working quietly in the prison sewing room. Alas, this proved to be yet another stratagem, and her job was replaced with solitary confinement on a diet of bread and water when prison officials intercepted a letter from Eva to her daughter Marion. It seems Eva had been offered $50,000 for the film rights to her life story, and she schemed to use the money to engineer an escape. Some of the money was to be used to bribe the prison authorities but Eva was willing to have head matron Louise Mittendorf and her husband murdered if they proved resistant to bribery.

Eva's health began to fail in the late 1920s. A long-needed goiter operation helped some, but Eva refused treatment for a subsequent gastric tumor diagnosed in 1927, telling the doctors, "You want to kill me!" This may have been part of a deliberate strategy to win a parole for medical reasons but it spelled slow, sure doom for Eva. After 1929 her health declined alarmingly, and she was bedridden for the last few months of her life. The end came on April 12, 1931, just as the governor of Ohio was about to act on her latest parole request. Causes of death listed included lung complications, heart disease, and the stomach tumor, which was reported to weigh a whopping 150 pounds. She was 50 years old.

And what of the others involved in Eva Kaber's satanic plot? Well, Marion McArdle was found innocent in a subsequent trial, a verdict seemingly incomprehensible to anyone having knowledge of her complicity in her stepfather's murder before, during, and after the fact. Marion's immediate response to the verdict was to go clothes shopping. She was married a year later from her aunt's home in Lakewood and it would be churlish to pursue her personal history further, except to note that she was with her mother when she died and arranged for Eva's cremation in Portsmouth, Ohio. Grandmother Mary Brickel's indictment was quashed, due to her age and her cooperation with the prosecution. Salvatore Cala received a life term, as did Vittorio Pisselli in Italy, where he was pursued and brought to justice by yet more detectives hired with Moses Kaber's money. Mrs. Colavito, improbably, was acquitted at her own trial, despite evidence introduced that her "potions" had been effective in ridding a number of woman clients of their husbands. In 1926 she was finally convicted and sentenced to prison for her part in a 1920 poisoning of an unwanted husband named Marino Costanzo. She died in Marysville 46 years later in 1972 at the age of 86. Ethel Berman was last heard of in September 1921, when she went into hiding due to death threats stemming from her Kaber testimony.

Why did Eva Kaber murder her husband? We may never really know. Whether she was a Lady Macbeth from the Cleveland slums from the start or an American Madame Bovary with a glandular disorder remains an intriguing, unanswerable question. In the end, however, you can at least say this, recalling the fate of Cala and Pisselli: Eva Kaber got her money's worth.

Chapter 5

STREETS
OF HELL

The 1944
East Ohio Gas Company
Explosion and Fire

It happens very suddenly, as you drive north through the neighborhood straddling St. Clair Avenue near East 55th Street on Cleveland's northeast side. Where residential housing still persists in the upper 50s, there are mostly modest frame dwellings of turn-of-the-century vintage—small houses on postage-stamp lots, so crammed together as to give passersby claustrophobia just looking between them. Unless you know the dire history of this place, however, you aren't prepared for the abrupt architectural change that begins north of St. Clair on East 63rd Street and persists westward to East 55th. Little by little, and then suddenly, the frame houses disappear and in their stead one finds modest, brick dwellings of a post–World War II character. And the closer you get to the property of the East Ohio Gas Company, the more modern brick homes you find—until residential housing ceases completely at the peaceful green border of Grdina Park, today the southern perimeter of the once-enormous gas company grounds. There's a reason for that park, and there's a reason for that eruption of modern, brick homes. For this is the Norwood-St. Clair neighborhood, once and still the heart of Cleveland's Slovene community and the site of Cleveland's worst industrial disaster: The East Ohio Gas Company Explosion and Fire of 1944.

How bad was it? Well, in terms of the bald body count, it wasn't the worst Cleveland area disaster: at 130 known dead it barely surpassed the Cleveland Clinic Fire of 1929—by a mere five corpses—and fell more than 40 short of the 1908 Collinwood School Fire death toll. But for sheer horror, its effect on a large community, and the physical destruction involved it would be hard to beat. Of its 130 dead, 61 were so badly burned or pulverized that identification, sometimes even as to the sex of the corpse, proved impossible. Seventy-three of the dead were employees of East Ohio Gas. The disaster injured 225 persons badly enough to require hospital treatment, 23 of them Cleveland firemen. It totally destroyed 79 houses, 2 factories, 217 automobiles, 7 trailers, and 1 tractor, and partially destroyed another 35 houses and 13 factories. It did extensive damage not only to the Gas Company #2 works but also to property or facilities owned by Bell Telephone, the Cleveland Transit System, the New York Central Railroad, the Pennsylvania Railroad, and Western Union. The total damage amounted to between $6 million and $8 million. Not to mention the cost of repairing the surrounding streets and sewer systems, largely smithereened into a splintered landscape of cavernous craters, and the promiscuous wreckage of subsidiary gas explosions.

Dollars, of course, don't tell the real story. The explosion and fire that turned most of East 61st, 62nd, 63rd, Lake Court, and Carry Avenue into neighborhood holocausts burnt out the heart of a deeply rooted, cohesive, supportive, ethnic community. That community would proudly recover and rebuild—but no one involved could ever pretend that things would be the same.

Again, how bad was it? It was the force of 130 billion British Thermal Units (BTUs) unleashed within 30 minutes on a mere 160-acre area, much of it congested residential housing. It was 25 millions of horsepower suddenly vented to destroy hundreds of homes, families, and lives. It was searing, scorching flames, reaching heights of 2,800 feet and 3,000 degrees Fahrenheit in streets where children played and retirees sat on their front porches of a sunny October afternoon. It comprised the destructive force contained in 10,000 tons of coal or, say, the energy of 120 minutes' worth of all the hydroelectric power west of the Mississippi devoted to the cause of blowing up and burning down the Norwood-St. Clair community.

After it was over, everyone agreed—*surprise!*—that it *never* should have happened. East Ohio Gas Company officials argued, quite correctly, that the explosion should not have occurred, given the laws of probability and the precautions taken to prevent it. City and neighborhood leaders excoriated both the gas company and city fathers for allowing such a lethal facility to be built so near a residential neighborhood. The fact of the matter is that the East Ohio Gas Company fire came, like Carl Sandburg's fog, on little cat feet. Decisions, both residential and industrial, unwittingly taken over decades of development, quietly and steadily made it almost inevitable that the East Ohio tragedy would happen just the way it did. All it took was a dangerous facility located close to a fragile, congested neighborhood. The East Ohio Gas Company #2 plant, located cheek-by-jowl to the Slovenian neighborhood of the East 60s, provided just such a site . . . and the exigencies of World-War-II energy production and distribution ensured that the disaster would occur in a certain way in that very particular place at that precise time.

The East Ohio Gas Company works located north of St. Clair and east of East 55th (formerly Willson Avenue) was one of the oldest industrial sites in Cleveland. Developed originally by the Cleveland Gas Light & Coke Company in the mid-19th Century, the gas works became a part of the extensive East Ohio Gas Company properties shortly after the turn of the century. Known eventually as the #2 works, the 10-acre gas company grounds east of East 55th and north of St. Clair became a major nexus for the storage and distribution of natural gas to East Ohio's many thousands of customers throughout Ohio. Meanwhile, just to the south of the #2 works, a vigorous ethnic neighborhood was developing simultaneously, and with little coordination to its industrial northern neighbor. Most of the housing stock was built between 1895 and 1905, predominately modest, working-class houses on very narrow, short lots, many of them two- or even four-family homes. This predominately Slovenian community stretched along the axis of St. Clair Avenue from the East 30s well into the East 70s, with the emotional focus of the community centering on St. Vitus Church, a Catholic nationality parish created in 1893.

It was only in the 1940s that the character of the #2 works changed in a manner threatening to the actual existence of the neighborhood. Owing to fluctuations in the rate of supply and limited storage capacity, East Ohio Gas was having trouble meeting the needs of its customers, especially during times of peak demand, such as prolonged winter cold spells. Supply problems were further aggravated by the war, and gas service to East Ohio customers had to be curtailed a number of times in the early 1940s. Something had to be done, and the solution chosen was a gas liquefication-regasification facility. And it was to be located at the heart of the utility's service area, the center of Cleveland's East Side.

The technology of natural gas liquefication had been under development for a half century, with most of the technical advances made by German chemists. The scientific concept was simple and its practical advantages were obvious: transformation of natural gas to a liquid state at minus 260 degrees degrees Fahrenheit involves a volume reduction ratio of 640:1. To be able to store 640 times as much natural gas as could be stored in its gaseous state, for regasification and use at peak demand times, was an irresistible option for East Ohio Gas, and they exercised it by constructing three liquid storage units of spherical design.

Built at a cost of $1.5 million, the three tanks were completed in January 1941. Their total capacity was 150,000,000 cubic feet. An adjoining regasification plant could convert the liquid back to gas at a rate of 3,000,000 cubic feet per hour. Storage commenced on February 7, 1942, and the plant quickly proved its commercial worth. But there were still shortages as wartime production demands increased, so East Ohio Gas Company received permission from the War Production Board on August 3, 1942 to build a fourth tank of 100,000,000 cubic feet capacity, double the size of its existing #1, #2, and #3 tanks.

There were some critical differences in the design of the fourth tank. Unlike the first three tanks, it was of cylindrical design. The first three tanks, in fact, were designed as spheres-within-spheres, the inner gas-holding sphere being insulated from its outer containing sphere by cork, with the entire 57-foot-high structure supported and suspended by steel supports. The fourth tank was a cylinder-within-a-cylinder (technically called a toro-segmental two-cylinder) and its inner insulation between the cylinders was composed of rock wool. The contrasting designs reflected, mainly, wartime economies. Despite its higher capacity, the #4 cylinder tank used 100 fewer tons of steel than a comparable spherical design, in part because it required fewer steel supports. Since cork was a critical war materiel, rock wool was chosen as the substitute insulation. As was the case with the other tanks, the inner gas-holding shell of the 50-foot-high #4 was constructed using a three-and-a-half-percent nickel-steel alloy to construct .

Designed and built by the Pittsburgh-Des Moines Steel Company, the #4 tank went into service in March 1943. But not for long.

Melted coins and keys from unidentified victims of the East Ohio Gas Company Fire.

While being filled for the first time, the bottom of the inner steel shell cracked because of uneven cooling, and it had to be rebuilt. It was soon back in service, although it seems that the cooling problem was not corrected. Neighborhood air-raid wardens would complain periodically over the next year and a half that there was frequent "frosting" on the surface of the tank, obviously caused by settling of the rock wool insulation, which allowed outside moisture to settle on relatively uninsulated spots between the inner and outer shells of the #4 tank.

Friday, October 20, 1944, arrived and waxed as a beautiful, crisp fall day in Cleveland. Things were humming at the #2 works. In anticipation of the coming winter, the L.S.&R. crew of 24 was topping off the last of the four tanks, #1, and expected to finish the job about 2 p.m. As that hour came, no one, later, remembered anything unusual. East Ohio Gas Company Assistant Chief Engineer John R. Feightner and Engineer Hugh O'Donnel were underneath the #4 tank searching for a steam hose about 2:15, and noticed nothing out of the ordinary. Mrs. Charles Flickinger, 36, of 5614

Carry Avenue, was cleaning house and was just about to plug in her sweeper. Mrs. Thomas Komor, also of Carry Avenue, was walking with her two-year-old daughter, Judy, to a grocery store on E. 61st Street. Mrs. Julia Torok, 44, of 1162 E. 58th Street, was on her way to her husband's barbershop on the south side of St. Clair at East 55th Street. And Marcella Reichard, 16, of 5473 Lake Court, was mopping the kitchen floor. Most school-age neighborhood children were in classes at Willson Elementary School on East 55th, anticipating the end of the school day and their return home in 20 minutes. The sun was shining and the wind was between 10 and 16 miles per hour. The time was 2:40 p.m.

No one will ever know with certainty just why and how the #4 cylindrical tank blew up at that moment. Most of the witnesses close to the initial disaster were killed, most of them the very East Ohio Gas Company technicians whose expertise might have most aided the ensuing investigations. But various witnesses in scattered locations later reported "heavy, white, steam-like vapors creeping and rolling" in the #4 vicinity about 2:30 p.m. Some of them thought the leak started about 10 feet off the ground and went halfway up the #4 tank. Two expert witnesses saw the blast preliminaries. H. J. Hense, of the American Gas Association Laboratories on East 55th, across the street from the liquid gas tanks, looked out the window about that time and noticed a leak in #4, with snow-white vapor or liquid gas streaming out. Seconds later he saw a second stream. John R. Feightner, the chief engineer of the L.S.& R plant, reacted immediately to what he saw. Standing in the center north door of the gas compressor building, he spied the cloud of white vapor and said, even as he began to run for his life, "My God, Number Four has let go!"

The first explosion came at about 2:41 p.m. The billowing clouds streaming out from #4 were suddenly illuminated at various points by rapid, yellowish-orange flashes. Seconds later came a tremendous blast, which shook the ground as far away as Shaker Square, and the flames of which were seen in Chagrin Falls. Almost instantaneously, a good deal of the 29-acre area including and surrounding the #2 works was on fire.

Outside the immediate blast area, waves of heat began to blow southward. Automobiles travelling on East 55th had their tires suddenly blown out from the heat radiating through the asphalt, and workers at the Warner & Swasey plant all the way down on Carnegie Avenue had to shut their windows against the intense heat. Meanwhile, young reporter George Condon was talking to the men's fashion editor on the 6th floor of the Plain Dealer building when, suddenly, over the editor's shoulder, he saw an immense pillar of flame rising on the northeastern skyline. He and his fellow reporters immediately left the building, heading east.

The first alarm was pulled at 2:41 p.m., and by the time the first Cleveland Fire Department company arrived at 2:43 many of the houses on East 61st and East 62nd were burning like torches. Fire officials and other witnesses later reported that many of the houses closest to the #4 tank at the northern end of East 61st seemed to be burning from the inside out. The reason for this soon became horrifyingly clear. Apparently in the minutes between the initial gas leak and the first explosion, a lot of liquid gas had seeped into the sewer system in the St. Clair area. Thousands of gallons of liquid fuel had already penetrated residential plumbing and drainage systems when ignition came, and shocked eyewitnesses watched as streams of flame raced up and down the neighborhood streets from catch basin to catch basin.

Aside from the force of the initial explosion, two factors increased the intensity of the initial inferno. One was the nature of the gas itself. As it was transformed back into its gaseous state by contact with the air, it became flammable, not to mention expanding to 640 times its liquid volume. Its presence in the sewer system and area house basements guaranteed that each home became an expanding holocaust as soon as ignited. The other factor was the unforeseen agency of the rock wool insulation, blown into countless liquid-gas-soaked fragments by the initial blast. Many of the rock wool pieces became flaming incendiaries that soon ignited numberless subsidiary fires.

Those who survived the first few minutes of the explosion and fires had terrible, touching stories to tell. One of them was Mrs. Berta Ott of 5472 Lake Court. As she later recalled:

> "Out of my window I see everything all red right after I hear the big noise. When I open the door the grass was burning in the yard already. So hot was it I didn't know whether to open the door or not. All the children but Geraldine were at school. We ran out . . . We run through the field. All was burning. My back was so hot I thought I was myself on fire already. I took so good care of everything. My dog Tootsie—she was to have puppies—my three cats, my chicken all gone. My poor Tootsie."

Cleveland Press collection, Cleveland State University.
**Distraught relatives, Willson School, October 20, 1944. Mrs.
Janice Komar, Judy Komar and Mrs. Charles Flickinger.**

Another woman with memories of instant hell was Mrs. Charles
Flickinger of Carry Ave, the housewife who had just been about to
plug in her carpet sweeper at 2:40 p.m.:

> "Suddenly it seemed like the walls turned red. I looked at the
> windows and the shades were on fire. Just like that. The house
> filled up with smoke. I think the furnace had blown up. Then I
> go out and see the fire all around."

There were many heroes and heroines in the first few minutes
after the #4 explosion. One was Jack Bogarty of 6357 St. Clair,
who had no idea what was going on when the doors of his house
suddenly blew in:

> "I thought we had visitors. A second later we heard the explo-
> sion. A hot wave of air filled the house. I grabbed little Georgene
> off the couch and ran outside."

Bogarty's experience was typical of the dozens of residents who conquered their initial fear of a world on fire to concentrate on helping others get to safety. Perhaps the most celebrated of this breed was Marcella Reichard, 16, of Lake Court. When the first blast knocked the mop out of her hand, she ran outside and saw that not only was the grass on fire but even the pavement, too. Marcella knew what to do, though:

> "I grabbed my mother and my little sister and we knelt and prayed. Mother went out the back way, and I told her she would be running right into the flame. I told them to hold their hands over their eyes and run toward the lake. Then we just ran."

Marcella also tried to save an elderly next-door neighbor without success, not to mention a cache of letters from her soldier boyfriend overseas. She ended up badly burned all over her face and left arm, but she managed to save her family. She was also responsible for, perhaps, the most eloquently homely description of the disaster, "The whole kitchen looked as if the sun were setting right in the room."

The local residents weren't the only people with horrific stories to tell. Seventy-three of the 130 people who died that afternoon worked for the East Ohio Gas Company, and the surviving utility employees and those at neighboring businesses had terrible memories of what they saw as they fled the spreading holocaust. Within seconds of the #4 blast, virtually *everything* in the area was on fire: buildings, vehicles, utility wires, asphalt streets, grass, sewers, and a large number of human beings and animals. (In addition to dogs and cats, many area residents raised chickens; only the area cats had a high survival rate). Or as Mrs. Frank Mervar, of Mervar Cleaners at 5372 St. Clair, put it:

> "Everywhere you looked, every little leaf, every twig branch, the telephone wires, everything was a mass of flames. I was sure we were being bombed."

A very lucky East Ohio employee was engineer John Feightner. He had already started running when the first blast knocked him off his feet, but he got up and managed to make it into the #9 Water Seal Holder, which was a water-well area within a nearby gas drainage container. Seconds later, Feightner saw fellow employee Dale Keller running by, enveloped in flames. He managed to get his attention, and Keller jumped into the well with him, extinguishing his flames. Meanwhile, another employee ran by in flames, but Feightner and Keller were unable to get him into the well. They watched until he stopped running, fell down, and burned to death. After some minutes in the well, Keller and Feightner got out and started running north toward Lake Erie. They had just gotten to the New York Central railroad tracks when the #3 tank exploded.

It isn't surprising that #3 blew up at 3 p.m., about 20 minutes after the first blast. Given the force of the #4 blast and the temperatures of up to 3,000 degrees Fahrenheit, it is surprising only that it took 20 minutes to melt the steel supports of #3 enough for it to collapse and detonate. More surprising still, however, was the fact that the #1 and #2 tanks *did not* blow up, despite their proximity to the two exploding tanks and the intense heat. For hours, virtually helpless firefighters watched and waited for #1 and #2 to blow . . . but it never happened.

Only the pen of a Dante could do justice to the sights and sounds that occurred in the St. Clair-Norwood neighborhood that hellish afternoon. Many of the human casualties were later found where they had died on the streets and in the houses adjacent to the #2 works. In the years to come there would be legends of completely cremated bodies found in the metal lockers of the East Ohio Gas Company Meter building, where terrified humans had locked themselves in to escape the heat—but such stories are apparently apocryphal. Thousands of birds, mostly sparrows, were instantly melted out of the sky and off telephone wires, as flames arced thousands of feet high, releasing temperatures usually not encountered outside a blast furnace. Meanwhile, the streets—East 55th, East 61st, East 62nd, East 63rd, St. Clair Avenue, Carry Avenue, and Lake Court—were littered with the pyres of burning human beings and the homes they had once inhabited.

As might be expected, the disaster did not bring out the best in everyone. Although initially Sea Scouts from local Coast Guard units and, eventually, the National Guard were put in place to prevent looting, not much could be done to defeat the ingenuity and ghoulish interest of many Clevelanders in the tragedy rapidly unfolding on the city's northeast side. There was a reported incident of children being trampled by a crowd of rubberneckers, who panicked when the wind suddenly shifted the flames toward them on East 55th. And there is a memorable photograph of crowds waiting for the trolley on Saturday, October 24, at Marquette and East 79th. Many of them repeatedly rode this line back and forth all day, as it afforded the best view of the otherwise sealed-off neighborhood.

The response of safety officials was rapid and well organized, but there was little they could initially do, except to rescue the rescuable and to seal off the neighborhood. Because of the release of liquid gas into the local sewer system, much of the water system was soon destroyed by a series of subsidiary explosions which continued to blow craters in the streets and pop manhole covers hundreds of feet high throughout the rest of the day. Many of the newspaper reporters who covered the catastrophe would remember the latter phenomenon best, especially their frenzied panic as exploding manhole covers chased them up and down the smoldering streets. *Cleveland Press* reporter William Dapo remembered:

"The exploding sewers for a time seemed worse than the fire itself. I was standing at Norwood Ave. and St. Clair when the blast so buckled the street a fire truck was buried in a huge crater. There was a hissing sound, then a roaring blast lifted the truck into the air. Flying bricks and glass flew all over the intersection. Too scared to run and too scared to lie down, I managed to move about three feet—to see beneath those feet another manhole cover. I took off then, but fast."

In practical terms the multiple sewer and street explosions meant that there was little water with which to fight fires that already encompassed an eight-block area. Thanks to the lakefront presence of the Coast Guard, however, a 1,500-foot hose was soon rigged up from a lake tug and water began to pour onto fires from the south side of the New York Central Railroad tracks. Meanwhile, the area from East 53rd east to Addison Road and south from Lake Erie to St. Clair was evacuated of more than 10,000 residents and sealed off.

The timing of the neighborhood quarantine was full of pathos, as it was accomplished just as neighborhood children were let out of Willson Elementary on East 55th. They arrived at the perimeter of their neighborhood to find it in flames—and probably their loved ones, too—and were sent back to Willson, where the Red Cross quickly established a disaster relief center. That night, 680 area residents slept on cots there, most still ignorant of the fate of their loved ones back in the burning inferno they had called home. Meanwhile, the County Morgue down on Lake Avenue at East 9th was besieged by a hysterical, weeping mob, desperate for news of missing relatives.

It is hard to say when the fire was brought "under control." Cleveland firemen claimed mastery about midnight (Saturday morning). Residents were allowed to return to most areas on Sunday morning, October 22nd, although some fires continued to smolder for days, and small, exploding pockets of gas continued to make life interesting for reporters and safety forces for some time after the flames had dissipated.

As in all disasters, there were some oddities that were never accounted for. Given the intensity of the blasts and the heat of the flames, a great number of homes on the streets nearest to the #2 works were completely destroyed, as even a casual drive down East 61st, East 62nd, or Carry Avenue makes manifest today. Homes many blocks away had paint blistered and stripped by the volcanic temperatures. Yet some homes relatively near the center of the disaster escaped damage almost entirely, and the same could be said for some lucky human beings, who inexplicably survived a catastrophe that killed most of their neighbors. Not to mention such freakish events as the death of Minnie Schwebs of 1011 East 61st St. Burned over her entire body, her clothes burnt off completely and her charred flesh hanging in grotesque shreds, Schwebs apparently walked from East 61st to Glenville Hospital, where she collapsed and died. Physicians could only conjecture that extreme shock kept her going long after she should have succumbed to her burns.

If forethought was lacking in the period leading up to the East Ohio Gas disaster, the aftermath certainly afforded careful hindsight and recrimination. After the flames were brought under control, some rather intrepid gas workers began to drain the liquid gas out of Tanks #1 and #2. This took several days, as there was no power available in the area and three locomotives had to be brought in on the New York Central tracks to provide power for the drainage operation. Meanwhile, Coroner Sam Gerber supervised the grisly task of searching for the many missing bodies and the accumulation and classification of evidence.

Pumper #7 in crater, Norwood & St. Clair, October 20, 1944.

It was ghastly work, somewhat hampered by poor early-November weather and the unsafe condition of many of the damaged buildings which contained the bodies of the missing. Of 130 bodies in the official tally, 61 were so badly burned or pulverized that no identification could be made. Most of them, like the 69 corpses identified, were either neighborhood residents or gas company employees. But some of them were just unlucky souls who happened to be in the wrong place at the wrong time. People like Louis Ringhoff and Joseph Meidler, roofing contractors, who just happened to be repairing the roof of a #2 works building that Friday afternoon when they were instantly incinerated. Likewise, James A. Conforti, 23, of Cornell Road, survived the blast but suffered severe burns. It seems he was putting himself through chiropody school by giving driving lessons, and he had unluckily picked the Norwood-St. Clair area for his student's lesson that Friday afternoon. Conversely, there were lucky individuals like George P. Binder. Superintendent of the liquid gas units, Binder, 45, was out in the field when the disaster struck. Virtually everyone in the office where he usually worked was killed as he watched from afar in horror.

Many of the neighborhood residents had to cope with the loss of their life savings, in addition to losing their families and homes.

Cleveland Press Collection, Cleveland State University.
Aerial view of East Ohio disaster, October 20, 1944.

Among the saddest sights of the disaster, observers remarked, were the many scenes of returned residents weeping over burnt tin boxes and cans. Like many Americans who had lived through the Depression, area residents were suspicious of banks, all the more so as a large neighborhood bank had failed during the 1930s. So when the fire came, it incinerated numerous boxes and lard tins of cash and war bonds that householders had stashed under their mattresses and in their basements. The bonds would be replaced eventually by the U. S. government but the currency was redeemable only if still largely intact. More complex financial problems were presented by the estates of victims whose wills had also been destroyed in the fire. Not to mention the difficulties of probating cash and silver found on the bodies of the dead.

East Ohio Gas Company, for its part, moved toward settlement of claims as rapidly as possible. It had good reason to do so, as hungry lawyers were already swarming like a Biblical plague on Norwood-St. Clair, hot on the heels of the vulnerable, returning residents. An office was quickly opened to process claims against the utility, and the company astutely sought to protect itself from bogus claims by conducting a thorough photographic inventory of every structure and vehicle in the affected neighborhood. This proved a prudent precaution, as in one case where a claimant came in with only a license plate, claiming all evidence of the vehicle it had belonged to had been destroyed in the fire.

By mid-November the search for the dead, conducted by 80 men with picks and shovels from the County Engineer's Department, was complete. More than half the casualties were represented only by bone fragments or body stumps. On November 14, 1944, a mass funeral and burial for the 61 unidentified dead was held in Highland Park Cemetery. There, before a crowd of 2,000, each body or body part was buried in a separate casket in an individual concrete vault. Each body received an individual grave number and the remains were carefully inventoried. Later, a simple, moving commemorative marker within a quiet garden was erected at the gravesite. All caskets, hearses, and the services of the funeral directors were donated.

And that was that, except for the rebuilding of the neighborhood—and the pleasures of the recriminations to come. Thanks to some insurance money, the eventual proceeds of almost 2,000 fire-loss claims filed against the gas company, and—above all—the efforts of the local Slovenian community itself, the neighborhood was rebuilt. The indomitable Slovenian residents would settle for nothing less. Mrs. Frances Skully, a 68-year-old widow, may well have spoken for the neighborhood as she returned to the ruins of her home at 1036 East 61st Street:

> "I'd be willing to set up a cot in my chicken coop and go back again. I couldn't think of living anywhere else. I could go through the neighborhood blindfolded. I know every step of the way. All my friends are there; where else would I want to go?"

In addition to its $3-million neighborhood settlements, the East Ohio Gas Company also paid more than a half-million dollars in settlements to the families of its injured and dead employees.

The nine separate investigations ensuing from the explosion and fire were less productive. The most ambitious probe was launched by Mayor Frank Lausche within 24 hours of the disaster. Lausche, who had grown up in the Norwood-St. Clair neighborhood, knew every inch and resident of the afflicted area, and he expected his appointed 12-man committee to produce some answers. Meanwhile, Coroner Gerber, never shy of publicity, launched his own probe, while the National Board of Fire Underwriters also sent a team to investigate.

The committees made heroic efforts to get to the bottom of the #4 blast, but the conclusions of the Lausche committee and its kindred bodies were neither very conclusive nor impressive, given the expectations placed on them. Virtually everyone agreed that the "location of the plant was poorly chosen in view of the surroundings and potential destructiveness of the stored liquid." In addition, the committees faulted the diking and drainage systems at the #2 works as inadequate. Gerber spoke for the future, if not, alas, for the past, when he concluded that no plant of the #2 type should be built in a "residential, semi-residential, business, or congested area." Apropos of this conclusion was a moment of probably unintended and undetected black humor, which came during the interrogation of a steel company official. When asked if he thought it would be a good idea to build any future L. S. & R. works so near a residential area, the official thoughtfully averred, "Well, just from a public-relations point of view, it would not be a very good idea."

None of the committees ever got to the bottom of the #4 failure.

Perhaps the one person who came out of the tragedy best was sly Sam Gerber, the perpetual county coroner of Cleveland in the mid-20th century. His rapid and assured handling of the mass autopsies and body search enhanced his already prominent political profile and *his* report astutely avoided conflict with a local utility giant by blaming . . . the Pittsburgh-Des Moines Steel Company, for overestimating the stability of its cylindrical design. Interestingly, no one ever seriously pursued the question of why area sewer lines— in contrast to standard practice—were not sealed to prevent the infiltration of gas.

East Ohio Gas Company shut down its remaining works at the #2 site soon after the disaster, and at the former site of the lethal tanks, Grdina Park stands today. The company still maintains its handsome office building on East 55th, just north and west of the fatal scene. All the residential streets were eventually reconstructed—except for that area taken up by Grdina Park, and Lake Court, where 27 houses burned to the ground. The latter street was abandoned as a residential area and today is given over completely to commercial and industrial use.

Cleveland Press Collection, Cleveland State University.
Mass grave burial service for East Ohio Gas Company fire victims at Highland Park Cemetery, November 14, 1944.

The last words, of course, belong to the victims, or at least to those with the most right to speak for them. Those words, somewhat ambiguous, are found on the plaque affixed to the monumental obelisk to the unknown dead of the explosion fire at Highland Park Cemetery:

SOCIAL PROGRESS
ATTUNED TO INDUS-
TRIAL ACHIEVEMENTS
FOR THE BENEFIT OF
THE LIVING SHALL
BE A MEMORIAL TO
THESE WHOSE LIVES
WERE UNWITTINGLY
SACRIFICED
OCT. 20, 1944

On the reverse of the monument is another plaque identifying the dead as those of the Norwood-St. Clair disaster. The East Ohio Gas Company is not even mentioned.

Chapter 6

"GOD, THE DEVIL, MAN OR BEAST"

The Incredible 1923 Saga of John Leonard Whitfield

You could call John Leonard Whitfield a cold-blooded killer. You'd be right: he murdered Patrolman Dennis Griffin in cold blood, burned his uniform, and buried his corpse under a tree. You could call him an oversexed pervert: aside from an unknown number of "wives," the middle-aged Lothario also captivated—and impregnated—a 14-year-old grammar-school girl, and made her his companion in a five-state flight from a nationwide manhunt. You could call him a self-loathing psychological mess: a mulatto of mixed parentage, he insisted for most of his life that he was white and devised a secret potion of chemicals, buttermilk, and lemon juice to lighten his skin color. And you could call him a glib and habitual liar: he never told the same story twice, often contradicted himself in every other sentence, and inveigled too many people into schemes that ruined their lives. Call him a thief: he stole sparkplugs and automobiles alike with reckless abandon and considerable skill. You could call him all these things—and you'd be right. But call him a man of cunning with nerves of steel, too. Because before his wild ride was over, John Leonard Whitfield led the police of a dozen states a merry chase and eluded capture with a brazen daring that captured the imagination of the nationwide audience that followed his escapades in sensationalistic newspapers of the day. All in all it was one wild ride, an incredible story which today reads like something out of Richard Wright by way of Chester Gould.

It started mundanely enough with missing sparkplugs. Sometime in early 1923, A. A. Probeck of the Reflex Ignition Company at West 105th and Lorain Avenue started getting reports of a glutted market for his company's product. Salesmen were reporting that midwestern customers seemed well supplied with Reflex Spark Plugs, and at a cost they couldn't match. Probeck put this fact together with some missing inventory reports and concluded someone was stealing and selling Reflex sparkplugs on the sly. The trail soon led to Nelson Cathcart, a Reflex engineer, who in turn fingered seven men who fenced the plugs. All that was missing was the identity of the ringleader, a master salesman reputed to have a persuasive manner and a flashy car. In early May 1923, a warrant was issued for that man, John Leonard Whitfield.

Carrying a warrant for Whitfield's arrest, Patrolmen Dennis Griffin and Harry Hughes staked out Whitfield's garage at 10607 Elgin Avenue on Cleveland's East Side early on the morning of May 11. Shortly after 6 a.m., Whitfield pulled into the garage in his customized blue Jordan. As he alighted from the auto, Patrolman Griffin arrested him and told him he had to come with them to the station at East 138th and St. Clair. Whitfield, blandly professing innocence, asked if he could say goodbye to his wife. The three of them entered Whitfield's house.

Retreating to his bedroom, Whitfield quickly grabbed a .45-caliber revolver and stuffed it in his hip pocket. His wife—a Mrs. Mary Becker who lived with him as "Mrs. Whitfield"—saw him do it and said, "Leonard, don't do that." Whitfield replied, "They're not going to get by with this," and followed the policemen out to the garage. There, the lawmen decided to take both cars, as both were filled with cases of stolen sparkplugs. Griffin and Whitfield got into the blue Jordan, while Hughes took the wheel of another Jordan. They probably left the Elgin Avenue residence about 6:30 a.m.

The car Hughes was driving had a tire low on air, and so he stopped at a filling station at Parkland and St. Clair. Minutes later, he arrived at the St. Clair police station. Griffin and Whitfield had not yet arrived in the blue Jordan.

An hour later they still had not arrived and an all-points-bulletin was flashed out all over the nation, while Cleveland-area police spread a dragnet for the missing car and men. It was the beginning of an amazing chase that involved thousands of fascinated Americans and would not finally end until March 1928 in a blaze of gunfire.

Griffin and Whitfield's whereabouts would not be determined for some days but various clues eventually told the morning's terrible story. With Griffin holding a gun on Whitfield from the passenger seat, the Jordan proceeded to Shaw Avenue. There, near the intersection of Hartford Road, George Dixon saw the auto drive by. A man he later identified as Griffin was slumped in his seat, "foaming at the mouth." Dixon thought he was drunk.

The blue Jordan was also seen about the same time by a 13-year-old paperboy, who thought he heard a shot or backfire as the car passed. He returned home and told his father he thought he had seen a policeman being shot. His father said, "I don't think so." Richard Knight, also out on Shaw Avenue that morning, heard the same shot or backfire.

Minutes later, Carl Gilbert, who knew Whitfield, saw him driving on Mayfield Road. About 7 a.m. he was spotted in Gates Mills near the Myron Herrick estate. Several hours later, about 9 a.m., Whitfield came on foot to the door of Mrs. Agnes Briel on Chagrin River Road near South Kinsman Road. Claiming he was trying to extricate a truck stuck in the mud, he borrowed a shovel from her and disappeared. About an hour later his blue Jordan was seen by Mrs. Charles Cermack on Pettibone Road near Geauga Lake, and still an hour later, Whitfield's blue Jordan roared at high speed through Chagrin Falls.

It was eventually discovered—too late—that Whitfield drove the Jordan to Stop #7 on the A.B.C. interurban line about 11:30 a.m. Making arrangements to store it for the day in William Koring's coal shed there, Whitfield returned to the city and made his way to 1562 East 93rd, the residence of a "Mrs. Leonard Whitfield."

She was no such thing. She was Marie Price, Whitfield's 14- or 15-year-old mistress from Ft. Wayne, Indiana. Seduced by Whitfield's flashy car and personable manner during his 1922 summer sojourn in Ft. Wayne, the 8th-grade student had been brought to Cleveland in January 1923—apparently with the compliance of her mother—and set up as his mistress, first at a Coit Road address, and eventually on East 93rd. Whitfield usually spent the night with Marie when in town, returning days to the accommodating other "Mrs. Whitfield" on Elgin Avenue, who provided home cooking, an element lacking among Marie's charms. "Mrs. Whitfield" had confronted Marie some months earlier but had backed down when the pert Miss Price boasted she "had John under her thumb" and "could break up her home anytime she liked." The first "Mrs. Whitfield" then backed down, even to the point of letting Marie live with

Cleveland Press Collection, Cleveland State University.
Wanted picture of John Leonard Whitfield.

her for some weeks and sewing clothes for her. Marie, a stocky, well-developed girl was by now almost seven months pregnant. Before she turned on him, Marie would later describe the tenor of this period with Whitfield as "swell."

Breezing into her East 93rd flat, Whitfield muttered something about some "trouble" over sparkplugs and told Marie to pack her things. Marie saw Whitfield pick up a .45-caliber revolver from the dresser as they left, and within minutes they were on their way downtown, chauffeured by Lucius Smith, a friend of Whitfield's who did not know that he was wanted by the police.

Whitfield's legendary luck began that day. About 2:30 p.m. he walked into the State Banking & Trust Company to cash a $150 check. Just ten minutes before, bank officials had been told by Cleveland police to watch for Whitfield. So when Whitfield presented his check to Teller Ira C. Finneran, the latter turned to head teller Walter A. Birr to ask if it was all right. Birr replied, "Why, surely, Ira, Mr. Whitfield is a good customer of ours." Whitfield departed with his cash, just minutes ahead of the police and Lucius Smith drove Whitfield and Marie to Stop #7 on the A.B.C. line.

By now, hundreds of Cleveland-area and Ohio policemen were searching everywhere for Whitfield and Griffin and hunting down hundreds of false leads that placed Whitfield in New York, Cleveland, Toledo, and Pennsylvania. The truth was undramatic and painfully simple. Whitfield retrieved the blue Jordan from Koring's shed, without even bothering to change its license plate. He drove back to Maple Heights, down Turney Hill Road to Schaff, Broadview to Denison, Lorain towards Rocky River. That night he and Marie slept in the car in front of a schoolhouse some miles out of Toledo.

Meanwhile, one of the largest police manhunts in U.S. history was taking shape as thousands searched for Whitfield and the still-missing Patrolman Griffin. The description broadcast of Whitfield was mostly accurate: a swarthy, 5-foot-8-inch, 200-pound man, 42 to 45 years old (he was actually 44), dark brown hair, medium brown eyes, gold front teeth in upper jaw and two knife scars below the heart. Although he had previously sported a mustache, Whitfield had shaved it off just before leaving Marie's East 93rd flat.

Along with the physical description went a summary of Whitfield's personal history which didn't augur well for the fate of Patrolman Griffin. Whitfield was born about 1878 in Jefferson or Waukesha, Wisconsin, where his father was a horse doctor. First convicted in 1900 for the theft of a buffalo robe, Whitfield had paid a fine of $20. Convicted again in 1903 of petty crimes, he was sentenced in 1906 to a 14-year term for robbery, gaining parole in 1914. He had stated his personal code vividly in a 1922 conversation with W. W. Franklin, a newspaper editor in Norwalk, Ohio. He told Franklin that he always carried a gun and that he was "not afraid of God, the devil, man or beast." Chillingly, he also said, "No one will ever get me. I'll shoot up the whole town first." The first Mrs. Whitfield, who was cooperating with the police search, further depressed hopes with her mournful statement: "He has an awful temper and never liked to trust himself with a gun. I believe that if the girl with him stands in the way of his escape that he'll kill her also."

Meanwhile, the hunt for Dennis Griffin also went forward. After

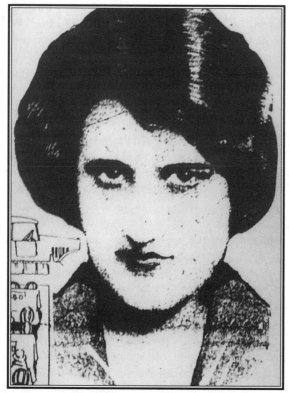

Cleveland Press Collection, Cleveland State University.
Marie Price.

hundreds of volunteers searched the Bluestone Quarry area for two days, the first break came with the discovery of charred remnants of Griffin's police uniform in the remains of a campfire near Petti-bone Road in Geauga County, an area where Whitfield's blue Jordan had been spotted on the morning of May 11. The next day, about 12:30 p.m., Dennis Griffin was found by Deputy Sheriff Lloyd Lafferty and others about 200 feet from the campfire under the roots of an uprooted tree. A little probing with a shovel quickly revealed a human hand in the mud, and Griffin's nude, decompos-ing body was dragged from its muddy grave. The autopsy revealed that he had been hit in the forehead, probably with Whitfield's pis-tol, and then shot through the neck, left to right, with a .45-caliber bullet. Griffin left a wife and nine-month-old son behind him. The day after Griffin's body was found, Whitfield was indicted for first-degree murder under Ohio's new cop-killer law. If caught and convicted he was going to face either the electric chair or life in prison. And where was the elusive fugitive? Hiding pretty much in plain sight, like some sort of human purloined letter. Although he repainted parts of the Jordan and soldered a Hudson ornament in place of the Jordan insignia, Whitfield still hadn't bothered to change his license plates. The morning after his flight he and Marie stopped at Mrs. Nora Whipple's grocery/filling station near Toledo. Mrs. Whipple fed them pancakes, later remarking that the bedraggled, quite pregnant Marie "looked like she had been puffed through a knothole." Meanwhile, the police, "ludicrously befuddled" (in the accurate phrase of the *Cleveland Press*) in their search for Whitfield, issued statements of hollow bravado and shallow scorn of the man who was making a fool of them:

> Whitfield, although he has eluded capture thus far, is held by
> police to be a blunderer. Only by the grace of good fortune, they
> say, is he at large today.

The Cleveland Automobile Club offered $500 for Whitfield's capture, swelling the total rewards offered to $2,850. The amount might have risen much higher had not Mayor Fred Kohler vetoed City Council's appropriation of $10,000, saying, with typical Kohler panache and disdain for grammar: "The reward now offered, $1,000, is more than ample to attract any stool-pigeon or squealer who would double-cross you or I, if he would protect a murderer of this description." A number of councilmen expressed outrage at the mayor's action—especially William Potter, who himself would meet an evil fate eight years later—and the hunt went on.

Whitfield was "seen" in Columbus, Toledo, Salem, Akron, Bedford (in a tree house, no less), Linndale, Hudson, Lima, and Cuyahoga Falls; in Meadville, Pennsylvania; Cedar Grove, West Virginia; Omaha, Nebraska; and Albany, Utica, and Rochester, New York. Not to mention appearances on a Great Lakes freighter and at Ontario, Canada. He and Marie actually were in Chicago, where they arrived about 5 p.m. on May 12. Marie by now was becoming suspicious. Whitfield had always insisted to her that he was Spanish; he now introduced his Chicago brother to her as a West Indian.

Cleveland News headline.

For the next seven days she and Whitfield criss-crossed the states of Indiana and Ohio, where Whitfield plied his trade as sparkplug salesman with his usual success. Then it was up to Wisconsin, the state of Whitfield's birth. After stopping at Kenosha, Racine, Milwaukee, Burlington, Edgerton, and Janesville, Whitfield and Marie pulled into Madison on the evening of May 23.

Madison should have been the end of the line for Whitfield. By now his untreated skin was darkening by the day, and descriptions of the fugitive and his very pregnant mistress had been broadcast in every newspaper and even projected on many movie screens throughout the United States and Canada. Nonetheless, the brazen Whitfield tempted fate on the evening of May 23 and took Marie to dine at "Chili Al" Felly's restaurant in downtown Madison.

The odd couple would have been out of place in this popular University of Wisconsin student hangout anyway, but "Chili Al" himself "made" Whitfield and Marie almost as soon as they walked through the door. Spotting them in a mirror, he casually walked over and took their order for steaks. He then went into the kitchen, told the cook that if he took less than 45 minutes to cook the order he would fire him, and called the Madison cops.

Several minutes later the police arrived and plainclothes Sgt. James Smith entered the restaurant, went up to Whitfield, and put a gun to his head. "You're John Leonard Whitfield and you're coming with us," said Smith. Whitfield, claiming mistaken identity, arose and followed Smith and the other policemen out the door.

Amazingly, the Madison police had already made the same kind of mistake that had cost Dennis Griffin his life. Although they had searched Whitfield for weapons, he was not handcuffed as they led him out to the street. As they walked toward the police wagon on State Street, a street car came down the middle of the street. Suddenly breaking free—as in some cliched movie chase—Whitfield ran in front of the speeding streetcar and escaped to the other side as the trolley temporarily blocked the view of the police. When the streetcar passed, they could just see Whitfield running down a side alley. They fired several futile shots and began to run after him. Although Madison police would come in for caustic criticism for not shooting more aggressively at Whitfield, their understandable defense was that they had imprudently shot a student to death during a "cap-burning" graduation festivity several years before.

Whitfield later claimed that he boarded that trolley and rode it several stops out of town. It seems more likely that he simply outran the police for several blocks. In any case, it is indisputable that he stole a green Buick roadster in Madison that same afternoon. He was spotted speeding through Okee, Wisconsin, at 4 a.m. the next day.

Marie Price was no fool. As her erstwhile lover fled down the alley, she grabbed the arm of a University of Wisconsin student and said, "Please walk down the street with me. The man the police just took and shot at was my escort." Quickly scooped up by the police, she immediately began her disingenuous and ingenious metamorphosis from Whitfield's moll to victim. The police also impounded Whitfield's prized 1917 custom-made Jordan. One of only two built, it was a highly souped-up racer, sporting a nickel-plated radiator and two spare wire wheels on the back. Whitfield had painted the red wire-wheels white, had the initials "A.A." painted on the side, and put the Hudson logo on the hood—but it still had the same license plate and some telltale bloodstains on the right front passenger side. Inside, the police found Whitfield's secret gun

Cleveland Press Collection, Cleveland State University.

compartment and, as expected, hundreds of sparkplugs.

Meanwhile, Whitfield was on the run again. Tracked and seemingly surrounded by hundreds of vigilante pursuers carrying a variety of firearms to a marshy area near Green Bay, he nonetheless eluded them, leaving only the evidence of his tire tracks as he escaped in his green Buick under cover of a dense fog. Several days later, he showed up at the Chicago garage of Dewey Biggs, an alleged "chopshop" for automobile parts. Here, Whitfield had some work done on the Buick, giving Biggs his .45-caliber revolver as payment. By May 28, his trail was completely cold.

Almost a month went by. Marie Price was tearfully united with her mother, who was about to become a grandmother at 33. As to her own responsibility in letting a 44-year-old man romance her adolescent daughter, she piously disclaimed, "I trusted him, and if he deceived me, is it any wonder he deceived my little girl?" Is it any wonder, either, that Marie, for her part, now vilified Whitfield? In particular, she seemed offended by the public disclosure that he was black, saying, "If he is what they say he is, I don't want anything more to do with him . . . . I am through with him. He certainly didn't give me a square deal and I am glad of the opportunity to tell all that I know." When pressed further, Marie guilelessly burbled, "I didn't know what to think, so I put it out of my mind. Gee, we had a nice time."

The long-awaited break in the case came in late June. Edward A. Haerl, a foreman at the Ternes Coal & Lumber Company at 6312 Michigan Avenue in Detroit, confided to his employer, A. P. Ternes, that he suspected their new barn boss, a well-liked and valued employee named "Sam De Carlo," was actually John Leonard Whitfield. Ternes, anxious for the reward, wrote a letter to Cleveland Police Chief Jacob Graul. Graul took it seriously—unlike the Detroit police, who had decided after a previous tip that this man was not Whitfield—and dispatched Detective Charles O. Nevel to Detroit. He got there on the afternoon of June 26 and immediately led a five-man police squad to the lumber yard. They spotted Whitfield almost immediately and accosted him with drawn guns. Nevel immediately made it clear that he was taking no chances: "Put up your hands. Any move and you will be riddled. Put handcuffs on him." As Nevel subsequently discovered, they had arrived just in time: Whitfield was about to leave in his new Hudson, and had previously installed a hidden trapdoor in the lumber yard office and altered the door locks to assist him in any sudden getaway.

The return, arraignment, and trial of John Leonard Whitfield provided the greatest show for Clevelanders since the trial of Eva Kaber in 1921. Although he was taken secretly off the train in Elyria to avoid crowds, a mob of 1,000 was nevertheless on hand as Whitfield was brought into the Cleveland Police Station on June 28. Reportedly shaken and fainting after his initial interrogation by Prosecutor Edward Stanton, Whitfield immediately went on a hunger strike. Meanwhile, Mayor Fred Kohler gloated over the turn of events: "It makes me laugh. I've saved the city $10,000. I laughed when Whitfield was captured without a reward, as I predicted, and I'll laugh when he is electrocuted." Whitfield was arraigned on Friday, June 29, and his trial was set for July 23. He had not yet lost the bravado that had carried him so far, so fast:

> I'm telling you—you may think I'm off, but I'm just telling you, you'd never got me if I hadn't wanted you to. Why, I've been all over this country. I know some mountains in Mexico where you'd never found me if I'd gone there. I just want to tell you something—it may sound funny, but I've been around a lot, and I've forgotten more than a lot of people know. Don't forget that. . . . We ought to make some money by taking movies of my trial.

Cleveland News headline.

As for Marie's comments on his racial identity, he had this to say:

> I have no negro blood in my veins, in spite of statement of the prosecutor that I have. I am not as dark complexioned as Marie Price.

This, despite his almost simultaneous boasts that it only took 6 or 10 drops of his secret potion to turn his skin from black to pink.

Considering his background and crimes, Whitfield had good legal counsel for the times. The long-suffering but forgiving "Mrs. Whitfield" hired lawyers Arthur H. Day (former candidate for Ohio governor), Blase A. Buonpane (former assistant county prosecutor), and Alfred De Lorenzo to defend Whitfield. While Whitfield continued a hunger strike that lasted six days, allegedly for fear of being poisoned, his lawyers tried to delay his trial. Their ploy was the claim that they needed to secure the testimony of a "Peter Milan" for their client's defense. Whitfield's claim was that Griffin had been accidentally shot with his own revolver, and that Peter Milan had kindly volunteered to dispose of the body for his friend John Leonard Whitfield. The motion to delay was overruled and the trial got under way on July 23.

Wearing a blue pin-striped suit, purple tie, and Oxford shoes with "fancy tan tops," Whitfield watched over four days as successive pools of 103 jurors were whittled down to a final panel of 10 men and 3 women; the jury was the first one picked under a new Ohio law allowing for an extra alternate juror. Among questions asked jurors were their opinions on capital punishment, and, more critically, "Will the fact that [Whitfield] is a member of the colored race prejudice you?" Throughout the two-week trial, hundreds of spectators fought for places at a spectacle that attracted national attention.

The prosecution was conducted by Edward Stanton, assisted by James T. Cassidy and Henry Williams. Calling more than three dozen witnesses, they constructed an almost seamless net of circumstantial evidence around Whitfield. Although Mrs. Whitfield's statement about his taking a gun with him when arrested was suppressed by Judge Frank C. Phillips—leaving moot the defense's contention that she was his common-law wife—both Marie Price and Dewey Biggs identified the .45-caliber revolver left with Biggs in late May as Whitfield's. Almost a score of witnesses placed Whitfield near the scenes of the burned evidence—including clothing identified by Marie as his—and Griffin's burial site near Pettibone Road. Virtually the only defense witness called—other than some negligible character witnesses—was Dr. Philip Jacobs, former Cuyahoga County coroner, who disputed current coroner A. P. Hammond's contention that only a .45-caliber bullet (Whitfield's gun, as opposed to Griffin's .38) could have made the wound in Griffin's neck. However sincere or weighty such testimony may have been, it was undermined by the defense's contention that Griffin had accidentally shot himself with his pistol in his *left* hand, when Whitfield tried to stop him from prodding him with the gun. Griffin was right-handed, as numerous witnesses testified.

Marie Price was a devastating witness against her former paramour. She blithely claimed ignorance of Griffin's killing, testifying that Whitfield had pacified her curiosity with the story that he had bribed Griffin to leave him alone. Her testimony, most crucially, tied Whitfield directly to the probable murder weapon and to frag-

Cleveland Press Collection, Cleveland State University.
Cleveland Press **headline, March 10, 1928.**

ments of his clothing found in the abandoned campfire. Defense attorney Blase Buonpane probably hurt his client's chances further with his aggressive interrogation of Miss Price:

> Buonpane: Isn't it a fact that your mother forced you to lead an immoral life in Ft. Wayne?
>
> Price: (angrily) No, it is not!
>
> Buonpane: Isn't it a fact that when you met Whitfield you were suffering from a disease?
>
> Price: (angrily) No, it is not!
>
> Buonpane: Isn't it a fact that your mother forced you to live a life of shame in Ft. Wayne?
>
> Price: (angrily) No, it is not!

We may never know the truth about the nature of the Price-Whitfield relationship; no one was about to take the word of a mulatto felon against an adolescent white girl in 1923 Cleveland. Whitfield asserted in his testimony that he initially came to Marie's home on a friend's recommendation as a "house of enjoyment." The weight of Marie's guileless testimony probably also benefited from increased public sympathy for her "victim" status; her child by Whitfield had been stillborn in early July.

Whitfield certainly didn't help himself on the stand. Virtually the only defense witness, he had already hopelessly compromised his credibility with numerous and conflicting statements. His first story, told to Detective Nevel after his arrest in Detroit, was that Griffin had shot himself accidentally with his own gun, and that Whitfield had let him out of the car to seek medical help. His second story, told in Cleveland on the night of his arrival, was that Griffin had prodded him repeatedly with his .38, and when he pushed it away, the gun had fired, killing Griffin. Whitfield's third story, told to Edward Stanton, included the "accidental" shooting incident, but added the detail that Griffin was drunk, and that the mysterious "Peter Milan" had kindly offered to take the dead policeman's body off his hands on Taylor Road Hill. "You know you are not a white man and you will get the worst of it," said the now-missing Peter Milan. For the record, Patrolman Griffin, a decorated World War I veteran, was a teetotaler—and Whitfield subsequently admitted that "Peter Milan" was a complete fiction. ("Say, did you believe that, too?") Judge Phillips himself was disgusted with the ever-mercurial content of Whitfield's testimony, and Prosecutor Stanton's frequent correction of Whitfield's testimony with excerpts from his previous statements finally prompted the enraged and confused defendant to shout: "I never told you nothing, man! I never said anything!"

The final blow to the defense came on August 2, when three boys playing near Stop #7 on the A.B.C. line found Patrolman Griffin's pistol where Whitfield had hurled it into Mill Creek. Identified by its serial number, it was yet another circumstantial item that tied Whitfield to the dead policeman. And it could have been worse: Judge Phillips disallowed introduction by the prosecution of photographs of the mud-spattered, decomposing policeman's corpse. He also threw out Coroner Hammond's contention that Griffin could not have been shot with his own revolver.

The jury went out at 3:35 p.m. on Tuesday, August 7 and returned with a verdict of Guilty—with a Recommendation of Mercy—at 2:35 p.m. the next day. The jury's decision on their fifth ballot was a compromise: some jurors had initially voted for acquittal and they threatened to hang the jury if the other jurors insisted on the death penalty. Judge Phillips was shocked by the verdict and let Whitfield know it:

> I would have had a measure of satisfaction sentencing you to die—disagreeable though it might be. I never knew of a more conclusive case, a more heartless crime, or more reckless, indifferent, depraved conduct following a brutal murder. This jury's failure to return a death verdict leads me to believe that no jury will ever return such a verdict where the evidence is circumstantial.

The three prosecutors refused to give the traditional thanks to the jury and Stanton did not hide his anger at the unexpected outcome:

> It has done more to encourage crime in the community than any one case I have heard of in years. It will embolden the criminal to violate the law flagrantly even to taking the life of those trusted with its enforcement.

Whitfield, for his part, was ungrateful and inconsolable. Despite the efforts of his attorneys to convince him he had been lucky, he complained bitterly, "I don't think I got the worst of it—I know it. . . .I'd rather have had them send me to the electric chair."

Whitfield, manacled between two guards, left for the Ohio Penitentiary the next day on the 12:05 p.m. train. His parting words to the crowd at the station were: "To hell with the people of Cleveland—they don't mean anything to me!" Three hours later he walked into the Ohio pen as Prisoner #52137 and responded to the warden's welcome with, "Go to hell!"

Even that wasn't quite the end of the story. Whitfield was a bad prisoner, earning disciplinary punishment at least once a month during the next five years for "crookedness, disorderly conduct and disobeying orders." But he hadn't lost his con-man talent, and he put his mouth in high gear again when a new guard, Oren Hill, came to work at the prison in January 1928. Within six weeks Whitfield had persuaded the gullible Hill to help him escape, based on the promise of an imaginary 48-acre farm and several equally illusory thousands of dollars. At 2:30 a.m. on the morning of Saturday, March 10, Whitfield went over the wall, using a 30-foot rope he had fashioned from mattress ticking, and wearing civilian clothes smuggled to him by Hill. The rope broke when he was ten feet from the ground, but he managed to limp his way to Hill's house nearby.

Whitfield was found missing at the 6 a.m. roll call, and Warden P. E. Thomas quickly wrung a confession out of Hill. Warden Thomas also sent Detectives Daniel J. Bonzo and W. E. Folk to Hill's house. Given prior experience of the police with the fugitive, their orders were unequivocal: "Shoot at sight."

Arriving at Hill's house, they brushed past a protesting Mrs. Hill to see Whitfield fleeing up the stairs and out onto the roof. A shotgun blast by Bonzo through the window brought Whitfield back into the house, but he hit Folk with a chair and then came at him with a butcher knife, knocking him down. As Whitfield lunged for a second time with the knife, Bonzo blasted him with a shotgun at point-blank range. Whitfield fell, his gall bladder shattered and his liver fatally damaged. His last words, worthy of a man who had prided himself on being a glamorous, criminal, movie-style "sheik," were "You got me!" He died of his wounds at 11:45 that night, and lies buried today in Harvard Grove Cemetery.

Chapter 7

"FIVE MINUTES OUT OF NOWHERE"

The 1932
Ellington Apartments Inferno

Arson is, perhaps, the most odious and repellent of crimes. Like poisoning, it is an act most often done in secrecy and stealth. It is difficult to prove, for, like most egregiously cowardly acts, it is not usually done in front of witnesses and therefore must be brought home to its perpetrators by strictly circumstantial evidence. The 1932 arson-for-hire torching of the Ellington Apartments complex at East 9th & Superior was just such a craven affair. Before it was over, it killed 12 people, injured more than 30, and sent one man to prison for life on the strength of predominantly—but overwhelming—circumstantial evidence.

Although generally unremembered now, the Ellington complex—today the site of McDonald & Company's architectural epitome of perpendicular brick—was once a microcosm of Depression-era Cleveland. Built by prominent Clevelander Morris Bradley in the 1890s, the Ellington was actually two linked residential hotels. The "Old Ellington," built in 1893, was a six-story structure of 80 apartments, while the "New Ellington," a one-story building behind it with access to Superior, was erected in 1897 and comprised 24 suites. Built before the era of steel frames, both Ellingtons were constructed of brick, mortar, and wood and divided into suites of two to five rooms.

The Ellington wasn't just a building, it was a way of life for most of its residents. Many had lived there since the turn of the century, and their characters and fortunes mirrored life in Depression-era Cleveland. They were predominately the not-yet-prosperous young and the still-bravely-struggling old. Miss Mary Gaughan, 22, and Miss Catherine Malloy, 28, were typical residents of the former class. Roommates, they worked at the nearby Hollenden

Hotel by day. Only too representative of the latter category of tenants—and the times—was Vera Bates, 60. Her story, as the *Cleveland Press* told it, was sad enough: " . . . a story in which a woman, once prosperous, had been thrown on her own resources in her older days—and had accepted the challenge." It was much worse than that. After her husband had gone into a retirement home, Mrs. Bates had tried to run a rooming house. It failed, as did her hopes of getting a job in a Cleveland department store. Eventually, she took a roomer in her three-room Ellington flat . . . and then another, as the wolf prowled yet closer to her 1932 door. By day she would store her bed under the stove in the kitchen where she slept, and attempt to peddle her homemade home preparations (silver polish and the like) from door to door.

In addition to its rental units, the "Old" Ellington contained a number of retail outlets on its first floors running down both East 9th and Superior. These included the Standard Drug Store on the corner, the Eglin Book Store, the Markowitz Hungarian Restaurant, the Cleveland Savings & Loan Company, the United Cigar Store, the Fluffy Pop Popcorn Company, and a barber shop. Most fatally, it also contained the American Beauty & Barber Supply Company.

"Five minutes out of nowhere" is how one witness characterized the Ellington holocaust and that is how it arrived for its hapless victims. At 26 minutes past midnight on June 7, 1932, John Linger, 38, was walking down the south side of Superior Avenue between the old Hollenden Hotel and the Ellington. Mrs. Evelyn Kilwine, a waitress at the Hollenden, was sitting in her automobile parked in front of the Ellington. Fred Bottomer, a *Press* reporter, was sleeping in his bed at the Doan Apartments, just south of the Ellington on East 9th. Jimmy Foxx, star slugger for the Philadelphia Athletics, had just retired in his room at the Hollenden. Meanwhile, Clark Sweeney and Fred Fisher, night elevator men at the Ellington, were searching through the building for the source of a strong odor of gasoline. It seemed particularly strong in the back courtyard, on the sixth floor, and especially in the airwell above the barber supply store. At about this time, Margaret McGreal, a second-floor tenant, returned to her suite. She woke up her roommates, Mary Gaughan and Catherine Malloy. She explained to the sleepy women that she was afraid they would get headaches from the gasoline odors wafting through the windows. Catherine already had one, and just as

Cleveland Press Collection, Cleveland State University.
Ruins of the Ellington Apartments, June 7, 1932.

she stepped into the bathroom to get an aspirin . . . the Ellington Apartments blew up.

The blast knocked John Linger up into the air, and as he came down on the sidewalk he saw the Ellington swell out like a fan and the roof seemed to lift right off. Evelyn Kilwine, sitting in her car, saw several of the Ellington storefronts on Superior suddenly explode, heard a tremendous blast, and then watched horrified as clouds of blue-green, then thick black smoke poured out of the Ellington. The thickest smoke seemed to be coming from the American Beauty & Barber Supply Company at 818 Superior.

Fred Bottomer was thrown out of his Doan Apartment bed by the force of the blast. He ran into the Ellington, already a mass of flames and smoke, and helped Fred Fisher rouse tenants and lead them to available windows and fire escapes. In some cases they had to break into vacant suites to get access to fire escapes. After saving all the lives he could, Bottomer ran back to the Doan, got his camera, and started taking pictures just as Cleveland firemen arrived and went into action.

The first alarm had been turned in from a Greyhound bus station on East 9th at 12:28 or 12:29. Within minutes, the fire had escalated to a multi-alarm fire, and four hook-and-ladder companies and 16 engines were at the scene. As perhaps as many as 10,000 gawking Clevelanders watched, they fought a desperate battle for hours with a raging fire that seemed curiously unaffected by water as it reduced the six-story Ellington to a smoldering shell of wreckage and ruin.

The first minutes after the initial explosion were a panorama of horrible scenes and desperate moments. Shrieking men and women appeared at apartment windows, screaming for help as the flames and smoke enveloped them. Some were saved by fire ladders or jumped safely into nets below on East 9th. Four of the 200 or so Ellington tenants were rescued by Philadelphia Athletics catcher Mickey Cochrane and a Philadelphia sports reporter, who grabbed a ladder and joined firemen in the first desperate minutes. Others, perhaps the majority, fled down flights of stairs or fire escapes to the street below. Several dozen escaped with their lives, albeit injured by burns, smoke, or flying glass and other debris.

Like all large fires, the Ellington inferno had its oddities. One of most memorable sights of the night was 78-year-old Dames Desnoyes. Blind, he was carried from a window by a fireman, still clutching his $60,000 Stradivarius violin. Many women jumped into the firenets below, but some were too petrified with terror, as the June 7th *Press* recounted:

> A woman appeared at a sixth floor window on the E. Ninth Street side. Smoke poured thru the window. Firemen stretched a net for her. "Jump," the shout went up to her. She screamed and ran back into the room, In seconds she reappeared. The woman refused to jump. Firemen stretched a ladder to her and a fire lieutenant climbed up and carried her to the street.

Mrs. Leida Chase Duncan and Mrs. Minette Stahl had lived at the Ellington for more than 30 years. They managed to flee in their nightclothes, also carrying their pet canaries, Pete, Betty, and Teddy Roosevelt, to safety down a fire escape. Meanwhile, above the noise of the fire, the wails of sirens, and the screams of the trapped could be heard the cacophony of neighborhood dogs adding their doleful baying to the melancholy scene.

Twelve persons, ten of them women, didn't make it out of the Ellington alive. Several, like 70-year-old Anna Mitchell, the

Ellington janitress, leaped to her death from a third-floor window. Others, like Conrad Werner, 55, a National City Bank guard, were found where death came upon them in their rooms. Werner had escaped—and then reentered the burning building to retrieve his bankbook. He was found suffocated the next day in his flat—still clutching his useless bankbook.

It was obvious from the beginning to shrewd observers that something not merely tragic but unspeakably evil had occurred. Cleveland Safety Director Frank J. Merrick and Fire Chief James E. Granger met at the fire scene within 20 minutes of the initial blast. Months later, Merrick would recall Granger's first words to him that night: "It's been set. This is murder!"

The suspicions of Granger, Merrick, and others focused from the start on the American Beauty & Barber Supply store on the Ellington's Superior side. The store's owner-manager, Ray I. Turk, a 39-year-old man from Cleveland Heights, professed to be completely puzzled as to the source and nature of the conflagration when questioned some hours after the blaze. But by this time fire investigators had already collected the testimony of several Ellington residents that there had been a strong odor of gasoline coming from the airwell above the barber supply store on the day of the fire. They also had the statements of elevator operator Fred Fisher and others that the initial column of flame had appeared in that same airwell. Furthermore, investigators found it curious, to say the least, that the force of the explosion in Turk's store had been so powerful as to blast its sturdy front door to untraceable smithereens. Two days later Fire Warden Patrick E. Barrett ripped up 15 feet of flooring in the store. Underneath, he discovered a badly burned 16-inch beam and rafters—and the overwhelming stench of gasoline. At the inquest, held a week later, Cleveland fire officials unanimously echoed the conclusion of State Assistant Fire Marshall Val Hafner:

> My investigation shows that the explosion was set. The explosion would not come from artificial or natural gas. The fire was fed by a highly inflammable liquid.

But fed by whom? Despite heroic inquiries, the investigative trail grew cold in the months that followed. Ray Turk cashed in his store insurance policies, totalling $15,000, with the Manhattan Fire & Marine Insurance Company. The Ellington was quickly rebuilt

Cleveland Public Library Photograph Collection.
Crescendo of Ellington Apartments blaze, June 7, 1932.

by the Bradley brothers as another residential hotel. And Fire Warden Barrett and Chief Granger continued to pursue their inquiries
about the American Barber & Beauty Supply Company. They had
a witness who had noticed workmen delivering some mysterious
cartons there early on the morning of the day before the fatal fire.
And they had information that much of the barber supply store
stock—valued by Turk at $18,000—had been secretly removed
between Friday, June 3 and Monday, June 6 and trucked to Pennsylvania. Turk had admitted to police that he had sold some stock
on Saturday, June 4 to a man and woman named "Mr. and Mrs.
Hirsch of Akron." But he could not explain why he had taken a
promissory note instead of cash for the purchase, and subsequent
attempts by the police to trace "Mr. and Mrs. Hirsch" proved fruitless. Clearly, something was rotten at the American Beauty & Barber Supply Company, but police and fire investigators lacked the
missing piece to confirm their dark suspicions about Ray Turk and
his barber supply company.

That missing piece came in January 1933 from Beaver County, Pennsylvania and was owing to the efforts of its county prosecutor, a thirtyish Javert with the unlikely name of A. B. De Castrique. De Castrique had been rousted out of bed on Christmas Eve of 1931 to look into a fire at the Better Shoe Shop in Ambridge, Pennsylvania, owned by a man named William Lazor and managed by his nephew, Daniel. De Castrique was intrigued by the fire, a clumsy arson triggered with pine shavings, oil-soaked rags, and a candle. He was even more intrigued, however, by the fact that Samuel Neamons, the insurance adjustor for the policy on the Better Shoe Shop, was at the fire scene that night . . . *even before the store's owner had been notified of the fire.* Something was rotten in Beaver County, and De Castrique began to lean on the Lazors. Within several months they confessed, and several months later—only weeks after the Ellington fire in June 1932—De Castrique had six men under suspicion and the criminal threads in his hands that would eventually lead to the solution of the Ellington tragedy.

Applying pressure to the jailed Lazors was the key. They led De Castrique to four members of an arson gang that had been responsible for at least $2,000,000 worth of fires in five midwest states during the early 1930s. By the end of 1932 De Castrique had secured convictions on all six, and it was just a matter of time before Cleveland officials, still nosing around Ray Turk's Pittsburgh connections, linked up with De Castrique's probe.

That time came on January 20, 1933, when warrants were issued for the arrests of Ray Turk, Samuel Neamons, Paul Childs, Benjamin Hirsch, and L. J. Kamons. The warrants were for first-degree murder charges in connection with the Ellington arson and most of the suspects were quickly scooped up. Neamons and Childs, the alleged insurance adjustors for the arson ring, turned themselves in to the police in Pittsburgh. L. J. Kamons, the alleged leader and mastermind of the ring, was already behind bars in the Rockview Penitentiary in Pennsylvania for his role in the Better Shoe Shop blaze. Ben Hirsch, the "Mr. Hirsch" who had signed a note for Turk's suspicious stock two days before the fire, went on the lam but was arrested in Pittsburgh on February 26, having been lured there by a fake telegram. Ray Turk was apprehended in Akron at the end of a two-day flight that took him to Ashland, Mansfield, Youngstown, Lodi, and Akron. Brought back to the Central Police Station jail in Cleveland, he sputtered with claims of innocence, rage and threats. To Detective John Corso of the Arson Squad, he said: "You're a married man and have several children. You think a lot of them. So do I think a lot of mine. I'll remember you a long time, pal." But Turk reserved most of his anger for Fire Warden Patrick Barrett:

> "You're the guy I've got to thank for all this. You've been going around trying to fix me with all my friends. Just wait until Pat Mulligan [Turk's lawyer] gets a hold of you. I've got plenty to talk to you about and don't forget it . . . ."

Getting ever more personal, Turk then told Barrett that he only had one day to live, as he was going to be "put on the spot" for arresting Turk.

Owing to Ohio law, each of the five men charged had separate trials. Turk's, beginning on June 15, 1933, was an entertaining, two-week legal battle. Judge John P. Dempsey presided over a jury of nine men and three women. Frank T. Cullitan led the prosecution and Frank G. Jones defended Turk.

As far as the fire itself was concerned, the state had only limited circumstantial evidence, none of it linking Turk directly to its setting and ignition. But thanks to a star witness, Abe Redlich, the state was soon able to establish that there had been a probable conspiracy to torch the Ellington; hence, Redlich's testimony about third-party hearsay incident to the conspiracy was admissible evidence. And Redlich had quite a story to tell.

Brought out of a Pennsylvania prison, where he was serving a term for his part in the Ambridge shoe store arson, Redlich told the court of his prior life as "business agent" for the Kamons arson ring. Travelling throughout the midwest to troubled small businesses, he and Kamons would pitch their services to entrepreneurs with poor cash flow and tempting fire-insurance policies. For a set fee covering the overhead of the arson (including travel expenses and the cost of a hideaway after the fire) and a percentage of the eventual insurance payment, the ring would torch the business in question. As an added convenience, they could also fence business stock (such as Turk's hair lotions) before the fire, replacing it in the targeted store with already fire-damaged goods from previous jobs.

Sometime in February or March 1932, Redlich testified, he and Kamons had met with Turk in Cleveland to arrange a fire. As a sort

Cleveland Public Library Photograph Collection.
Firemen pouring water on the Ellington Apartments blaze, June 7, 1932.

of "prospectus," Kamons had brought along a copy of the Better Shoe Shop insurance claim and the faked inventory that he had prepared for same. Despite Turk's claim at his trial that he had never met Redlich in Cleveland, the latter was able to pick him out in a lineup and also—more impressively—to take authorities directly to Turk's house on Belmar Road in Cleveland Heights. Redlich's memory was that Kamons had muttered that Turk was "not yet ready for the fire" when they met in February or March, but changed his mind after missing the store rental payments in May and June. Turk also claimed that he had never met Kamons in Cleveland. But Jeanette Cope, an Ellington resident and last-minute "surprise" witness recalled sharing a ride with Kamons in the Ellington elevator just two or three days before the fire. She picked him out in court without hesitation.

Small pieces of circumstantial evidence gave cumulative support to Redlich's story of a deliberate plot. Fred Streyle, a painter, testified to seeing four laborers unload a truck full of cartons and bring them into Turk's store at 6:55 a.m. the morning before the fire. There was additional testimony about some suspicious gasoline purchases from a Rockwell service station, and George E. Schmiel, one of Turk's salesmen, testified to "something missing" from the store that same afternoon—which corroborated the claim that Turk had transferred stock to a Pittsburgh warehouse in anticipation of the fire. And there were receipts from local trucking companies, Erie Cartage and Standard Loading, introduced in court to support that claim.

Turk did not help himself much on the stand. Affecting complete indifference to most of the proceedings, he only showed emotion, a brief spate of tears, when two of his four young children testified in support of his alibi for the night of June 6. His claim that Alva Bradley and Safety Director Merrick had "framed" him to avoid liability for the fire was preposterous and unsupported by any evidence. Turk actually tried to claim that he had 10,000 to 15,000 gallons of "highly inflammable" hair tonic in the store at the time of the blaze, a possible explanation for the ferocity of the explosion there. But he was contradicted completely by fire experts, who noted that the entire volume of the store could not hold that much liquid. Not to mention the testimony of Cleveland Fire Department officials who reported on tests they had conducted on Turk's "highly inflammable" hair tonics. The store's ruins contained completely unburned jugs of the stuff and in repeated tests it *extinguished* flames rather than burning. The final nail in Turk's legal coffin was the testimony of Webster Seely, another surprise witness and veteran *Cleveland News* reporter. While poking around in the ruins of Turk's store on the day after the fire, Seely had found something missed by arson investigators: an electric flatiron and an electric toaster—with four feet of wire attached to it. It is not known to this day what fluid was used to torch the Ellington, but it seems likely that Seely discovered the triggering mechanism. The state's case did try to place Kamons at the store in the minutes before the fire, but without success.

It didn't take the jury long to decide Turk's fate. Sequestered from the beginning of the trial, they began deliberations at 9 a.m. on July 1. Four hours and 50 minutes later they reached a verdict of "Guilty—With a Recommendation of Mercy," and Ray Turk

Cleveland Press Collection, Cleveland State University.
Cleveland Press headline: "Hold Turk, 3 Others in Death Fire."

was sentenced to life in prison by Judge Dempsey. As his family sobbed behind him, the still-passionless Turk said: "All I've got to say is that I was wrongfully arrested, wrongfully confined in County Jail for five and a half months, wrongfully indicted and wrongfully convicted."

After Turk's conviction, the Ellington case petered out in episodes of fitful anti-climax. L. J. Kamons, described as the "merciless and inhuman" mastermind of the arson ring, went on trial on October 2. No sooner was the jury sworn in than the announcement came of a mistrial; it seems one of the jurors had imprudently gone and talked to fellow-defendant Paul Childs at the County Jail. Kamons was reindicted on November 17, and his second trial before Judge Samuel Silbert, again with Abe Redlich as the state's star witness, ended on November 23 in a verdict of "Not Guilty." William R. Myer, foreman of the six-man, six-woman jury defended the surprise verdict with these words:

> "I think I can say without violating the confidence of any of the other jurors that each of us felt that Kamons was guilty of setting the fire. But [the] vague and indefinite testimony of Abe Redlich ... created a doubt and the judge's charge [emphasizing 'reasonable doubt'] left us with no other verdict than acquittal."

Kamons and Redlich returned to prison to serve out their convictions on the Better Shoe Shop rap and Cuyahoga County prosecutors quashed the indictments against Childs, Hirsch and Neamons. They had each served almost a year in jail.

In June 1934, Ray Turk's first-degree murder conviction was reduced to manslaughter by the Appellate Court. Its legal reasoning was that Ray had not intended to kill anyone when he conspired to commit arson. On April 15, 1935, he was resentenced to a term of 1 to 20 years by Common Pleas Judge George P. Baer. Described as "still fat and unworried" by *The Plain Dealer*, Turk's last recorded comment was, "I'm as innocent as a newborn babe." The rebuilt Ellington Apartments endured until 1967, when they were torn down for construction of the Central National Bank, now the headquarters of McDonald & Company. Today, the Ellington Apartments and their horrific history are virtually unknown to Clevelanders.

Chapter 8

"COLD LEAD FOR BREAKFAST"

The 1870 Galentine-Jones Melodrama

It has been said that it is difficult, despite unimpeachable evidence, for us to believe that our ancestors had sex lives. Hence our picture of behavior in past eras tends toward the passionless and bland. This is notoriously true with respect to the Victorian era, an epoch its critics would have us believe was brimming with sexual repression. It is therefore with pleasure that one turns to contemplation of the Galentine-Jones melodrama. Feminists may justly decry its unwitting exposure of period hypocrisies about female sexuality, but Cleveland scandal buffs and all right-minded aficionados of the ridiculous should treasure every last gory detail of this four-month Victorian sensation. Nineteenth-century Clevelanders may have been reticent about their biological urges, but the Galentine-Jones mess certainly demonstrated their throbbing, pulsating existence.

As Napoleon remarked of mating, the chief necessary condition for a good homicide is proximity. Such proximity came to Cleveland in November 1869 in the person of Dr. Jay F. Galentine. Twenty-four years old, Galentine had been around much in his young life. Born in New York to the family of a physician, Dr. C. B. G. Galentine, in 1846, Jay had come with his parents in 1862 to Brooklyn Township in Cuyahoga County. A few scant months later, he enlisted as a private in the Ohio 103rd Regiment, where as company clerk he saw war service in Kentucky, Tennessee, Alabama, and Georgia. Mustered out in early 1865 while on furlough in Brooklyn, he immediately sought out the company of a Miss Mary McArthur of Cleveland.

Mr. Galentine and Miss McArthur had met rather quaintly. During the war, lonely Jay had advertised for female correspondents in

Cleveland-area newspapers. Miss McArthur had responded, and under pseudonyms the two had vigorously corresponded to the end of the war. Their actual courtship was quick. Jay finally met her in the flesh on June 7 or 8 and they became engaged less than a fortnight later on his 19th birthday, June 22. Married two months later, they commenced on the path of marital discord that would lead to murder only five years later.

Miss Mary McArthur may be forgiven if she had motives other than a grand passion for accepting Mr. Galentine's proposal. In her late teens, she was a product of what would now likely be called an abusive family. Her father had deserted her mother while the latter was sick some years previously, returning eventually to become what the newspapers described as an "unkind" father to Mary. He had subsequently remarried, but by the 1870s his second wife had left him and he was a fugitive from justice on a warrant for raping a tenant's wife at his Brooklyn farm.

The Galentine pairing was not a marriage made in heaven. Testimony at Jay's 1871 trial disclosed that there had been conjugal discord from the beginning. After a stint as a schoolteacher, Jay pursued dentistry, more or less unsuccessfully, over the next four years in Brooklyn, Parma, and Oberlin. While in Oberlin, he deserted Mary for several weeks. The warring couple was eventually reconciled, but not before Jay told acquaintances that his wife was a "shrew" and Mary advertised to all that her husband was a dissolute wastrel. A telling example of her marital disdain was her alteration of a note Jay left to inform patients of his absence on business: "Out of town, gone to Berea, on a spree, will be back in a week or two." One can only hope that Dr. Jay was intermittently consoled by his wife's recorded charms: blonde hair, blue eyes, dimples, high forehead, and a front-braided hairstyle known as a "bandeau."

Be that as it may, the Galentine family moved to Cleveland in the fall of 1869, specifically to the Foote Block, a new commercial development at the intersection of Detroit Street and Pearl Road (now West 25th Street). A good commercial location, the building contained a stationery store and a drugstore on the ground level. Upstairs, via a central staircase, was Dr. Jay's dentistry office and living quarters. Unfortunately for everyone involved, there was also room for the office and home of Dr. William H. Jones.

Whether Jones was an outright villain or a mixture of frailties is

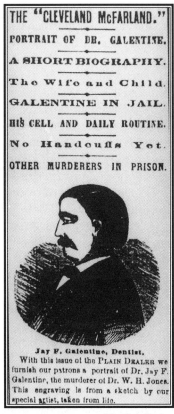

The Plain Dealer.
Portrait of Jay F. Galentine.

The Plain Dealer.
Portrait of W. H. Jones, M.D.

for the reader to decide. Whatever he was, he must have seemed—especially to the former Mary McArthur—like a successful version of her struggling dentist husband. Thirty-two years old, over six feet tall, and by all accounts markedly charming and virile, Dr. Jones was well on his way to becoming a successful physician. Born in Stowe, Ohio and having served as a surgeon with the 115th Ohio Regiment in the Civil War, Dr. Jones was already an ornament of the northeast Ohio medical profession. Considered one of the best anatomists in the country, he had a flourishing practice and held a chair in the Charity Hospital Medical College. To his professional lustre, he added the personal attractions of assurance, suavity, and flowing conversation, all well-attested to by his friends in the wake of his death. True, even his obituarists would admit that "he was not without peculiarities or faults and his reputation was not unspotted." But let us not anticipate our story.

On July 29, 1870, Dr. Jay Galentine left on a trip east. His explanation was that he was looking for a better dental practice; Cuyahoga County prosecutors would later claim that he actually meant to desert his family but there is solid evidence that he stayed in touch with Mary and sent her both letters and money. It is definitely known that Mary wrote Jay, and an easy conjecture that two sentences in one of her letters hurried him speedily homeward: *"What I am or what I may become, you have made me. . .What is there for me but to be bad, remember whatever becomes of me, you drove me to it."*

What Mary had become, Jay Galentine soon found out. Although she disclosed nothing upon his return from the east, he sensed a distance between them and started to become suspicious about Mary's frequent and unexplained absences. Sometime, probably in early October, his suspicions took definite form. Writing in a disguised hand, he wrote a note to Mary and slipped it under her door: "Mrs. G., can't you send your husband away?"

Jay's fake letter did the trick. Realizing that he was in some way on to her, Mary opened up a full heart to her mate in bed that night. It was a terrible story, wrung out of her with much seeming reluctance, shame, and tears.

According to her story, neighbor Dr. William Jones had been most attentive to her during Jay's absence. She had, eventually, per Jay's instructions, tried to consult with him on some property matters. But Dr. Jones put her off, suggesting instead that they take a moonlight buggy ride. Mary demurred on the grounds of propriety and the rebuffed Dr. Jones politely agreed.

Hours later in the middle of the night, Mary was awakened by Jones, who demanded she admit him to her flat so he could tell her something "important." She refused, and the next thing she heard was the sound of Jones opening the outer door with a key. She fled into another room and locked the door, imploring him to leave.

Minutes or hours may have gone by. Finally, thinking he had given up, Mary unlocked the door and stepped out . . . only to be seized by Dr. Jones and dragged to a lounge, where he pushed her face down into the cushions, almost suffocating her. The next few minutes weren't pretty:

Having held her in this position for a time he let her raise herself a trifle. She again begged him to leave her, but he made no reply to her entreaties except to bid her be quiet as her screaming would avail her nothing . . . no one would believe her story. . . . He lifted her from the lounge, dragged her to the bed, and bidding her be perfectly quiet, accomplished his purpose. This done he returned to his own room . . . [while] Mrs. Galentine lay all night upon the bed weeping bitterly and thinking of the outrage.

Adding no doubt to her bitterness was the memory of Dr. Jones's earnest assurance, uttered in the moment before he "accomplished his purpose": "Trust me, Mrs. Galentine, on my honor as a Mason, I will do you no harm."

Dr. Jones's initial nocturnal rape was just the beginning. He apparently had a key to the Galentine chambers, and in the days that followed continued his outrages against Mary Galentine— sometimes, she later confessed, forcing her to minister to his passion "four and five times a day." The days and nights went by, her husband returned from the east . . . and still she said nothing. Why?

Mary would later claim that she kept silent out of shame and for fear of what her husband would do—either to Dr. Jones or to himself—if she revealed the state of affairs. The subsequent range of opinion, predominately male, was, of course, skeptical of Mary's silence. The New York *Democrat* put a cynical "she asked for it" spin on the story:

We do not quite believe the story. . . . A man may be attracted to a woman; he may go to the fence and look over into her possessions, so to speak, but here he must stop, unless there be a look, a word, a wink, a nod, an insinuation, a motion of the head, a slight motion of the body, an unexplainable look or something of that sort.

In any case, we know that she was silent, apparently until early October, when her husband tricked the truth out of her.

The day after Mary's tearful revelations, Dr. Galentine confronted Dr. Jones with her accusations. Jones calmly denied the charges and refused to speak further except in Mary's presence. She was brought into the room and Jay repeated her story. Jones

THE WEST SIDE TRAGEDY.

THE STATEMENT OF MRS. GALENTINE.

The History of the Affair.

Nothing which has happened in Cleveland within the history of the city has created such excitement as the shooting of Dr. W. H Jones, on Saturday morning last, by Dr J. F. Galentine. A great many stories are in circulation, the most of which are mere creations of the imagination and wholly un reliable.

The particulars of the shooting were given in the PLAIN DEALER on Saturday. The prisoner, Dr. Galentine, has been removed from the Central Police Station to the County Jail where a coll has been assigned him

The Plain Dealer.

now admitted sex with Mary, smugly insisted it was mutual attraction, and offered Jay a cigar. Declining the smoke, an angry Jay asked Mary if she had not cried and begged Jones not to have his way with her. She insisted she had, but the impassive Jones simply sneered that he "had known women to cry harder and beg worse."

If Dr. Galentine had shot Dr. Jones at this point, the story would have ended there; no jury in the United States would have questioned Galentine's immediate execution of the "unwritten law" against the accused violator of his wife. Unfortunately for himself and Mary, Jay merely repeatedly threatened to shoot Dr. Jones "down like a dog." Jones reminded Jay at this juncture that he was an expert marksman who could snuff a candle at 20 paces, and would welcome an armed confrontation with Jay. And that was that: Dr. Jones left, presumably with a key to the Galentine flat still in his pocket, and Dr. Galentine was left to consider alternative measures.

It took him a while to make up his mind. After contacting his attorney to institute a lawsuit for rape against Jones, he approached the latter with the proposition that the good doctor marry Mary after she secured a divorce from Jay, "to keep her out of the gutter." It is not recorded whether Jones laughed in his face but he did refuse and warned Galentine that he "held the honor of your wife and child in the hollow of my hand."

Jay now tried a new tack. He wrote an anonymous letter detailing the particulars of Mary's version of events and took it to the *Cleveland Leader* for publication. The letter named no names but stated that legal action was under way which would soon expose the name of the perpetrator. Publication of the letter was somewhat delayed by the press of news about the Northeast Ohio State Fair, but it eventually appeared in the October 6 edition of the *Leader.* Surely, Dr. Galentine believed, Dr. Jones would now "come down" and make a deal to save Jay's reputation and Mary's honor.

He would not. Several more meetings with Jones produced only more sneers and defiance. The last straw for the humiliated Jay— who apparently suspected that Mary was still submitting to "criminal conversations" with Dr. Jones—came on Friday, October 7. That night, after a meeting between Mary and Jones, on which Jay eavesdropped, Mary and Dr. Jones agreed not to testify against each other in any lawsuit brought by her husband. Presumably, it was at that moment, as Jay later put it, that he "became convinced . . . that her sorrow was the sorrow of being found out." For her part in the bargain, Mary would later claim only the highest motive. According to her statement, Jay had offered her one-third of his money if she would testify that Jones raped her; she piously—or so she later said—replied: "It is only a blackmailing operation and you know it." It now seemed to Jay that he had run out of options.

Except one. He had been publicly threatening all week to shoot Jones "like a dog" and on Friday, October 8, he bought a single-shot pistol and practiced with it on the near West Side lakeshore. Finding it unreliable, he borrowed $10 from a grocer and bought a seven-shot revolver. His dental patients that afternoon found him unnaturally agitated, laughing inappropriately at everything, they later testified. That Friday night, after his frustrating conversations with Jones and Mary, Jay went to sleep on a couch in the Galentine apartment.

Jay was awakened at about 7 a.m. by the sound of a door leading to his wife's bedroom clicking shut. When he arose and found it locked, his suspicions were immediately excited, and he waited in the common hall outside with his revolver. His patience was rewarded minutes later when Dr. Jones emerged from a door, apparently pulling up his pants. That was all Jay had to see—although the layout of the building was such that Jones *could* have been coming out of the water-closet, not Mrs. Galentine's bedroom. Approaching close to Jones, Jay fired once. The bullet entered just below the fourth rib on the right side, smashed through the right lung, entered the right auricle of the heart, continued through the left heart muscles, and came to a stop near the fifth rib on the right side. Jones, stunned, turned into the door of his office, spun around, and slammed the door shut.

The shot was heard by Frank Hurd, who owned the drug store below. Looking up, he remarked to M. C. Beardsley, who owned the adjoining stationery store, "Sounds like somebody got cold lead for breakfast." The shot was also heard by two men in Dr. Jones's office, who now watched as he lurched unsteadily into the room. One of them was W. B. Donaldson, his cousin from Geauga, in town for the State Fair. The other was W. F. Oldroyd, a medical student interning with Dr. Jones. To Donaldson's stunned question, "Doctor, are you hurt?" Jones could only mutter, "I . . . don't . . . know." Jones and Donaldson took him to a bed, where he died eight minutes later.

Meanwhile, Jay Galentine stumbled down the stairs in his stocking feet, the smoking revolver in his hand. "What's the matter up there, Doctor?" inquired Beardsley. "I have shot the son of a bitch!" said Galentine. When asked who he had shot, Jay replied, "I have shot Jones, the god-damned seducer!" Returning upstairs to don shoes, Jay came back down and wandered down Detroit Street hill towards the river. On the way he met Patrolmen John Faran and John Eberhardt and delivered himself up to their custody. He repeated his remarks about Jones, expressed pleasure at the news of his death, and was led away to be booked for murder on the East Side.

It is hard to appreciate now the effect the Galentine-Jones murder had upon 1870s Cleveland. Spoiled and satiated as we are by such spectacles as the Sheppard murder and the O. J. Simpson extravaganza, it is difficult to appreciate the voyeuristic joy it brought to Clevelanders of that era. Cleveland was just beginning

Shocking Murder on the West Side.

Doctor J. F. Galentino Kills Doctor W. H. Jones.

The Victim Lives Eight Minutes.

A WOMAN SAID TO BE AT THE BOTTOM OF THE TRAGEDY.

PROBABLY ANOTHER McFARLAND CASE.

FULL PARTICULARS OF THE BLOODY AFFAIR.

THE RUMORED CAUSES WHICH LED TO THE DEED.

Doctor W. H. Jones, a young and prominent physician of Cleveland, was fatally shot at an early hour this forenoon, on the West Side, by a young dentist, named J. F. Galentine. The following article, which ap-

The Plain Dealer.

to become a big city, and its newspapers were beginning to craft the kind of sensationalistic crime reporting that would make the names of Hearst, Pulitzer—and Louis Seltzer—famous. The murder and its ensuing trial dominated Cleveland newspaper coverage for weeks, and every effort was made to squeeze the last scintillating drop of sex and gore—always masked in prose of hypocritical prudery—out of the affair.

Nor did the trial disappoint an expectant audience, many of them women who crowded the packed courtroom where Jay was tried for first degree murder in January of 1871. Wearing a suit of plain black and a black silk hat, Jay was led in, looking, *The Plain*

Dealer stated, "bleached perhaps, but not pale." For his defense he had good legal talent: Samuel E. Adams and Judge S. Burke. Facing them for the state were Prosecutor Edwin T. Slade and his younger brother A. T. Slade, assisted by lawyers Charles W. Palmer and Homer B. De Wolf.

Burke and Adams relied on a two-pronged defense of their client. On the one hand they appealed to the "unwritten law" as a justification for Galentine's admitted shooting of Jones. Burke wasn't subtle about it:

> I say the hand of the Almighty was in it. . . . Why is it the universal answer of all mankind, on hearing of the killing of a seducer [is] "Served him right."

It was clear, of course, that by stressing the word "seducer" instead of "rapist" that Adams and Burke were, at best, ignoring the question of whether Mary was telling the truth. Or as Adams slyly characterized her behavior after the first alleged outrage, " . . . however cheerfully she may have at length yielded." And the defense continued to pound away with the emotional force of the "unwritten law"—and to blacken Jones's name—right up through the final arguments:

> It is not for me to say here that if he had not ever been stricken down by this man, the pistols of other husbands would have been pointed at his breast. . . . If this tragedy, with all its fearful incidents, shall teach the libidinous scoundrels who mock chastity that female virtue is not a mere bagatelle . . . it will be the noblest shot fired since Sumter.

Burke and Adams also unsuccessfully attempted to put Mary Galentine on the stand, implying that only she could support her husband's supposed belief that he had shot Jones coming out of her bedroom. Burke and Adams doubtless knew that her testimony was inadmissable, but it was a nice way of reinforcing the alleged precipitating scene in the jury's mind.

Their other perfect non-witness was Dr. C. B. G. Galentine, Jay's father. The senior testified to numerous cases of insanity in the family and then suffered an incapacitating stroke, preventing his cross-examination.

The other prong of the defense was a claim of temporary "emotional insanity," a novel legal strategy for the time.

The prosecution was straightforward. The state's case was that Galentine had tried to blackmail Jones and had only turned to murder when Mary's refusal to cooperate with the scheme pushed him toward disgrace. Or as Slade put it, he had shot Jones only:

> ... when he found it was impossible that his avarice could be satiated by the price of his wife's virtue. . . . The spirit of avarice held high carnival in his heart. He was willing to riot in a brother's blood because he could not get the almighty dollar.

The state also argued, quite reasonably, that there was no substance to Galentine's plea of temporary insanity: his acquisition of a revolver, his recognition of Jones in the hallway, and his straightforward explanation of his actions (*"I have shot Jones, the goddamned seducer!"*) showed that he had "reason, memory, and judgment" at the time of the shooting. And whether Jones was a rapist or seducer was irrelevant; the trial was about his murder, not adultery or his moral character.

It was clear where presiding Judge Robert F. Paine's sympathies lay. In his instructions to the all-male jury, he noted that a husband catching his wife with another man *in flagrante* was one thing, specifically second-degree murder. But if the husband were to wait awhile before seeking retribution, it suggested premeditation, i.e. first-degree murder. And after quashing a last-minute attempt by two female spiritualists to introduce a spirit communication from the deceased Dr. Jones into the record, Judge Paine sent the jury to its deliberations.

Judge Paine was not very happy with the verdict. After only about six hours the jury came back on the evening of January 30, 1871, with a verdict of manslaughter. It was rumored that the voting on the first ballot had been six for complete acquittal, four for First Degree Murder, and two for Second Degree Murder. At Jay Galentine's sentencing three days later, Judge Paine peevishly commented that it was a "very aggravated case of manslaughter" and sentenced Jay to the maximum ten years in prison. He was also fined $1,100 in court costs. It is recorded that several women sobbed aloud as Jay Galentine arose and thanked Judge Paine and the jury for a "fair and impartial trial."

THE MURDER TRIAL.

Trial of Jay F. Galentine for the Murder of Dr. W. H. Jones.

THE VERDICT.

"GUILTY OF MANSLAUGHTER."

A CARD FROM THE JURY.

The crowd of spectators in the court room at 4 o'clock Tuesday afternoon remained patiently waiting until, about 6 o'clock in the evening, hoping for, yet scarcely expecting the verdict. At the hour last named, the court took a recess until 10 o'clock at night, and the room was soon cleared.

Long before the appointed time for the

The Plain Dealer.

Judge Paine was not the only party disgruntled by the verdict. In the *Cleveland Leader*, correspondent "H" waxed eloquent on an aggrieved populist theme—the disparity in sentencing between Galentine and a less well-born wife slayer:

> Because William Schallenberg was poor, ignorant, and knew nobody, he was sentenced to death for the slaying of his wife. The more polished Galentine, who is educated and well informed about the law, shoots his victim with malice purposely, deliberately, and premeditatedly, and is found guilty only of manslaughter. What a mockery of of all our notions of justice! Is not the law equal? Is it not for all?

The *Leader* also saw fit to point out that Galentine had been friends with Andrew J. Bauder, whose trial at Toledo for the murder of his wife had just ended in identical fashion:

They were intimate friends before the war, enlisted at the same time, fought in the same battles, were mustered out together, and came to Cleveland. They both had trouble with their wives, were indicted for murder, found guilty of manslaughter, and soon will be together again in the penitentiary.

What happened to Mary Galentine is unknown. One hopes that she recovered from her misadventures in a more sympathetic venue. She was only 22 years old, after all, at the time of her domestic unpleasantness, and she had to look after the welfare of her child, Bertha. Her last distinct appearance in history came in 1874, when her husband divorced her from prison on "grounds of adultery." Larry Hawkins, who authored a previous account of the Galentine-Jones tragedy, asserted that she survived her ex-husband, was never bothered by men again, and bequeathed $2,000 to a pet canary.

Jay Galentine fared pretty well in later life. Paroled before serving his ten years, he returned to the West Side, set up his dental practice again, and married into a well-to-do family. Dr. William H. Jones sleeps yet in a Hudson, Ohio, churchyard. And the final word belongs justly to the *Cleveland Leader*. After weeks of swimming in a sewer of journalistic sensationalism with the rival *Plain Dealer*, it concluded the trial with this reproving comment on the spectators, especially female, who had thronged the trial throughout its fortnightly run:

> There certainly has been no good for them to do there, no virtuous but unfortunate woman to sustain and encourage by their presence, nothing for them to see or learn but what would have been far better unlearned.

Chapter 9

"HORROR OF ALL HORRORS!"

The 1895 Central Viaduct Disaster

There are several good places to begin the story of the 1895 Central Viaduct tragedy. One of them is down in Cleveland's "Flats." A walk or drive through its maze of crowded, truncated streets offers a quick appreciation of the transportation challenges Clevelanders faced before the construction of high-level bridges in the early 20th century. Cross-town traffic was perpetually stymied by congestion in the Flats' crowded streets and the constant interruptions caused by drawbridges being raised to let river traffic pass. If only a high-level bridge could be built . . .

Another place to begin the Viaduct story is down by the Cuyahoga River itself. Although cleaner now than in 1895, the river at the disaster site is still crooked, muddy, and relatively shallow. It does not look like a friendly place to fall, and one's eyes instinctively gauge the yawning distance from the massive Innerbelt Bridge above to the river below. Perhaps the best place to begin the Viaduct tragedy, however, is in the air, or more exactly, on the tracks of the RTA Rapid Transit bridge situated but a few feet from where the Central Viaduct once thrust across the Cuyahoga a century ago. Sometime on a dark and stormy night, say in November, you might want to take a Rapid and watch, carefully, as it rolls across the steel truss span over the Cuyahoga River below. Look down, then, and think: *Yes, that would be a long way to fall . . . and what if I hit something hard on the way down?*

Like most of Cleveland's civic improvements, the Central Viaduct did not come easily. Agitation for a bridge to Cleveland's expanding South Side preceded completion of the Superior Viaduct and was intensified by South Side resentment of the civic

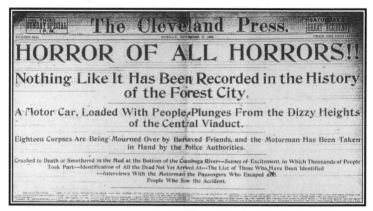

Cleveland Press Collection, Cleveland State University.

and commercial advantages enjoyed by its neighbors to the north. South Side Councilman James M. Curtiss first introduced a Council resolution in March 1879, asking that the city engineer investigate the best location for a south viaduct. This being Cleveland, however, years of bickering went by before construction finally began on April 26, 1886.

As developed by City Engineer C. G. Force, and later by Walter W. Rice, the Central Viaduct was actually a series of two complementary bridges. The first, the "Central Viaduct" proper, was a 2,839-foot series of spans that stretched from Central Avenue (today a point just south of the juncture of Ontario Avenue and the Hope Memorial Bridge) in a straight line southwest across the Cuyahoga valley to Jennings Avenue (today West 14th Street). The second bridge, a stretch of 1,088 feet, ran over Walworth Run and connected Abbey Avenue with Lorain Avenue—a section still in use today. The Central Viaduct proper was a "stilt" bridge: a series of 20 steel pan-shaped spans supported on stone piers; the length of the spans varied from 30 feet to 236 ½ feet. Elevation above the Flats was 89 feet over land, 101 feet over the Cuyahoga River.

A problematic feature of the bridge was its pivoting center span which crossed the Cuyahoga River. Built on a pier which jutted up from the center of the river, the center span rested on a turntable which allowed turning to permit river traffic to pass by. Completing the bridge furnishings were 2,000-candle-power electric arc lights, spaced 270 feet apart on 32-foot-high poles. From the very beginning, it was assumed that electric street car tracks would occupy the main 40-foot-wide roadway.

In later years it would be claimed that the Central Viaduct was an "unlucky" bridge from the start. It is undeniable that its fearful reputation began with a bang on the afternoon of January 5, 1888. Two men, Harry Burton and Daniel Ockel, were crushed to death when a heavy derrick at the edge of the bridge fell on them. the *Cleveland Press* did not stint on the gory details:

> Ockel's head was severed from his body above the lower jaw. His heart and lungs were lacerated and torn out near the left shoulder which, with the left arm, was mangled and hung by shreds of flesh to the neck. The whole upper part of the body was crushed in. The right leg was fractured above and below the knee, and the left leg was fractured at the ankle.

Not to be outdone, *The Plain Dealer* reported:

> A double handful of brains stained an iron support which had crushed the skull of a victim, and a pool of human blood lying underneath the confused mass marked the place where another had fallen.

The dead were buried in Erie Cemetery and construction continued.

December 11, 1888, was the happy, if cold day on which the Central Viaduct was opened and dedicated. It began with a parade at 2 p.m. and climaxed with a palatial banquet at the Hollenden Hotel. That evening's paroxysm of civic boosterism, with its unmistakable tone of Cleveland-on-the-make was, perhaps, best captured by William R. Rose, then a journalist for the Cleveland *Sun and Voice,* in some doggerel composed for the occasion, which concluded with fulsome praise for James Curtiss, the tireless champion for the South Side bridge:

In coming generations when
Our children's children tell
The famous stories of the past—
The tales they love so well—
With cheering and with laughter
One deed they'll keep alive,
How well brave Curtius saved his bridge
In eighteen eighty-five!

But not everyone was happy with the Viaduct, as this satirical *Press* reply to Rose's paean demonstrated:

> I stood on the bridge at midnight
> And nobody stood with me,
> As the moon rose over the City
> With a tax rate of 2.83.
>
> I saw the moon's reflection
> In the river flowing free,
> And it looked like the plat of some real estate
> In a city taxed 2.83.

The Central Viaduct opened just at the time Cleveland's street railways were undergoing full conversion from horse-drawn to electrically-driven cars, and soon the bridge was carrying thousands of Clevelanders per day on the Cleveland Electric Railway's ("Big Consolidated" or "Big Con") Cedar-Jennings line. And the bridge seemed, immediately, to fulfill the expectations of its proponents. But three years after its opening, sometime in late 1892, another "unlucky" incident occurred. Two crowded, speeding streetcars were crossing the Viaduct when one of them jumped the tracks and crashed point-blank into the other. The cars were totalled and there were a large number of dead and wounded.

As with the Superior Viaduct, the main drawback of the Central Viaduct was the bottleneck at its pivoting center draw. Owing to river traffic, it had to be opened and closed several hundred times a month. Jammed streetcars, pedestrian traffic, and horse-drawn vehicles simply had to wait, fuming and fretting, for three to six minutes while the draw was opened and closed. It was frustrating to both river and bridge users—and as Clevelanders would discover, extremely dangerous.

In theory, the Central Viaduct tragedy should never have happened. There were a number of safeguards designed to prevent bridge traffic from entering the open draw. There were a pair of four-foot gates located about 14 feet from both the western and eastern ends of the draw. In addition, there were—or were supposed to be—red warning lights on the gates. When the draw was opened, the bridge tender would hoist an additional red warning light on a pole 10 feet high over the gates.

Sketch of car #642 falling through the draw.

Additional safeguards had been installed on the viaduct by 1895. About 200 feet from the eastern end of the draw and about 170 feet from the western end were derailleur switches. In order for a streetcar to proceed any further, the conductor or motorman had to stop the car, disembark, and manually pull the derailleur switch. Should they fail to do so, the streetcar would automatically be diverted to a dead-end stop at the side of the viaduct, well short of the gates and the draw. There was also an electrical "cut-off" switch located more than 500 feet from the draw that automatically shut off all electrical power to streetcars when the draw was open. But sometime during the first week of November 1895 the cut-off on the eastern side of the draw shorted out. It is not known to this day whether the employees who daily drove the cars of the Cedar-Jennings "Big Con" line were ever told that the cut-off was out of order.

Dusk comes early to Cleveland in mid-November. It was already dark as many weary travellers trudged or drove to and across the spans of the Central Viaduct around 7 p.m. on November 16, 1895. It was Saturday, always a busy shopping day for Clevelanders, and an opportunity to visit relatives in other parts of the city. Thousands were out on the streets, on horses, and in streetcars despite the dark and a mild drizzle that fell throughout the evening. Let us mingle with them as the chill fall mist falls on what will, for 17 of them, be the last evening of their lives.

Edward Hoffman is the car conductor on Car #642 of the Cedar-Jennings line this evening. Born in Germany and only 23 years old, he has worked for "Big Con" for two years, mostly at the car barns, and before that at John D. Rockefeller's Forest Hills estate. Popular with passengers, Edward has a wife and small child waiting up for his arrival home at the end of the evening. Running from the East End (near Lake View Cemetery), Car #642 leaves Blue Rock Spring (a popular mineral springs resort then located near where the RTA tracks now cross Cedar Avenue in University Circle) about 6:50 p.m. and arrives, via Cedar most of the way, at Public Square at 7:22 p.m. Several passengers get off there and several more get on; more will disembark and embark when the car reaches the Central-Ontario stop just before the viaduct. Fifty-two fares in all will be collected by Conductor Hoffman on that #642 run; only about half of the passengers will be on the car as it lurches onto the Central Viaduct at about 7:30 p.m.

Edward Dahlke is the commander of the tugboat "Ben Campbell" on the Cuyahoga River that night. As 7:30 p.m. comes, his boat is towing the "Abram Smith," a loaded lumber barge, upstream. As the tug approaches the bridge, Dahlke blows his tug's whistle to alert the bridge tender to open the draw and let him pass.

Captain Charles Brenner is the officer in charge of the draw this night. From his booth on the north side of the Viaduct, located near the safety gates, he hears the tug's whistle and rings five bells to signal the bridge engineer in the draw pier to open the draw. He then (or so he and Agust Inon, his opposite number on the south side of the viaduct, will later testify) raises a red lantern on a pole 10 feet high to alert the tug that the viaduct is about to open. Brenner and Inon then close the safety gates. Car #642 pulls up to the derailleur switch.

Cleveland Public Library Photograph Collection.
Spectators crowd Central Viaduct to gawk at
search for bodies, November 17, 1895.

Augustus Rogers is the motorman at the controls of Car #642 that drizzly evening. As he brings the car to a stop at the derailleur, Conductor Hoffman jumps down, pulls the derailleur switch and then signals Rogers to proceed. He moves the car controls and #642 began to accelerate toward the draw.

John Stringer is one of four or five men standing on the rear platform of #642 as it moves toward the draw. Like his companions, he is standing outside the car door because he wants to smoke. As the car begins to move, he throws away his cigar stub and prepares to reenter the car. At that moment, someone asks him for a light, momentarily distracting him . . . and inadvertently saving his life. The cast is in place; the tragedy occurs.

Captain Brenner saw the whole thing happen. As car left the derailleur, picking up speed, he ran out of his booth, screaming, "Stop! Stop!" at Rogers the motorman. Within seconds, the car reached the gates, and, as Brenner and another bystander tried to hold the gates, it smashed through and rumbled straight towards the open draw only 14 feet away.

Motorman Rogers may have been the first on the car to realize the mortal peril approaching. As #642 approached the gates, he suddenly noticed that they were closed, and screamed "Jump!"— suiting the action to the word and landing in a bruised heap at the edge of the open draw.

John Serringer was another smoker on the rear platform of the doomed car. He had boarded #642 at Public Square and was paying little attention as he watched Hoffman throw the derailleur switch and felt the car start up again. The next thing he remembered was someone shouting, "Jesus, Stop! Stop! For the love of God, Stop!" Serringer lunged for the safety gates as Car #642 tipped over the edge of the draw . . . and the sudden upward lurch of the trolley's rear as it pitched over threw him to the safety of the Viaduct deck.

Passenger John Mendik, a professor of athletics at the Sokol Nova School, had an even closer call. Seated in the third seat from the rear of the car, he heard the cry of "Jump!" and saw men on the rear platform leaping for the bridge deck. He would long remember the faces in #642 as Death announced its arrival in the car:

> The grewsome picture of startled, death-staring faces, and what transpired in that one dread moment, would take up hours of painful description, and baffle my attempt. All were on their feet, save the mother and child, and whether it was cool self-possession, unconcerned despair or resignation to God's will that prompted such remarkable composure in the face of such danger, I am at a loss to know.

Mendik somehow got through the rear door, onto the platform, and was hurled five feet into the air by the sudden tilt of the car's plunge over the side. He landed on the deck, badly bruised, severely gashed on the head, but alive. Charles Clark, Andrew Radke, G. O. Ross, and Jacob Heller also leapt to safety from the rear of the trolley. Seconds later, they heard a terrifying crash, far below.

James Patterson, the viaduct engineer inside the draw pier, did not actually see the accident, but that was only because he covered his face in horror as he watched the car careen over the edge. But many witnesses had a clear view as the car, travelling between four and six miles per hour, crashed through the safety gates and went over the precipice. It must have been terrible to watch. The car, impelled by its forward motion, did not fall at once, but continued its horizontal progress for a few seconds. Then, as its interior lights went out (when it lost contact with its overhead wire), and as its passengers screamed in terror, it plunged 101 feet, almost hitting the tugboat "Ben Campbell," and smashing into the foundation of the draw pier, sending a 100-foot column of water into the air. Then came a sizzling sound as the broken car settled at a 60-degree angle in the muddy water. And then . . . silence.

Rescue efforts began immediately. Oddly enough, the first alarm was turned in by Harry Rebbeck, a Cleveland fireman, who had also turned in the first alarm on the January 5, 1888 viaduct construction tragedy. Within minutes Captain Dahlke, Motorman Rogers, and other witnesses had gotten in touch with Cleveland's safety forces and aid converged on the accident scene by land and water.

The scene they discovered there was a ghastly one. Clothing was floating in the river, including four ladies' hats, three men's hats, a large fur cape, a black lisle thread glove, three aprons, an olive-green waist, and a coffee-colored canteen. The smashed-up car was sticking up several feet out of the river, and groaning and gurgling sounds were coming from the frightful wreckage. The groaning came from Patrick Looney. Seated in Car #642, he had noticed the agitation of the other passengers, and managed to make it to the rear platform as the car went over the edge. Incredibly, he survived the ride down, clinging to the car railing, and he remembered the collision with the draw pier. That impact, fracturing his skull, knocked him out for a few seconds. When he came to, he was under water and he was conscious of a humming in his ears. He came to the surface and began to moan. As rescuers tenderly transferred him from the wreck to a makeshift raft, he screamed, "My God, won't you take me from this death? Don't let me die here! Help me to safety!"

The gurgling sound didn't last long. It came from Mrs. Eliza Sauernheimer. Trapped in the wreckage with a crushed right arm and skull, and internal injuries, Eliza lived only five more minutes, as rescuers J. F. Brown and John Welch of the tugboat "Spranckel" held her bleeding head above water while others frantically worked to free her body from the debris. Everyone else in the car—16 people—had already drowned or been smashed to pieces. Several physicians, including Dr. A. B. Schneider of nearby Jennings Avenue, made their way to the river that terrible night to offer aid, but there was nothing for them to do but watch as rescue attempts quickly turned into retrieval of the dead from the ruined streetcar.

That unspeakable task went on for almost two days and was hampered by a number of factors. Chief among them was the condition of the car; it had broken up badly on impact and many of the bodies were trapped under the wreckage. Several early attempts to raise the car succeeded only in breaking it into more pieces. The muddy bottom of the Cuyahoga River was an additional impediment: city diver Walter Metcalf spent many hours wandering amid its mucky depths, while city police and firemen grappled with hooks, mostly in vain, for corpses.

Matters were not helped by the behavior of the populace. Within minutes of the accident, thousands of curious Clevelanders converged on the scene, some of them pickpockets who plied a lucrative trade amid the milling rubberneckers. All streetcar lines to the area became jammed with passengers and crowd estimates throughout the night and the following day ranged from 50,000 upwards. They swarmed all over the Flats and lined the bridges above, seeking the best available vantage points. Seventy policemen were needed to control the surging mob, and a terrible accident was miraculously avoided when a spectator-covered lumber pile shifted, pitching dozens of rubberneckers onto more gawkers below.

One by one, the bleeding, muddy, broken corpses were fished out of the river and taken to one of six private morgues. Owing to the competitive relations among the latter, disgraceful scenes occurred as rival morgue employees fought each other and even grieving relatives for possession of the bodies. One such macabre episode was the recovery of the body of Miss Martha Sauernheimer, as recounted by a *Plain Dealer* reporter:

> Friends telephoned for an ambulance, and in a short time two of Heffron's and Hogan and Sharar's appeared. Heffron's arrived first, and his men made a rush for the body. As they neared the edge of the pier they were seized by the brother and

Cleveland Press Collection, Cleveland State University.
Car #642 races toward Death.

brother-in-law of the dead girl, and commanded not to touch the body. They tried to shake the enraged relatives off, and quite a little struggle ensued. Young Sauernheimer said that he had given orders to Undertaker Mattmueller to come for the body, and any other person would touch it at his peril.

It was only after another hour, while thousands gawked at the bleeding, bedraggled corpse that Mattmueller's ambulance arrived and bore off poor Miss Martha's body.

With the last known corpse, that of Matthew Callihan, recovered at 2:15 on Monday afternoon, November 18, two tasks now provided further diversion to expectant Clevelanders. First came the funerals of the deceased—seven of them on Tuesday alone— pathetic spectacles all reported in every sobbing detail by Cleveland's daily newspapers. Prizes for most bathetic media coverage and disgraceful conduct went to, respectively, *The Plain Dealer* and the spectators at the Hoffman family funeral. Mrs. Annie Hoffman, 30, had been on #642 with her son Harry, 7, and daughter Gertrude, 4. All journalistic stops were pulled out for the wake at the Hoffman home at 1508 Pearl Street in paragraphs that put Dickens's description of Little Nell's demise to shame:

> The funeral obsequies held over this mother and her two babes were sad. Sad because of their simplicity, infinitely sad because of the grief of the only survivor of the little family. In the modest home on Pearl Street the three sleeping forms were laid out in caskets of purest white. On the right reposed the little, golden haired girl, her features as beautiful as an angel's, nestling in its satin pillow, while the ringlets of gold fell round the face, making a halo which completed a picture of the rarest beauty. On the left the body reclined, a few red scars—mute witnesses of the awful calamity—marring the otherwise peaceful expression of his face. And in the middle the mother slept— slumbering in eternal sleep, while on her face also naught but happiness was to be read—happiness in eternity with her children! Glancing from those sleeping forms to the beautiful floral offerings, only a sharper pang shot through one's heart. There was a beautiful design of "Gates Ajar," with two large, white floral gates standing half open, waiting to receive the spirits of the dead: an anchor surmounted by a dove of purest white told of hope and peace; a harp with a broken string of a life departed.

Hundreds of ghoulish spectators turned the Hoffman funerals into a shameful spectacle. When the crush at the entrance of St. Paul's Church became so great as to require the intervention of the police, the frustrated mob made a frantic rush for the rear entrance of the church. While the morbidly curious filed past the three open caskets—some of them two, three, or more times—others fought, fidgeted, and elbowed in the aisles and staircases until their din could be heard above the peal of the church organ.

Other victims of the viaduct horror were an interesting cross-section of Cleveland's turn-of-the-century population. Miss Bessie Davis, 22, was a second-grade school teacher at the Sackett Street School, assistant Sunday School librarian, and enthusiastic member of the Scranton Avenue Free Baptist Church. She was returning from a visit to her uncle on the East Side and on her way to Saturday night choir practice when she met her fate.

Henry Mecklenburg, 35, was a tailor, easily identified at his autopsy by the packet of needles in his pocket and his right club-foot. Unmarried, he had lived with his mother and sister and had only been in the United States for a few years.

Marie Nettgen, 22, had been visiting her brother that Saturday afternoon. A domestic servant, she had emigrated to the U.S. about 1890, and was a devout member of St. Michael's Church on Scranton Avenue.

Minnie Brown, 40, was head cook at the Broadway Cafe on St. Clair, near the Cleveland Theater. Married twice, she had been recently widowed for the second time and left with five children. Her son Daniel, 15, when called upon to identify her corpse at McGarry's Morgue, could only sob, "My God, it is my mother. And there are four children depending on me for support!" Minnie's autopsy revealed a fractured skull and she rests to this day in an obscure corner of Riverside Cemetery, beneath a humble stone labeled simply "Mama."

James McLaughlin also sleeps in Riverside, amid a plot occupied by family and in-laws. Mildly less obscure than the other victims, McLaughlin, a union printer by trade, was known around Cleveland as an excellent amateur baseball pitcher and had pitched a year of professional ball in the old American Association. Examination of his body at McGarry's morgue disclosed a fractured skull, a broken neck, and much broken glass ground into his clothing. There was $1.10 in his pockets, two memoranda books, buttons, and two keys. He would have celebrated his 35th birthday on Monday, November 18.

Louis Hueltz, 28, was a well-liked U.S. mail carrier on his West Side route. Diver Walter Metcalf had to cut his body in two to get it out from under the trolley wheels at the bottom of the river. He left a wife and two children.

Curt LePhene was only 15. The son of a German army officer, he had immigrated to Cleveland just the previous month, when his widowed mother came here to be with her new husband. When hauled out of the Cuyahoga he was wearing an overcoat and vest, a checked brown coat, and trousers.

Harry Foster, 19, had been a timekeeper in the millinery department at Root & McBride's Bank Street (West 6th) store for the previous 18 months. Identified by a card on his body, Harry, whose skull was crushed by the accident, was on his way home from a football game at Oberlin when death took him. By sheer luck, the catastrophe spared his acquaintance, Mark L. Thompsen, who had also attended the same game. Although both had returned to Cleveland via the Erie Railroad, only Harry had won the footrace to make the 7:30 car at Broadway & Ontario.

One of the sadder casualties was Mrs. Martha Palmer, 59, of 165 Kenilworth Street in the Flats. Abandoned by her husband in 1886, she had struggled to make a living as a dressmaker since. Her daughter Lida broke down completely while identifying her mother's body at the morgue: "Oh Mama, can't you speak to me? If you could only speak one word. She can't hear me—she is dead!"

The official inquest into the Viaduct disaster opened at 9 a.m. on Tuesday, November 19. Hundreds of spectators were packed into the coroner's courtroom. Like virtually all inquests following Cleveland disasters during the last century, it opened with high expectations and closed with muttered, inconclusive, and harmless recriminations. The chief witness was motorman Augustus Rogers. He adamantly denied any knowledge that the electrical cut-off had been inoperative and he insisted that there were no red warning lights, either on the safety gates or posted above. About a dozen eyewitnesses subsequently gave conflicting testimony about the warning lights, leaving the question moot. A shattered red lantern was recovered from the depths of the Cuyahoga—but unfriendly rumor had it that parties friendly to Bridge Captain Brenner or interests sensitive to the potential liability of Big Con in the disaster had thrown several similar lanterns into the river after the fact. While Cleveland City Council debated blustering and thoroughly silly legislation to prevent similar disasters, the inquest shuddered to its predictable conclusion, given its many hours of irreconcilable and even incomprehensible testimony. Or as the *Cleveland Press* cynically summarized matters:

> The testimony brought out before the coroner regarding the Central Viaduct accident indicates that people may see strange things when they are frightened. Some of the witnesses have declared that they saw red lights upon the safety gates; others say that they saw white lights upon the gates, and others are positive that there were no lights of any color. Other witnesses have sworn that the gates were shut; still others have testified that the gates were open, and some of the people who claim to have been

upon the spot at the time of the accident are positive that no one who stood more than 50 feet away from the draw could have seen whether the gates were shut or not. It has also been asserted before the coroner that a lighted lantern was thrown into the river several minutes after the accident occurred; and one witness asserted upon oath that he knew that a lantern found in the river two or three days after the accident was the one . . . .

The final verdict, delivered by Coroner George W. Arbuckle on December 9 satisfied no one, except perhaps the officials of Big Con. Arbuckle's judgment was that no one involved in the accident had technically committed an "unlawful act," so his finding was that no one was to blame.

More decisive action, however, had already been taken on other fronts. On the Monday morning, November 18, some "Big Con" employees showed up at the viaduct and installed a new electrical cut-off. And when another disaster almost occurred on the Superior Viaduct on November 22, Little Con officials in charge responded immediately. With three streetcars waiting at the western end of Superior draw at 2 a.m., several of the motormen had left their cars to gossip with each other. The rearmost car, driverless, suddenly bumped the next car, which in turn pushed the front car toward the draw. It stopped just a foot short of the safety gate, and Motorman R. A. Dittrick and Conductor R. R. Patterson were subsequently fired for leaving their vehicles.

The later history of the Central Viaduct was not a happy one. The draw span was removed in 1912, and replaced with a high level truss-bridge that eliminated the draw entirely. One of the worst fires in Cleveland history, the Fisher-Wilson lumber conflagration on May 25, 1914, destroyed 300 feet of the Viaduct. It was rebuilt but became increasingly unsafe and hard to maintain as the years went by. Upkeep problems, as with the Superior Viaduct, were aggravated by continual sinking of the land under its western approaches. The opening of the Lorain-Carnegie Bridge in 1932 obviated much of the need for the Central Viaduct and it was finally closed and condemned in 1941. During World War II it was razed and its 500 tons of metal were converted into scrap metal. All that remains today are a few of its stone supporting piers on both sides of the river and several yards of its old trolley tracks, which can yet be seen in the street just south of the eastern end of the Lorain-

Carnegie bridge. That, and a copy of an 1895 ballad whose eighth and last stanza contains the last words on the Central Viaduct Disaster:

> The bridgeman claimed he did the work and he was not to blame.
> But someone must be punished or it will occur again.
> Who the guilty party is it's not for me to say.
> But God above will point him out upon the Judgment Day.

Chapter 10

DEATH TAKES A POWDER

The Strange Case of Hazel Gogan

The ideal murder story blends the novel and the familiar. It should have elements of the strange yet resonate with local color and the reassuring homeliness of the seven deadly sins. The ideal *Cleveland* murder story, additionally, should involve both East and West sides and partake of both high and low society. The weird tale of Hazel Gogan's death is just such an ideal Cleveland murder story. Before it was over it involved repeated violations of at least five of the Ten Commandments, resulted in a first-class murder trial, and provided months of titillation to Clevelanders and nationwide connoisseurs of criminous deeds. Better yet, despite an unequivocal jury verdict, it left a taint of unanswered questions and ambiguities that yet puzzle and entertain area murder buffs. Here follows—believe it or not—the bizarre story of Hazel Gogan's untimely demise.

Joe Gogan was a self-made man of the type that worships his creator. Sixty-three years old in 1950 and born Joseph Goga to a humble immigrant family of cabinetmakers in the East 49th-Broadway area, Joe had worked his way up from nothing to millionaire status over the first five decades of the century. One of seven children and a "graduate of the fourth grade," as he liked to say in later years, Joe began his financial ascent at the turn of the century as a $2.50-a-*week,* 13-year-old machinist for the Peerless Motor Company. Working in Cleveland, Youngstown, Akron, Pittsburgh, San Francisco, and Panama over the next two decades, Joe Gogan improved his engineering skills by hiring tutors to teach him by night the knowledge he needed to implement by day. Returning to Cleveland in the 1920s and rounding off his education with more lessons from a Case mathematics professor, Joe founded the Gogan Machine Corp. in 1924 with a capitalization of $10,000.

It is worth noting here the only trouble he ever had with the law until his 1950 murder trial was a judicial tongue-lashing in 1899 for hitting a boyhood acquaintance with an apple core.

By 1950 all of Joseph Gogan's hard work and shrewd effort had paid off handsomely. The Gogan Machine Corp., thanks to his inventive genius and astute marketing, was a successful manufacturer of railroad car springs and patented devices for testing the hardness of metals. Joe's days were now divided between long days at the Gogan plant at 1440 East 55th and hours of cherished leisure at "Three Oaks," his palatial 106-acre estate in Kirtland. Beautiful, well-groomed grounds showcased a 19-building compound that included swimming pool, pistol range, tennis court, pavilions, floodlit gardens, and mirrored stables housing Joe Gogan's cattle and blooded Arabian horses. Not the least splendid feature of the Gogan manse was an underground bomb shelter, complete with 12-inch steel walls, indirect lighting, forced ventilation, bar, a refrigeration room filled with meats and produce, fireplace, mirrors and expensive furniture. And, characteristically, a bronze bust of Joseph Gogan in front of the fireplace. In his occasional modest mood, Joe would allow that it really wasn't a bomb shelter at all:

> "It's not exactly a bomb shelter. I call it a bomb shelter, but we use it more as a rumpus room than anything else. Of course if you ever hear a real big noise, it is a real comfort to know you can go someplace that is safe."

Of course, it wasn't quite paradise, as nothing mortal can be. As we shall see, "Three Oaks" was troubled by vermin, most especially rats.

As is often the case, Joe Gogan had not accomplished his success alone. The partner and co-producer of the Gogan Machine Corporation miracle was his wife of 23 years, Hazel Matthews Gogan. Variously described in her 1950 obituaries and at Joe Gogan's trial as 45, 47, 55 or 57 years old, one's best guess is that she was at least the latter age. Starting at the beginning of Joe's firm in the 1920s as a stenographer, Hazel had married him in 1927 and together Joe and Hazel had built up the business to its multi-million dollar worth in 1950.

As is also often the case, success and a loyal wife were not

Cleveland Press Collection, Cleveland State University.
Portrait of Hazel Gogan.

enough for Joe Gogan. Perhaps his hard-earned success had gone to his head: there are diverting, gossipy tales extant of his imperious behavior as lord of "Three Oaks," including whipping his neighbors with a ready riding crop when they dared to object to his riding his horse over their shrubbery. In any case, there was unmistakable evidence by the late 1940s that Joe Gogan had succumbed to that common temptation of successful men: the Other Woman.

Her name was Leona Norbun. Although Cleveland newspapers reported that Joe Gogan met Ms. Norbun at an Akron horse show in 1941, he probably told the truth when he claimed he'd known her since she was in pigtails—which is likely, as Leona was the younger sister of two brothers, Charles and Steve Quinn, who had tutored Gogan in engineering decades before. What is even more likely, however, is that Joe and Leona's relationship quickened significantly during the 1940s. They were remarkably thick at that

1941 Akron horse show and, as various Gogan servants would subsequently testify at his murder trial, Joe entertained Leona on several occasions during the mid-1940s while Hazel was away. Clearly, the Gogan marriage was headed for a smash.

The smash duly came in 1948. Although a suspicious Hazel hired private detective Ray Manning at some time in the late 1930s to keep an eye on her husband, she apparently had decided to live with her marital situation. That decision changed in the summer of 1948 when she found two tickets for a Lake Erie cruise in her husband's wallet.

Egged on by her sister, Mrs. Pearl ("Pearlie") Heiser, Hazel booked three tickets for the same Lake Erie cruise. Accompanied by Pearlie and private detective Manning, the threesome shadowed Joe Gogan and his female companion—Leona Norbun!—as they retired to their stateroom on August 9 and confronted the pair as they emerged the next morning. Hazel forthwith sued for a separation and Joe returned to "Three Oaks" several days later to find Hazel and Pearlie decamping in haste with two automobiles crammed full of Gogan silver, furnishings, and collectibles.

Pearlie Heiser, to say the least, is one of the most interesting characters in the Gogan melodrama. Both she and her husband had been employed for some years by the Gogan Corporation—until Joe Gogan abruptly fired them in 1946. A matter not proven at his murder trial was whether Pearlie had been involved in the theft of some valuable blueprints from the Gogan Corporation. Be that as it may, there is no doubt that Pearlie took an enthusiastic role in the sugar-daddy-caught-in-love-nest scenario of August 9, 1948. Under vigorous cross-examination she would later admit that she "watched from a crack in a door two rooms away and would shout a warning to Hazel when anyone walked down the corridor." Some would say this was ungrateful behavior from a woman whose relationship with her sister's rich husband had brought her paid trips to Mexico, California, Florida, Canada, and Europe, not to mention three cars, a mink coat, silver fox furs, and a squirrel coat. But as she piously put it at the trial, "My sister was entitled to half of it. . . . I didn't consider them coming from Joe Gogan."

If Joe Gogan wanted Hazel Gogan dead after August 9, 1948, he certainly didn't act like it. Continuing to see her on a regular basis, he conceded to her a residence at 13870 Clifton Boulevard in Lakewood and continued to buy her lavish amounts of jewels and furs.

Cleveland Press Collection, Cleveland State University.
Joe Gogan and Mitzi.

They were seen together in public on numerous occasions, and many of their acquaintances did not even know that they were estranged, much less separated. Their separation was formalized in December 1948, and Gogan would later claim that he gave Hazel about $600,000 between their separation and her death. It is known with certainty that he bought out her interest in the Gogan Machine Corporation and that he also agreed to pay her $132,000 in nine payments. Interestingly, only three or four payments were made before Hazel's death—and it was a condition of their separation agreement that no payments would be due her estate *if she died before the fifth payment.*

It was an unexpected side of Joe Gogan that nearly put him in the electric chair. Although a man of little formal education, he had an almost childlike enthusiasm for the arts, especially painting. As did his wife Hazel: together they had spent thousands of Gogan dollars on expensively framed and individually lighted portraits and landscapes that decorated the walls of both "Three Oaks" and Hazel's home at 13870 Clifton. There were cynical souls who said that Joe and Hazel's collection was worthless kitsch and that art dealers around the world rubbed their hands in gleeful cupidity whenever they saw the Gogans coming, but neither Joe nor Hazel cared about such sneers. They knew what they liked and it didn't matter that an art collection they valued at millions was probably only worth hundreds, if that. What did matter, fatally for Hazel, was that that Joe and Hazel both wanted the same paintings.

It is a good guess that everyone except the dead woman herself lied about Hazel Gogan's last day on earth, so what follows is a most-likely scenario about her demise. It is at least uncontested that she was talking on the telephone in her second-floor bedroom at 13870 Clifton with Mrs. Katherine S. Whitney at about 11:50 a.m. on July 17, 1950. And just about that time, her estranged husband arrived at the house in a red pick-up truck. He had come to repossess three of his favorite paintings from the house. In the bed of the truck were some blankets to wrap the paintings in . . . and a bag of cyanide poison that his "Three Oaks" caretaker had asked him to get that morning to kill rats at the estate.

Joe would later insist, and probably sincerely believed, that the three paintings, which included an oil portrait of himself, were worth $35,000. Testimony at his trial suggested that their value was negligible to nil, but Joe nevertheless desperately wanted them back.

Arriving at Hazel's Clifton Boulevard house at about 11:50 a.m., Joe tried the front door. His story later was that Hazel shouted at him to go to the back door. There he briefly conversed with a Halle's delivery man and tried the door. It was locked and Hazel shouted that if he wanted to get in, he would have to break in. Which he did, smashing a pane in the front door and another in an inner door. Gaining access to the living room, Joe deployed his blankets and began removing the desired paintings from the walls.

What happened after that was disputed—and the substance of Gogan's indictment for first-degree murder. Mrs. Whitney testified that Hazel interrupted their telephone conversation to say that two men with a pick-up truck were breaking into her house. Hazel then screamed and hung up, and Mrs. Whitney called the Lakewood police.

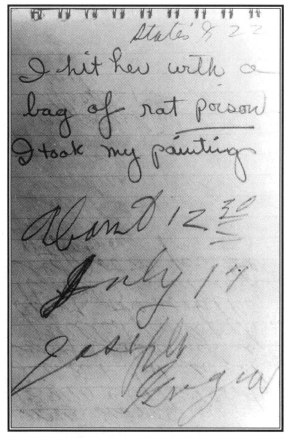

Cleveland Press Collection, Cleveland State University.
Joe Gogan's signed "confession."

Meanwhile, Hazel descended to the first floor where she confronted Joe in the act of wrapping the three paintings in blankets. He changed his testimony about what happened next but the most probable scenario is this: while grappling with Hazel over one of the paintings, Joe hit her with one of the blankets he had brought. Inside the folds of the blanket was the large bag of cyanide rat poison . . . which burst on contact with Hazel's flailing arm . . . and showered the unhappy couple with a brown, poisonous powder.

What happened next was witnessed by two 16-year-old Lakewood girls, Mary O'Neill and Nancy Dugan, St. Augustine Academy students who were waiting for a downtown bus across the street from Hazel Gogan's house. They saw Joe and Hazel arguing out on the front porch and they saw Joe push Hazel down as he attempted to wrest his paintings away from her. At this point, Albert Lisowski, a truck driver, was flagged down by the frightened girls and he approached the porch, where Hazel lay. When he got there Hazel was daubing her face with a washcloth, and Joe Gogan asked him if he lived there. When Lisowski said no, Joe told him to "get the hell out of the place." As Lisowski retreated, Gogan turned to his prostrate wife and repeatedly demanded—according to Lisowski—to know where she kept "the loose jewels." Receiving no answer, Gogan loaded his three paintings in his truck and prepared to depart. Interestingly, he took only the three paintings: left intact in the house were $10,700 in cash, several hundred thousand dollars' worth of furs and jewelry, and about $500 in loose change.

At this point, or possibly sooner, Gogan's plant superintendent, Martin P. Steg, showed up in Gogan's Buick. Martin's story evolved over time. His original statement was that he followed Gogan because he was afraid of what the temperamental industrialist might do to his estranged wife. According to him, Gogan's first remark when he saw him was "What the _____ are you doing here?" It seems more likely, however, that Steg was there by prearrangement with his boss to help him take the paintings away. In any case, Gogan and Steg exchanged vehicles and Steg drove the paintings off to his North Olmsted residence while Joe returned to his East 55th plant. Significantly, Joe stopped on the way at a Detroit Avenue garage, where mechanic Frank Blasius helped brush stray cyanide powder off Gogan's clothes. Neither Blasius or Gogan suffered from the experience.

Meanwhile, back at 13870 Clifton, things were not going well with Hazel Gogan. When Mary O'Neill and Nancy Dugan got to the porch, Hazel's eyes were streaming and she was daubing with a blue washcloth at the brown powder all over her face. She staggered to her feet and went into the house where, unwisely, she continued to wash her face.

Minutes later, the Lakewood police, alerted by Mrs. Whitney, arrived. When Police Sgt. Alfred Edwards got there he found Hazel Gogan unconscious on a davenport, her face streaked with brown powder and a lens from her glasses lying in a pile of poison. The front door glass was shattered, as was the pane in the inner door,

Gogan Admits Tryst in Philadelphia Hotel

By BUS BERGEN

The state disputed Joseph Gogan's testimony of a tranquil marriage today as it drew from him admissions he met Mrs. Leona Norbun 'three or four times" in a Philadelphia hotel and used aliases in registering at out-of-town hotels.

However, the trial was suspended when Prosecutor John J. Mahon, running a high temperature, caused an emergency court recess. Examined by Coroner S. R. Gerber, a trial witness, he was

year-old prosecutor's recovery. Before he was excused, Mahon worked from a detailed report of Gogan's activities as early as 1945, apparently gathered by a private detective.

Gogan denied he spent a night with the "other woman" on a boat trip to Detroit Aug. 9, 1948, as charged by state witnesses. He identified Mrs. Norbun as Eleanor Bradley, Philadelphia bridal consultant.

Stayed Overnight

he testified he last saw her "around Easter Sunday last year."

Gogan told Mahon he could not remember any of the aliases he had used.

Q.: Ever use J. G. Gordon?
A.: No, I never used that one.
Q.: Ever receive mail under that name at the Statler here?
A.: No.
Q.: Ever stop at the Barns Hotel in Logansport, Ind.
A.: Yes.
Q.: On Aug. 20, 1917?

don., 138 W. Grand Blvd., Detroit."

Q.: Did you sign that?
A.: Yes, for a friend of mine.
Q.: Who is this friend?
A.: A business friend.
Q.: Why would he ask you to sign a card in his name?
A.: That's his business, not mine.

Shows Another Card

Mahon then asked Gogan whether he stayed at Hotel Oliver in South Bend, Ind.

Cleveland Press Collection, Cleveland State University.

and a broken chain and chain holder were pulled loose from the doorjamb. Next to Hazel's body was the vigilant presence of her black-and-white Boston terrier, Mitzi.

Hazel Gogan was rushed to Lakewood Hospital. There, Dr. John R. Paradise and Nurse Mary Curtis labored heroically to save her. They administered oxygen, glucose, and caffeine and put a restraining strap on her legs to mitigate her convulsions. All their medical efforts were in vain and she died at 2:05 p.m. without regaining consciousness.

In the meantime, Mary O'Neill and Nancy Dugan had copied down the license number of Joe Gogan's Buick and within a few hours he was accosted at his plant by Detective Louis Bendo of the Lakewood Police.

Although initially uncooperative, Gogan seemed genuinely flabbergasted to hear that his wife was dead and that the police thought the cause was his rat poison. "That stuff won't hurt you," he insisted, "I can eat that stuff." He then willingly showed Bendo a can of the poison he kept at the plant and later that afternoon wrote, dated, and signed the following statement for Lieutenant Millard Roglin—which he would completely repudiate at his trial: "I hit her with a bag of rat poison—I took my paintings." He also stated to Roglin that "I did not hurt her and I did not kill her. The powder is harmless. I should know, I got most of it."

In retrospect, some would later wonder why Cuyahoga County Prosecutor John J. Mahon and County Coroner Sam Gerber were so anxious to push a first-degree murder indictment against Joseph Gogan, which was duly handed down on July 18th. Gerber and Mahon were going to have to prove that Joe Gogan had planned and committed murder with a bag of cyanide, surely a clumsy, if not baroque way to rid oneself of an unwanted spouse. Some would later speculate that Gerber wanted a celebrity-caliber conviction to bolster his campaign for financing a new County Morgue. Whatever the case, Joe Gogan was put in the County Jail with no bail while the County prepared its demand that he die in the electric chair. While in County Jail, Gogan continued to conduct his business affairs and befriended his fellow-inmates. For one young man who was there for spousal non-support, Gogan paid his arrears and got him a job at his plant. To the outside world he presented a brave front, saying, "I'm not a bit worried. I'm innocent. It was an accident." But reporters noted a "nervous twitching around his eyes and an inability to sit still."

Gogan's trial, which lasted a then-record-breaking seven weeks, began on December 4 before Judge Joseph A. Artl. Joining Mahon for the prosecution was Assistant County Prosecutor Thomas J. Parrino. Allied with them were Coroner Sam Gerber, his staff, and divers medical experts recruited for the case.

Joe Gogan could afford the best legal defense available in Cleveland—and he got it in the persons of William J. Corrigan and Fred W. Garmone (the same legal team that would defend Sam Sheppard at his infamous first trial in 1954). It was a classic Corrigan performance, perhaps his best. During seven weeks of testimony he hammered mercilessly away at the medical evidence presented by the prosecution and employed the full arsenal of his withering sarcasms to chip away at the state's witnesses and its presumptions about Gogan's alleged motives for murder.

It could be argued that the state's case was shaky, regardless of Corrigan's ability. Gogan's adulteries notwithstanding—and the jury was spared no detail of his trysts—the testimony of virtually all witnesses was that the Gogans, even when legally separated, acted like an amicable "couple" up to the day of Hazel's death. Joe had continued to lavish jewels, furs, and money on the woman he called "The Boss" and he had recently bought out her share in the Gogan Corporation And although he had lately changed the beneficiary of his $20,000 life insurance to his paramour and stood to gain $98,000 if Hazel died at the time she did, this must have

Cleveland Press Collection, Cleveland State University.
Photo of William J. Corrigan, attorney for Joe
Gogan (and also Eva Kaber and Sam Sheppard).

seemed like chump change to a jury deluged with copious testimony about a doting husband who had lavished hundreds of thousands of dollars on his wife, estranged or not.

Corrigan was particularly clever on the question of motive. Pearlie Heiser did not make a good witness in court, and the trial had to be temporarily halted when she physically collapsed under Corrigan's relentless cross-examination on January 3. Despite all the trips and gifts she had gained through her connection to Joe Gogan, she insisted to the end that she had considered her good fortune entirely due to Hazel, an unconvincing demurral to a jury that both prosecution and defense had labored to persuade that Joe Gogan was an inventor/genius entrepreneur. And that Pearlie denied all knowledge of her sister's estate—a matter of $565,000 of which Pearlie was the sole heir and for which she had signed an estate inventory—probably did not go over well with the jury. By the end of the trial Corrigan felt so confident of this angle that he used it as the climax of his final summation:

> Do you think Joe Gogan would make Pearlie Heiser rich? You think he'd go out and murder somebody to make that woman a millionaire?

Corrigan's attack on the medical evidence brought him into legal combat with his perennial adversary, Coroner Sam Gerber. Gerber insisted adamantly, despite evidence of a previously damaged heart, that Hazel's death was due to "cyno gas" resulting in respiratory failure. But all of Gerber's knowledge and experts were challenged and effectively mooted by similar medical experts for the defense. Corrigan, moreover, personally humiliated Gerber, repeatedly tripping him up over ambiguous medical terminology. In arguing over the Prussian blue test for the presence of cyanide, Corrigan noted that it had been marked "questionable" by the coroner's office. Gerber immediately rose to the bait and found himself trying to explain how "questionable" could be interpreted as "positive" by a layman. And Corrigan, after establishing Gerber's formal credentials firmly in the jury's mind, lured him into the following trap:

> Corrigan: Do not all the books say that in order to have cyanide you must have color blue?
> Gerber: Yes, but you need not.

Assistant Prosecutor Parrino probably didn't help the state's medical case, either, when he testified on December 27 that Hazel had aggravated the effect of the cyanide by trying to wash it off her face.

The final nail in the state's case was driven by neither the prosecution nor the defense. In mid-December, while in a Courthouse anteroom, *Cleveland Press* reporter Bus Bergen overheard several state witnesses mention the presence of Hazel's dog Mitzi at the death scene. Although the prosecution and Gerber had known of the dog's presence, they had not mentioned it either before or during the trial. After Bergen publicized the dog's presence at the death scene, Corrigan exploited his surprise canine witness to the hilt. Gerber et al. were arguing that the spilled poison powder was so lethal it had killed a 160-pound woman—and yet here was a 10-pound dog apparently unaffected by the "cyno gas"-filled room. In the end, Gerber could only sputter plaintively, "I can't understand it. You'd expect the dog to die or be very ill." He declined Corrigan's offer to put Mitzi on the stand.

It was well for Joe Gogan that Mitzi's presence testified so eloquently for him, as his own appearance on the stand was laughably unbelievable. Denying the ample evidence of his furtive adulteries, he claimed that he had only signed some hotel registers in question as a "favor" to unnamed friends. He insisted that he had not struck Hazel with the cyanide bag and denied their subsequent struggle on the front porch. He entirely repudiated his signed statement of July 17 and implied that Hazel had suddenly become unwell while he was removing the paintings. According to Joe, the bag had accidentally ruptured as it fell out of the blanket but Hazel had assured him that she would be all right. If Joe Gogan was telling the truth on the stand, virtually all the eyewitnesses to his philandering and Hazel Gogan's last moments were lying through their teeth. But in the end, as Corrigan made clear in his summation, nothing mattered except whether Joe Gogan was guilty as charged:

> I don't care if you find Joe Gogan threw his wife down the stairs, punched her in the mouth or hit her in the face with a bag. You still can't find this man guilty as charged in the indictment because it states she died of cyanide poisoning.

After a marathon of seven weeks, the end of the trial came suddenly. On January 24, 1951, the jury of seven men and five woman returned a verdict at 9:10 p.m. after only two hours of deliberation. There had been six ballots in all, and only one juror had even held out for manslaughter through the first five ballots. And it was clear what had been the decisive piece of evidence. Juror Mary Ingram remarked, "The dog was the deciding factor," a comment echoed by Juror Rose Marcus: "I just couldn't forget the dog in that room with Mrs. Gogan."

Joe Gogan certainly agreed. "Old Mitzi helped save Joe's life!" he enthused while kissing the dog for the benefit of photographers after the verdict was announced. "Best gift I ever bought!" That night, Joe Gogan returned to his Kirtland estate and began sorting through the 150 letters from lovesick women that had accumulated during his six-month legal ordeal. The next day he returned to work and filed suit to reclaim the three paintings that had brought him to 13870 Clifton Blvd. on July 17. A month later, he instituted vigorous legal action to recover some of Hazel's estate.

Our last glimpse of Joe Gogan is, alas, not a happy one. Shortly after his trial, he and Leona Norbun left for a world cruise. Married in Voras, Mexico, on September 8, 1951, they subsequently returned to settle down at "Three Oaks." But domestic tranquillity continued to elude Joe Gogan. In September 1953, Leona Gogan sued Joseph Gogan for divorce in Painesville Common Pleas Court. Her petition stated that Gogan had threatened her with a loaded pistol in their Kirtland home and, further, that her husband had once thrown a dish of coleslaw and a plate of peas in her face. One wonders if the second Mrs. Gogan was grateful for Joe's choice of weapon.

Chapter 11

THIRD MAN
AT HAMILTON

The Rise and Fall of
Judge William H. McGannon,
1920-1921

For those who like to see the mighty brought low, Cleveland has afforded many such exhibitions over the last century and a half. But for sheer duration, scandal, and almost unlimited shameless perjury, true connoisseurs of Cleveland crime among the high and mighty would probably rate the McGannon-Kagy affair as the best of breed. Before it ran its course it produced three major murder trials, a record number of perjury indictments, and the ruinous disgrace of a popular and well-respected judge. The real truth about this bizarre episode may never be known—except that almost everyone involved could not have been telling the truth for any length of time.

As any old-timer will tell you, downtown Cleveland was once a swinging scene at night. Especially weekend nights, and Saturday, May 7, 1920, was no exception. Traffic was dense, with streetcars running up Euclid every ten minutes, and throngs of pedestrians dotted downtown blocks from Public Square to Playhouse Square. Even as far north as the intersection of East 9th and Hamilton Avenue, it seems, there were dozens of Clevelanders enjoying the midnight sights and fleshpots of the Forest City during this Prohibition night. Dispute would develop later as to just *how* many Clevelanders were present at that particular intersection as May 8 arrived, but everyone allegedly present eventually agreed on one fact: three men were standing on the sidewalk near a parked Cadillac at the curb, just a few feet south of Hamilton on the east side of East 9th, when a shot rang out at precisely 12:27 a.m.

One of the three was Harold Kagy, automobile salesman and

owner of a nearby repair garage—and he had just been shot in the back with a .38. The slug entered at a 45-degree angle near his right tenth rib, punctured his right lung, bounced off his left fourth rib, and came to rest just below his left shoulder. Staggering toward a nearby garage, he cried out, "My God, I'm shot!" and fell to the sidewalk. Two men on the street, Patrick Gunn and Charles Kaiser, hearing his cry, ran to Kagy. He screamed, "For God's sake get me to a hospital before I bleed to death!" By this time, two plainclothes policemen, Walter Schuld and James Perko, who had also heard the shot, were on the scene. Commandeering a car, they and Kaiser helped Kagy into it, and a man named Harold Brunson drove them to Lakeside Hospital. Although Kagy had already told Kaiser at East 9th that he didn't know who had shot him, he now changed his story. At Lakeside Hospital, with Kaiser as a witness, he told Perko and Schuld that the guilty gunman was a man named Johnny Joyce.

Joyce was no stranger to Cleveland police. Dapper to a fault, he often sported flashy diamonds, was a Cleveland pioneer in the wearing of spats, and was reputed to have introduced the double-breasted Chesterfield overcoat to the Forest City. With a record of a dozen arrests stretching back to 1895, mostly on pickpocketing, public intoxication, and "suspicious character" beefs—and a charge just three days old for violation of the Volstead Act—Joyce had already been identified by witnesses as one of the three men present when the shot was fired at 12:27 a.m. Moreover, he had been seen fleeing from the shooting scene by several who knew his face well. But by this time, only minutes after the incident, Cleveland police were already after bigger game. The identity of the third man at the scene was still unknown, but the parked black Cadillac most definitely belonged to Judge William H. McGannon, chief justice of the Municipal Court.

Until this early 1920 May morning, Judge McGannon had been the Golden Boy of the Cleveland Bar. Born to Lake County poverty about 1870, he had come to Cleveland in 1890 after a stint at teaching school. Graduating from Western Reserve Law School in 1898, appointed County Examiner the same year, he was picked as assistant Cuyahoga County prosecutor by Sylvester McMahon in 1905. Elected Police Court judge in 1907, McGannon was elected as the first chief justice of the municipal court in 1911, and reelected for a six-year term in 1915. Celebrated by journalists for his "ability to arrive at the truth regardless of all red tape and subterfuge," he was seen as the man to beat in the Cleveland mayoral election of 1921.

All of which must have been on the mind of Charles Sterling, Joseph Matowitz, Joseph Burkhardt, and other Cleveland detectives as they arrived at the doorstep of Judge McGannon's home on East 116 Place about 90 minutes after Kagy was shot. For reasons never explained, the judge's wife, Anne, was awake, as were the judge's brothers, also present at this unseemly hour. Judge McGannon himself was apparently asleep. Detective Burkhardt would later testify that the awakened judge seemed the worse for drink, but that did not stop him from asking McGannon why his abandoned black Cadillac had been found at the scene of the crime.

Judge McGannon was not at a loss for a blandly told and simple story. According to him, he had met with Kagy earlier in the evening on East 55th so that the experienced garageman could troubleshoot his ailing Cadillac. After Kagy declared that the automobile's engine was "missing," he and the judge had taken it for a test drive out Lake Shore Boulevard to Willoughby and back. Stopping at a cafe, Kagy had eaten while Judge McGannon enjoyed two modest mouthfuls of brandy, despite his sworn duty to uphold the law of the land. Eventually, they had motored to Ferguson's Cafe at 12108 Euclid and Coltman Road in East Cleveland. There, they encountered saloon keeper/bail bondsman Johnny Joyce. Liquor had been summoned, but—so said the judge—had been consumed only sparingly by Kagy, heavily by Joyce, and not at all by himself. The three men had left Ferguson's about midnight with a sober Kagy at the wheel and McGannon had gotten out of his car at East 9th and Euclid, telling Kagy to drive Joyce wither he chose and to keep the car until it was repaired. McGannon had then crossed to the west side of East 9th and walked to Public Square via Superior. Catching a 12:30 streetcar in front of the May Company on Euclid, he had returned to home and bed about 1 a.m.

Meanwhile, back at Lakeside Hospital, a rather different story was being told by the critically wounded Harold Kagy. Although Kagy had demurred when Kaiser interrogated him minutes after the crime, he now unequivocally accused Johnny Joyce, as he would to his dying breath:

> There was no row preceding the shooting. Joyce was beefing about many things as we came downtown. His hat was off and he was using bad language. He got out of the machine, still

doing much talking. I got out of the machine to find out just where he wanted to be taken. I turned and he shot me in the back. Judge McGannon was not there. He got out of the machine at Euclid Avenue and East 9th.

The next afternoon Johnny Joyce, after negotiations with the police, turned himself in and was held on $7,500 bail. He was quickly rushed by Police Chief Frank W. Smith to Lakeside Hospital, where Kagy looked at him and said, "That's the man who shot me." Joyce replied, "I didn't do it, Kagy, You know who really did it. Why don't you tell them who it really was? Why don't you tell them the truth?" Finally, after Kagy refused to retract his identification, Joyce burst out:

> "I'm the goat in all this. I'm not going to be the only one to suffer, you'll see if I am. But I'm not going to tell anything till I get to court."

Joyce was as good as his word. He said nothing until his trial, except to deny shooting Kagy. Among the details he concealed was a meeting with Judge McGannon the afternoon after the shooting at Ferguson's "soft drink" cafe. There the following dialogue may have ensued:

> McGannon: John, I know you are as innocent as a a newborn babe. Keep your mouth shut. You will come out all right.
> Joyce: Keep my mouth shut for what? I didn't kill Kagy.
> McGannon: Go and get some sleep. I'm nearly dead.

Meanwhile, the search for the "third man" seen by numerous witnesses at the scene intensified. He was generally described as about 6 feet tall, 200 pounds, and wearing a light gray overcoat and soft hat. Rumors abounded that it had been Judge McGannon but he stoutly denied it and the police refused to subpoena him, evoking this stinging front-page editorial from the *Cleveland Press*:

> Judge McGannon can and should insist upon being called as a witness. HE SHOULD INSIST ON TESTIFYING!

As for police reluctance to subpoena any "third man," despite claims that they knew who he was, the editorialist had nothing but

Cleveland Press Collection, Cleveland State University.
Mary Neely.

the kind of scorn Louis B. Seltzer would later reserve for Sam
Sheppard:

> The police say they know who he is, but that they can't prove
> his identity, and hence they are not going to subpoena him as a
> witness at the Joyce hearing. In other words the police are insist-
> ing that they must have witnesses to prove who was a witness.
> Stuff and nonsense! Balderdash! Flummox-food! Bunk! Bull! .
> . . . STOP STALLING!

The hunt for the third man became more intense when Harold
Kagy died of complications of his infected lung wound at 6:35 p.m.
on May 23. The day before he died, his four brothers and father
took a statement from him, again implicating Joyce as the shooter
and denying that McGannon was the "third man" at the scene. On

June 4, Joyce was indicted on a charge of second-degree murder and again held on $25,000 bail.

Kagy's trial before Judge Maurice Bernon and an all-male jury did not open until November 9. By this time, the rumors that McGannon was the "third man" had become so widespread that he had to take a leave of absence from his court. Clevelanders were expecting sensational developments from the trial and they were not disappointed.

The raw substance of the trial was the violent conflict between the two versions of the night of May 7-8 recounted by John Joyce and Judge McGannon. According to Joyce, it had been a sodden evening, indeed. After an alcoholic binge of two or three days, he had arrived at Ferguson's cafe about 10 p.m. An hour later, Kagy and McGannon came in and the threesome retired to a private room where the judge drank brandy ("Three Star Hennessey") and Joyce and Kagy tippled bourbon ("Golden Wedding") from Joyce's quart bottle. About midnight they left Ferguson's in the judge's car, Kagy driving, Judge McGannon in the front passenger seat, and Joyce seated behind Kagy. Amply supplied with hootch, they stopped at University Circle to have a snort, and continued on down Euclid Avenue. Having finished their bottles at East 79th, they threw them out the window of the judge's Cadillac and continued on downtown.

Joyce admitted he had been quite drunk but he did remember McGannon and Kagy arguing about money during the ride downtown. When the car stopped at Hamilton and East 9th, McGannon and Kagy helped the intoxicated Joyce out of the car and he leaned drunkenly against a nearby telegraph pole. He then heard McGannon say to Kagy, "Where is that money? Come here. I won't stand for that!" Joyce then heard a loud noise—but staggered away from the scene without knowing that Kagy had been shot.

Joyce then recounted his meeting with McGannon at Ferguson's on Saturday afternoon to a rapt courtroom audience.

McGannon took the stand to offer a far more demure version of the evening of May 7. No, he had not been drinking at Ferguson's or on the ride downtown; indeed, he had been as sober that evening as, well, a judge. ("I did not have anything to drink. I am not a drinking man.") And he was not at Hamilton and 9th when the shot was fired; he had gotten out of his Cadillac in front of the Lennox Building, just north of 9th and Euclid some minutes after 12 midnight. And, no, he had never told Joyce at their May 8 meeting at Ferguson's that he knew Joyce to be as innocent as a "newborn babe."

Harold Kagy's testimony probably would have sent Joyce to the electric chair. But Kagy was dead and his "deathbed statement" implicating Joyce and giving the judge an alibi was disallowed by Judge Bernon on the arguable grounds that Kagy had not known he was dying when he made the statement—despite the fact that he cooperatively expired the day after he made it and that his fingers were turning blue at the time he signed it.

Which left the question of who to believe up to the testimony of the other witnesses, a motley crew to say the least. A possible motive and means for Joyce were introduced by Edward Rice, an employee at Ferguson's. He testified that Joyce arrived there quite drunk about 10:20 p.m. with a gun sticking out of his pocket and declared loudly, "I'm going to get the _____who knocked me off the day before," a vengeful reference to his liquor bust on May 5. In addition, Rice had later heard Ferguson say to Joyce, while in the private room, "Put that away," presumably referring to his gun. Joyce on the stand primly claimed what he "put away" was a bottle of whiskey, not a gun.

Charles Kaiser testified that he saw the heavy "third man" who fled from the scene but could not identify him. William Wilson, a Canadian war veteran, however, had also seen the third man and he identified him in court as Judge McGannon. Wilson also testified that he had been told by a stranger prior to the trial that "the best thing I can do is to remember as little as possible about the 'third man.'" Adrian Short swore that he had seen the third man fire the shot but couldn't identify him as McGannon. Dr. J. H. Gass, yet another bystander on that crowded corner, had also seen the third man fire the shot, and put something "shiny" in his pocket, and he now identified him as Judge McGannon. Policemen Perko and Schuld had seen three men at Hamilton, heard one of them say, "Let me see where you got your money, come here!"—but could not identify the third man at the scene.

The only solid eyewitness against Joyce was Jesse Holmes, a black man who was brought from the City Jail, where he was held on a "cutting to wound" charge, to testify. He claimed he had heard Joyce say to Kagy, "I have a way of making a man do what I want." Moreover, Holmes swore he had actually seen muzzle fire from the gun and he steadfastly identified Joyce as the gunman. Unfortunately for the prosecution, Holmes was taken apart by defense attorney Walter Meals on the stand. The climax of his cross-examination must have been a nightmare for Prosecutor Roland Baskin, as Meals argued the probable truth—that the "Jesse Holmes" on the stand was not even the witness by that name at the shooting scene.

The dishonest impression created by Holmes was aggravated by his claim that plainclothes officers Perko and Schuld had worn uniforms that evening—a delusion shared by William Wilson and other witnesses.

McGannon's alibi had not yet assumed the monstrous and populous proportions it would take in subsequent trials. Detectives Herman Burkhardt and John Skala testified to seeing the judge drunk in front of Weber's Restaurant on Superior about 12:38, supporting the claim of his roundabout journey to Public Square.

Neither the prosecution nor the defense, ultimately, had a strong case, as was reflected in their summations. Given the fact that no one except the questionable Jesse Holmes could identify Joyce as the triggerman, there was little in Joyce's account of the evening incompatible with his innocence.

The Joyce jury went out at 3:45 p.m. on November 17 and returned five hours later with a verdict of "Not Guilty." Joyce had never been in danger: the first of five ballots was 6 to 4 for acquittal, the second was 10 to 2, followed by two ballots at 11 to 1. After a final query to Judge Bernon about Kagy's deathbed statement—again disallowed—the jury unanimously acquitted Joyce. As the verdict was read, Joyce leapt to his feet and said, "Justice has been done. I knew you would free me."

That all thus far had been prelude became clear the day after, when Prosecutor Baskin reconvened the Grand Jury for further investigation of the case. Both McGannon and the prosecutor's office were frantically soliciting witnesses, and it was clear that the judge was now the target. William H. McGannon was indicted for Harold Kagy's murder on November 26. His $10,000 bail was immediately posted by Irene Kilbane, wife of Cleveland prizefighter Johnny Kilbane.

The trial, which opened on December 14 before Judge Maurice Bernon, was in part a recapitulation of the Joyce murder trial. The

Cleveland Press Collection, Cleveland State University.
John W. Joyce.

irony that the positions of the principals—Joyce and McGannon—
were now reversed was missed by no one. And most of the same
witnesses came forward to tell the same stories again. Perko,
Schuld, and Short reiterated their testimony about the "third man."
Wilson again fingered McGannon as the triggerman. Detective
Burkhardt again recounted seeing Judge McGannon intoxicated on
Superior—but some minutes *after* McGannon claimed to have
boarded a Euclid Avenue streetcar.

What was interesting at the second trial were the differences.
Patrolman Frank Brooks now came forward to swear he had seen

McGannon at Hamilton between 12:15 and 12:30 a.m. J. H. Gass now testified that he hadn't seen the third man's face, previously identified by him as McGannon's. Joyce's memory, too, had misted over somewhat, and he now couldn't remember whether he'd heard a shot or a car backfire. "I didn't know who shot Harold Kagy and I don't know today," he said.

The bombshell the prosecution had been hinting at for weeks exploded on Tuesday, December 21, when Miss Mary "May" Neely took the stand. A short, plain-featured, middle-aged practical nurse, Miss Neely had known the judge for 16 years and, she testified that December afternoon, had been following him around on that fatal May evening. Just *how* she knew the judge—she claimed to have seen him almost every day of that decade and a half—and *why* she had been following him around at midnight were not quite explained, although her quest seems to have had something to do with the judge's personal life, something that neither she nor McGannon's family was anxious to have disclosed. In any case, Neely's story was that she had been standing at East 9th and Oregon (now Rockwell Avenue), two blocks south of Hamilton, when she saw McGannon pull something from his pocket and saw a shot fired. Her story continued with McGannon putting something in his pocket and fleeing west down Hamilton Avenue.

There was worse to come for the judge. Miss Neely testified that sometime later she had met with the judge and that she had told him to get his story straight, tell the police there had been an "accident," or even allow Miss Neely to take the blame. The judge, she said, had rejected her noble offer to take the rap—but had offered her $500 with promise of more to come "if I would say I didn't see anything happen on Hamilton Avenue." (Miss Neely's sister, Louise Webb, incidentally, backed up Mary's bribe tale, having supposedly been conveniently positioned by a window to eavesdrop on the conference.) The judge, for his part, ended their alleged colloquy by musing, "If only I could get someone to say they saw me get out of the machine at East 9th Street and Euclid."

The judge's wish, if true, seems to have been answered beyond his wildest prayers. Perhaps it also had something to do with the money paid by the McGannons to the Walter J. Burns Detective Agency, which had been scouring the city for helpful witnesses. Mr. and Mrs. Harry Du Rocher of Lakewood took the stand and swore they had seen the judge walking north toward Superior on East 9th at the fatal moment. Louis Ross also saw McGannon at Superior and 9th. Guy Dwyer saw him in front of the Gaiety Theater on 9th. Joseph Johnson saw McGannon standing by his Cadillac at Euclid and 9th. Mrs. Catherine Fay said she had seen McGannon walking down East 9th near Superior. Demonstrating a fine fraternal loyalty, the judge's brother, Dr. A. C. McGannon, testified that he had conveniently seen his brother *twice* that evening—once walking north up East 9th and again on his way down Superior to Public Square. Not to be outdone, Charles Seaver, who had been making a film delivery on Euclid, claimed to have seen Judge McGannon standing 75 feet north of Euclid on East 9th—at a time when Seaver was standing on the north side of Euclid, 150 feet west of 9th. As the imposing Hickox Building loomed five stories high at the northwest corner, *Seaver would have had to see through it to catch a glimpse of Judge McGannon at those distances.* Seaver came to be known to Cleveland newspaper readers, perhaps cruelly, as the "man with X-ray eyes."

Better yet was the testimony of Henrietta Jouget. Suffering from insomnia at midnight, May 8, she had happened to be strolling in the vicinity of East 9th and Euclid. There she noticed a "suspicious"-looking man alight from a streetcar and step into a dark doorway. He transferred something to his overcoat pocket and pulled a hat over his eyes. Finally, just as the judge's Cadillac pulled away from the curb (having deposited the judge there for his much-witnessed walk north), Ms. Jouget saw her sinister man jump on the running board of the Cadillac and crouch there as it motored to its fatal rendezvous with death at Hamilton. Better yet, the crouching man fit the description of the "third man" perfectly—200 pounds, 6 feet tall, and wearing a light overcoat. Not knowing when to stop, Jouget added that her man "looked like he was mean and nasty—his nose was red like a tomato and his complexion light." A meticulous witness, to say the least, Jouget even produced the sinister "third man's" hat, which he had conveniently dropped for her to retrieve from the scene. Amazingly, her testimony about the crouching running-board rider was seconded by two other witnesses, Mrs. C. Beardsley and Miss Ethel Beardsley.

Several more witnesses were introduced to buttress Judge McGannon's story. James McCafferty, a cab driver, testified that he had been driving Miss Neely and two other women around Cleveland at the time she claimed to have witnessed Kagy's shooting, although he could not remember either their names or itinerary very well. (McCafferty was later the first witness in the McGannon-Kagy trials convicted of perjury). Four defense witnesses claimed—believably—that Miss Neely could not have made such a positive I.D. of Judge McGannon et al. from her vantage point two blocks away, especially at midnight. (One juror would later confess, "It was Miss Neely's testimony that stuck me, for I believed she said too many impossible things.") And Miss Rayta Middleton claimed she had chatted with Miss Neely on a Cleveland streetcar in July, during which conversation Miss Neely offered a far different version of the now disputed events. In all, the state called 18 witnesses, while the defense, swollen by the spectators who thronged the judge's alleged walk down East 9th, called 38.

The prosecution reiterated the evidence offered by credible witnesses, some of them policemen, that McGannon had been at the scene of the crime, not to mention such inconsistencies as why William McGannon had walked north to Superior to catch a streetcar at Euclid. The jury went out at 6:15 on December 29.

It came back in just before 6 p.m., December 31, still hopelessly deadlocked. From the beginning, two jurors had held out for acquittal, and after their 53 ballots of utter frustration, Judge Bernon declared a mistrial. Much of his decision was based on his feeling that the trial could not legally run over into the new year. Judge McGannon's new trial date was set for February 7.

By the time that trial commenced, Cleveland citizens were thoroughly aroused. The Cleveland Foundation, outraged by police corruption and such spectacles of farcical justice as the unsolved Kaber murder and the Joyce-McGannon trials, announced in January that national experts, including Felix Frankfurter and Roscoe Pound, would be brought in to survey the administration of justice in Cleveland.

Judge McGannon's second trial, under Judge Homer G. Powell before a jury of nine men and three women, was, notwithstanding one shocking development, far duller than his first. By now, memories had faded much, and only Johnny Joyce and Patrolman Frank Brooks would positively identify McGannon as being the "third

Cleveland Press Collection, Cleveland State University.

Judge William H. McGannon.

man" at the Hamilton corner. And then everything fell completely apart for Prosecutor Stanton and the state's case on February 11. With Miss Neely, wearing a sailor hat, once again poised to repeat her accusations, Stanton led her through the paces until:

Stanton: Did you see a machine?
Neely: Yes, I saw a machine.
Stanton: Did you see a car with a license No. 116363?
Neely: I don't remember.
Stanton: Were you at the corner at that time?
Neely: I don't remember.
Stanton: Did you get off the street car at that point?
Neely: I don't remember.

After five minutes of Miss Neely's progressively deteriorating memory, a frustrated Stanton asked for a recess. But the dialogue just got worse when his interrogation resumed:

Stanton: Did Judge McGannon get out of the machine?
Neely: I cannot answer other than to say that Judge McGannon did not kill Harold Kagy.

After some astonished probing by Prosecutor Stanton and Judge Powell, Miss Neely eventually blurted out that answering their questions "might tend to disgrace or incriminate me to answer it." Threatening her with contempt of court, Judge Powell asked her to tell him privately her reasons for refusing to testify. She whispered in his ear and then Judge Powell announced that Miss Neely did not have to answer questions asked at the previous trial. Her lapses of memory and refusals to answer continued through the remainder of her testimony and included a failure to remember her meeting with McGannon and his offer of a $500 bribe to forget anything she had seen on Hamilton. When queried later, Miss Neely coyly disclosed that she had given her answers without coaching; the legal phraseology about self-incrimination had just happened to be in a book she had recently seen—opened to the apt page!—in the courtroom.

More witnesses were called after Miss Neely's unexpected testimony, but the heart had gone out of the prosecution's case. With state witnesses' memories evaporating or uncooperative, and more persons coming forward daily to testify that they and an apparent cast of thousands had seen the judge on his alibi walk down 9th and Superior, defeat loomed. It came on February 18, 1921, at 11:20 a.m., when a verdict of acquittal was announced. It had taken eight ballots and 20 hours. Judge McGannon walked out of the courtroom a free man.

Or so he thought. After all, given the rule of double jeopardy, Judge McGannon could not be tried again for the murder of Harold Kagy. But Prosecutor Stanton, the legal community, and the citizens of Cleveland were outraged by what had been perceived as a carnival of perjury and undue influence in all three trials thus far. Both Judge Bernon and Judge Powell begged the Cleveland Bar Association for an investigation of "wholesale perjury" and the Bar

Association demanded that Judge McGannon resign his position. United States Secret Service agents poured into Cleveland and began to interview witnesses and collect documents. Within weeks, new indictments were handed down for perjury against nine persons: Joseph Johnson, Louis Ross, Guy Dwyer, Mrs. Catherine Fay, Charles Seaver ("the man with X-ray eyes"), and George Bobich for supporting Judge McGannon's alibi with preposterous fictions. William Wilson and Dr. Gass, for their testimony about Johnny Joyce, were likewise indicted. The ultimate total would reach at least 15 perjury indictments. And Chief Justice of the Municipal Court William H. McGannon was indicted on April 14 for lying about getting out of his automobile at East 9th. The last veil protecting the identity of the "third man" had melted away. McGannon announced on February 24th that he would resign from the bench on March 15. He and his family attempted to forestall the inevitable by having him committed to a sanitarium in April. After a couple of weeks, however, Judge Florence Allen had him arrested there—"nervous breakdown" or not—and taken to County Jail. He claimed he had no clothes to wear—until the deputies threatened to take him as he was.

Things went more smoothly for the prosecution at McGannon's perjury trial, which opened before Judge Allen in June 1921. The first jury summoned in late May had to be thrown out on May 31 just after the opening statements had been completed, due to some prejudiced comments by a jury member and a court bailiff. Once again, it was attorney William Boyd for the defense and Edward Stanton for the state, assisted—so that no one would miss the point—by a specially appointed representative of the Cleveland Bar Association, William David. Miss Neely, happily, was her smiling, cooperative self again, and almost immediately blurted out the magic words everyone had been waiting to hear for a year: "I saw Judge McGannon shoot Harold Kagy." (Judge Allen ordered the magic words struck from the record). And there was worse to come. Miss Neely also told of a secret meeting with the judge on February 10, just a night before his second trial opened. During that meeting, in Room 210 at the Hotel Mecca, thoughtfully provided by ex-*Cleveland News* reporter Charlie Burke, Judge McGannon had coached Miss Neely in her refusals to remember or reply that would so startle Stanton, Powell, and the jury at the judge's second trial. And what price did Miss Neely exact of the judge, considering her expected perjury, and their unspecified relationship of more than 16 years? Only that he "give up a certain friend, to be more attentive to his wife, to go to church, and to be a better man." Miss Neely also got $110 in cash from the judge. Not to stint on the largesse flowing from his moral reformation, Judge McGannon also paid cooperative Charlie Burke $1,025 for the use of his room. Burke, a genuine mental giant, had already filed suit against the judge, demanding payment of the balance owed him for opening his premises as perjury rehearsal space. The judge, for his part, was unable to explain the purpose of $700 in checks he had given to Burke. Another ex-*News* reporter, Edward Allen, who had worked with Burke in arranging Neely's perjury, also testified against the judge, disclosing that McGannon had also asked both of them to testify falsely that Neely had perjured herself at McGannon's first trial.

The feebleness of McGannon's personal testimony in rebuttal of Neely, Burke, and Allen's charges was a measure of the psychological attrition his year of scandal and trials had taken on him. Against Burke and Allen's sworn testimony and the physical evidence of the checks, he could plead only that he had been drinking heavily and was "mentally and physically sick" at the time of his actions. His explanation of his Hotel Mecca meeting was even weaker: according to his version, Miss Neely had come there "conscience-stricken" about accusing him and confessed that her reason for accusing him was, "You didn't treat me very kindly. You didn't let me ride in your automobile." Patrolman Charles Sarvach testified for the defense that he had overheard Miss Neely's alleged motive for turning against the judge: "Because you promised to marry the other woman." The Judge's attorney, William Boyd, demanded that the jury deem Neely's version of that fatal May night an "impossible" tale that "hinged on the insane."

The case went to the jury at 9 p.m. on June 24. After some hours of deliberation, the jury foreman informed Judge Allen that they found reaching a verdict "impossible." Judge Allen, however sent them back to the jury room and they reached agreement on their eighth ballot on the evening of June 25 after 27 hours of deliberation. No sooner had Judge Allen read the words aloud "guilty as charged in the indictment," than ghastly echoes of "guilty" came from McGannon and his mother in the courtroom. McGannon was

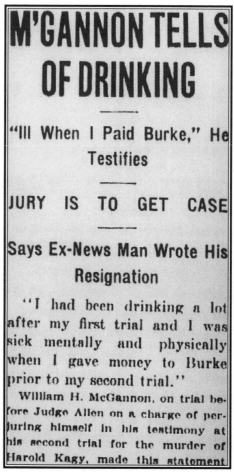

M'GANNON TELLS OF DRINKING

"Ill When I Paid Burke," He Testifies

JURY IS TO GET CASE

Says Ex-News Man Wrote His Resignation

"I had been drinking a lot after my first trial and I was sick mentally and physically when I gave money to Burke prior to my second trial."

William H. McGannon, on trial before Judge Allen on a charge of perjuring himself in his testimony at his second trial for the murder of Harold Kagy, made this statement

Cleveland Press Collection, Cleveland State University.

so crushed he could barely utter the words allowed him by Judge Allen before sentencing:

"I told the truth when I sat on that witness stand. Almighty God knows I told the truth. I know nothing more about the shooting of Harold Kagy than what I told when I was on the stand. God traced my footsteps on that night. He knows that I am innocent. This is the greatest miscarriage of justice in history."

Judge Allen sentenced Judge McGannon to 1 to 10 years in the Ohio Penitentiary. Just as he left the courtroom, McGannon momentarily stopped, and raising his right hand above his head, shouted:

> "As there is a Jesus Christ in heaven, he will make these people suffer as I have suffered. He will torture them and punish them as I have been punished. If they don't suffer as I have suffered, then there is no God."

Walking outside, Judge McGannon and his family stepped into the black Cadillac that Harold Kagy had piloted on their ill-fated ride downtown 13 months previous. Several days later he was found guilty of contempt of court for arranging Neely's perjury in his second trial and served 20 days in the County Jail before departing for Columbus.

Judge McGannon served 19 months in the Ohio Penitentiary before his conditional release on January 5, 1924, on medical grounds, specifically severe diabetes. The judge's many legal appeals proved fruitless, but he still tried to make a living from the practice of law. In the summer of 1928, he and his wife, Anne, who had steadfastly supported him through better and worse, moved to Chicago, where he toiled for a law firm. On November 17, 1928, he dropped dead from a heart attack as he was boarding a streetcar. He was somewhere between 58 and 62 years old.

Miss Neely had preceded him to the grave by six years, dying in Lakeside Hospital in Cleveland in May 1922. According to her friends, she had changed her name and tried to put her past behind her. She was only 42. Johnny Joyce died at the age of 53 in June 1929. He ran unsuccessfully for the Ohio Legislature in 1925; one wonders if he meant the words he said on the day he finished his 60 days in the workhouse:

> In the future, I'm going to live a clean, honest, upright life. I'll devote my attentions to helping the poor and downtrodden.

Rogue reporter Edward Allen drowned shortly before the judge's death. And Ferguson's, the "soft drink" cafe where it all started, was raided for violation of Prohibition on December 28, 1920. And that was that.

Or was it? To this day the question of who really shot Harold Kagy remains open. While it seems likely that Judge McGannon was present at the fatal scene at Hamilton and East 9th, no one has ever established a creditable means (i.e. a murder weapon) or a substantial motive for McGannon's shooting Kagy.

Which leaves a fascinating possibility. The author knows a man . . . who used to know a fellow . . . who ran a saloon many years ago down on Lakeside Avenue, near the old County Morgue. This saloon keeper insisted that the unknown truth of the Kagy shooting was simply this: Miss Neely, an estranged girlfriend of Judge McGannon, *was* tailing the judge on that fatal May 8 at midnight. But she wasn't at Oregon Avenue when 12:17 a.m. arrived. She was across the street from the parked Cadillac, on the west side of 9th Street near Hamilton, and she was mad as hell at the judge. It was she who drew a shiny object from her pocket and fired at her estranged paramour. Given the light at that hour and a poor aim, she unwittingly hit not her ex-lover but innocent bystander Harold Kagy. *Kagy, Joyce, and McGannon were not aware that it was she who fired the shot that hit Kagy.* This, if nothing else, would explain her alleged offer to take the blame in her meeting with the judge after the shooting, and it would also explain why some witnesses remembered an unidentified woman in a fur coat fleeing from the scene. Sneer if you will, and mutter *cherchez la femme,* but it is surely a more consistent and believable theory than any you will find in the voluminous trial transcripts, newspaper coverage, and police records on the McGannon-Kagy murder mess of 1920.

Chapter 12

RED DAWN IN CLEVELAND

The 1919 May Day Riots

Historians can't seem to make up their minds. One day they stress the cyclical, repetitive nature of human experience; the day after they emphasize the unrepeatable and quaint oddity of the past and its inhabitants. In one breath it's *plus ca change, plus c'est la meme chose;* the next wheeze out is L. P. Hartley's saw, "The past is a foreign country; they do things differently there." About the only thing most of them can agree with is William Faulkner's gloomy, fatalistic phrase: "The past is never dead; it's not even past."

These contradictory but equally true views could well be applied to Cleveland's 1919 May Day Riots. Although neither quite a murder nor a disaster, they were certainly a disgrace and a phenomenon that will probably never be repeated here: a primarily ideological conflict, aggravated to violence by lingering war-time tensions in a city with a large foreign-born, non-English-speaking population. Cleveland has changed much since 1919, and social conflicts since the Great Depression have usually played out here along racial fault lines. But the issues of nativism, patriotism, and free speech embedded and engendered in the May Day Riots are with us yet. If you don't believe it, consider the bitter animus directed in 1990–91 against local area protesters of the Gulf War. Consider the jail term handed out to Cheryl Lessin in 1990 for burning an American flag on Public Square. Consider, too, the still-seething groundswell of public demand for English-as-the-official-language, here and throughout the United States . . . and the tragically farcical events of 1919 Cleveland come into almost too-familiar focus.

Socialism and kindred "radical" ideas developed early in Cleveland. The Socialistic Labor Party had an active chapter in the Forest City by 1876 and gained six percent of the Cuyahoga County gubernatorial vote in the 1877 elections. Known as the Social Labor Party by the 1890s, the Cleveland affiliate flourished under the leadership of Max Hayes and Robert Bandlow, joining with the Populist party to support progressive candidates in local and state elections. The local peak for such movements probably came in 1911, when Socialist mayoral candidate Charles E. Ruthenberg won 10 percent of the vote.

Ruthenberg proved to be the central figure in early-20th-century Cleveland socialism and, ironically, the man most responsible for its demise. Born in 1882 to Germans of liberal political background, he left school at 14 and soon found work as a bookkeeper and sales manager. First inspired by the career of Mayor Tom L. Johnson, Ruthenberg veered more sharply leftward in 1908 after checking out Karl Marx's *Capital* from Cleveland Public Library. Joining the Socialist Party in 1909, he became recording secretary of the Cleveland chapter a year later. Running frequently for the mayoralty of Cleveland, Ruthenberg also ran for Governor in 1912, the highwater mark for Socialist electoral fortunes in American history. Opposing American entry into World War I, Ruthenberg was in and out of jail after 1917. As May 1919 arrived, he had just been released from a year's sentence at the Canton Workhouse on a charge of obstructing execution of the Selective Service law.

The precipitating cause of the 1919 May Day Riots was Ruthenberg's decision to hold a May Day celebration at Public Square. The ostensible reasons for the rally were Ruthenberg's candidacy for the mayoralty and to protest the jailing of Eugene V. Debs, America's best-known Socialist, for violation of the Espionage Act.

There was, of course, much more to it than that. It is hard to believe now, but in 1919 it seemed to Ruthenberg and other leftists that a Red Dawn of socialism/communism was breaking all over the world. With the Soviet takeover of Russia a fact, and leftists battling for power with governments in Germany, Poland, and Hungary, it seemed to many, both reactionaries, revolutionists, and lots of people in between, that World Revolution on the Marxist model was a real possibility. Or as Ruthenberg was reported by police as saying in early 1919: "Revolutions in Europe have been successful, why not here?" Both he and the controlling faction of the Cleveland Socialists saw a Red Dawn coming, and on March

May day riot photo with mounted policeman at right and trolley sign in middle, May 1, 1920.

30, 1919, he announced the conversion of the Cleveland Socialist chapter to the aggressive Leninist brand of revolution:

> By a practically unanimous vote, the members of the Socialist party of Cuyahoga County yesterday aligned themselves with the Bolsheveki of Russia and the Spartacans [sic] of Germany in adopting a Left Wing program. The important points of this program are repudiation of political action in favor of social reform measures and the indorsement of mass action thru organization of the workers in the industries and a Workers' and Soldiers' Council, to carry on the struggle for industrial democracy and the overthrow of capitalism.

Several days later, Ruthenberg began promoting a Socialist parade, to be held in Cleveland on May 1.

His timing could not have been worse—or better—depending on one's point of view. Events in the U. S. and abroad may have made Ruthenberg and his cohorts optimistic for the chances of revolution. But the same events spelled Red Terror to many middle-class Americans, and their fears had already begun to generate the phenomenon known as the "Red Scare." I.W.W. groups and other radical factions had already sparked political and labor disturbances in Seattle and elsewhere, and the publicity in Cleveland newspapers about Bolshevik excesses abroad and leftist letter-bombs and labor strikes at home had many persons, especially public safety officials, on edge. Add the lingering atmosphere of wartime hysteria in Cleveland—a hysteria (or "patriotic enthusiasm" if you will) still being whipped up during the spring of 1919 to sell yet more Liberty Bonds—and you had the ingredients for a popular bloodletting. All it would take was a suitable provocation, and Ruthenberg's rhetoric, at least as retrospectively interpreted by Cleveland Police, proved sufficient cause.

Ruthenberg's conception of the May Day rally was simple and hardly covert. Four columns of marchers (symbolizing the world-wide appeal of the Soviet experiment) would converge on Public Square for speechifying at about 1 p.m. on May Day. One would come from the west at West 25th and Lorain; the north column would proceed from 16th and St. Clair; the south column from East 55th and Scovill, and the east column from Acme Hall at East 9th and Euclid, the Socialist meeting place. Eventually, the four columns would merge at Public Square and listen to fiery rhetoric about World Revolution spouted by Ruthenberg et al. and then disperse.

It didn't work out that way. It may never be known *exactly* what happened. Ruthenberg's Bolsheviks (for that was the hard core of his march's organization, despite its boast of including 32 labor and political groups) were not about to admit fault after their bloody debacle. Nor were Cleveland's Finest, a police force already a scandalous byword in U. S. municipal corruption, willing to admit excessive behavior in the aftermath of the absolute worst of the many riots that occurred throughout the United States on May Day, 1919. So what follows is a narrative incorporating known facts and shrewd guesses, which is about the best history can hope to be.

The trouble started on Superior, just after Ruthenberg's column had turned from East 9th toward the Square. This was the main group, with Ruthenberg, clad in dark coat and black hat, leading about 300 men. About 30 of his marchers were discharged American soldiers, and some of them were carrying red flags. Police

Deputy Inspector Jacob Graul would later insist that Ruthenberg had *promised* that no red flags would be carried. Ruthenberg denied, of course, that he had made such a pledge, but the point was moot. Although the state of Ohio, already captivated by the Red Scare spirit, had outlawed display of black or red flags, the law did not go into force until July 1, 1919. Whatever his alleged promise, Ruthenberg's marchers were at least within the law's letter as they turned left on Superior and came abreast of the Colonial Theater.

Ruthenberg's "Reds" weren't the only ones who had come out to make a show that May afternoon. Although the total of all four columns of leftist marchers was estimated at about 5,000, at least twice that many spectators lined the routes of the march as the scarlet-festooned May Day marchers walked by. Many of the spectators were American soldiers, some discharged, some not, but most of them didn't like what they saw and heard as the parade went by.

An irony of post-riot analysis was that Cleveland authorities unanimously blamed the disturbance on "radical" foreigners. It was a foreigner who precipitated the first riot—but he was a Canadian and he was most definitely not in sympathy with Ruthenberg's marchers. Ex-Private James Stevens had served in the Canadian Army on the Western Front, losing both legs in action there. Now, sitting in his wheelchair in front of the Olmsted Hotel at the corner of 9th and Superior, he took in the sight of Ruthenberg's red-festooned column. Suddenly, wheeling his wheelchair into the street, he demanded that the red flags be lowered, while other spectators demanded that marchers in military uniform remove either themselves or their uniforms from the parade. As Stevens confronted the marchers, some of them began to jeer at him. Seconds later, he yelled, "Get those red flags! Get 'em, boys!"

Stevens's words seem to have been what the bystanders were waiting for. A white-haired man made a grab for a red flag and was clubbed and slashed by marchers. Two soldiers, U. S. Army Lieutenant Soweski and Virgil Cone of the U. S. Navy, jumped from their trucks and tore away the nearest red flag. Within seconds, the middle of Ruthenberg's Square-bound column was involved in a pitched battle with opponents and police. Blood began to spatter on Superior Avenue as knives, guns, umbrellas, and pieces of lumber were brought into play by the marchers and their antagonists. Minutes later, a squad of Cleveland mounted police waded into the melee, nightsticks flying.

Cleveland Public Library Photograph Collection.
Ruins of sacked Socialist Party office, May 1, 1920.

It may never be accurately known just what role the Cleveland police played in the May Day riots. Their post-riot claim was that they initially intervened in the Superior Avenue fight to protect the marchers; it was only when the latter—unprovoked—attacked them that they focused their efforts on breaking radical heads. But it was hardly a secret that Cleveland safety forces were itching for a showdown with Cleveland "Reds," and they joined the battle with enthusiasm as the fighting spread west toward Public Square and south down East 9th. Police Chief Frank W. Smith later volunteered another explanation for police intervention: one of his officers, Patrolman Robert Kern, had been attacked without cause by the marchers at East 6th and Superior. Only then had Smith sent in mounted police to ride them down.

Despite mounting casualties and spreading chaos, the head of Ruthenberg's column managed to make it to Public Square. But not for long. With their penchant for provocative symbolism, the marchers' goal was the northwest quadrant of Public Square. As that was also the scheduled speaker's stand for a Liberty Loan rally scheduled for later that day, the symbolism was hardly lost on the hostile crowd already gathered there. As two marchers in Army uniform raised red flags on the speaker's stand, Lieutenant Herbert Bergen of the 305th Ammunition Train demanded they "take off the uniform or throw away the flags."

The flag-bearers didn't get a chance to respond to Bergen. Within seconds, the angry mob surrounding the stand seized the two men, threw them off the platform, and tore the red flags to pieces. A general free-for-all now commenced with police, soldiers, ex-soldiers, and divers other Clevelanders chasing and beating up any "radicals" they could catch. Some wounded marchers managed to flee to the Marion Building on West 3rd; there, rioters caught them again and gave them another beating.

Lasting several hours, the May Day riots eventually spread southward along the axis of East 9th all the way to Scovill. At the height of the disorders, virtually all Cleveland police, assisted by Army trucks, a Renault tank (a promotional gimmick for the Liberty Loan), and hundreds of "patriotic" Clevelanders attempted to restore order—if beating anyone who looked remotely like a "Red" could be defined that way. The police apparently stood by quite effectively as a mob of several hundred men, women, and children efficiently sacked the Socialist Party Headquarters at 1222 Prospect Avenue. Breaking down a door, rioters smashed typewriters, office furniture, files, and all the windows. Oddly, the only thing left undisturbed was a money box, impounded by the police. When the police finally intervened, they supposedly sent the men, women and children there . . . home.

The first fatality came at Woodland and East 9th, where Detective Charles Woodring was attempting to control a hostile crowd. When his efforts seemed to have no effect, he warned that he would shoot the first one to come toward him. Seconds later, he shot 17-year-old Samuel Pearlman through the chin and neck at close range. Woodring claimed that Pearlman attacked him. The body lay unidentified at the County Morgue, until a newsboy notified Samuel's father, Louis, a Kinsman Road tailor, of his son's death. Louis claimed the body, insisting that his son had never been involved with politics, much less with the Cleveland Socialists.

An oddity of the May Day disturbances was their sporadic and scattered occurrence. There were isolated pockets of rioting and arrests as far east as East 55th and Scovill that long afternoon. And the second-worst conflict took place at Buckeye Road and East

89th, almost eight hours after the Superior Avenue donnybrook. About 9 p.m. Police Lt. Nelson G. Meeker and his men were attempting to hold off an angry mob there. But the crowd rushed the men, fracturing Meeker's skull, and the police began to fire at the surging rioters. Three of their bullets hit Joseph Ivanyi, 38, in the abdomen. Evidence does show that Invanyi was one of Meeker's attackers.

The worst of the rioting was quelled by 3 p.m. By that hour the casualties had almost climbed to their final total of two dead and more than 200 wounded. Most of the injuries came from police nightsticks deployed on Superior Avenue, East 9th Street, and Public Square. But a few more wounds were added that night, when police, aided by an angry mob, charged a radical parade at West 25th and Lorain Avenue, sending six to the hospital. Rounding off the night's work, the anti-radical mob, unhindered by police, stormed a Socialist meeting at the West Side Assembly Hall, expelled the "Reds" and unfurled American flags from the windows.

The aftermath of the Cleveland May Day riots was all that American enthusiasts of the Red Scare could have wished. At least 120 "radicals" were arrested and jailed at Central Police Station. Over the next few days most of them were brought before Police Court Judges Howells, Terrell, and McMahon and given the maximum sentences possible. Most were charged with disturbing the peace or assault and battery. Most were found guilty without much pretense of evidence or an adequate defense and given sentences ranging from 30 to 90 days in the workhouse and $25 to $200 in fines.

Some of the rioters had interesting defenses, whether true or not. Fred Brenner, secretary of the Cleveland I. W. W., had been arrested on the night before the riot for "overcrowding" a Socialist meeting hall. On Thursday, having paid a $5 fine, he was just coming out of the Federal Building on Superior "when a policeman grabbed me and shoved me in a patrol wagon." Judge Terrell did not buy his story and Brenner got 30 days at Warrensville workhouse and a $25 fine. Fellow Police Court Judge Sylvester McMahon expressed judicial and popular sentiment, no doubt, with words he addressed to those at whom he threw the book on Monday morning:

Cleveland Press Collection, Cleveland State University.

"Best Picture of the Bolsheviki Riot."

> It's a pity the city ordinance don't [sic] permit me to sentence
> you to long jail terms. You seem to think the Declaration of Inde-
> pendence gives you freedom to tear the government down, but
> you can't do it.

This, it should be remembered, was said to broken and bandaged
men and women who had spent three days and nights in jail. Their
fate was more honestly and succinctly characterized by a headline
in the *Cleveland News*, only hours after the riots: "REDS
CLUBBED BY POLICE IN RIOTS."

Abe Trotzky probably suffered for his name as much as anything. Arrested at East 55th on a disturbance charge, he claimed he
was passing by some soldiers when one of them exclaimed,
"You're a Bolshevist!" He insisted he was not a radical, had never
belonged to the I.W.W. or the Socialist Party and, more impor-
tantly, was no relation to Leon.

The fairer sex was not neglected by Police Court magistrates.
Helen Spector, 26, was charged with "being part of a noisy assembly," her fate for refusing to remove a red-colored decoration from
her person. She got $25 and costs from Judge Howells. More seri-

ous was the case of Miss Rose Charvat, 30, who was charged with assault and battery on Lt. Meeker in the Buckeye Road riot that led to Joseph Ivanyi's death. As Meeker still lay comatose in the hospital, Miss Charvat's case was continued.

Meanwhile, Cleveland authorities, newspapers, and organizations indulged in an orgy of overreaction, self-congratulation, and public belligerence. The official tone had been set only several hours after the bloodshed by Cleveland attorney, John J. Sullivan. Speaking from the very Liberty Loan stand that had been the focal point for Public Square rioting, he thundered to his now jailed opponents:

> Get right or get out! . . . May Day of 1919 will live in Cleveland history as the day the disturbers of the republic were crushed in their first attempt to promulgate principles opposed to our traditions and our institutions.

Accepting police characterizations of the riot as a radical attempt at insurrection, the *Cleveland News* reported on May 2 that the U. S. Government had mobilized two machine-gun companies to deal with further disorders, in the event local police could not handle them. Chief Smith, without warrant of law, announced on May 3 that no outdoor meetings of Socialists would be permitted, and police moved to stop those already scheduled. And while U. S. District Attorney E. S. Wertz consulted with officials of the Justice Department about summary deportation of any aliens jailed in the riots, Cleveland Council rushed through an ordinance on May 5 prohibiting display of the red flag in Cleveland. A month later, another ordinance requiring police permits for parades became law. Passed unanimously, both ordinances provided $200 fines and 60 days in the workhouse for violators.

Such seemingly draconian provisions weren't enough for some Cleveland guardians of public safety. Police Chief Frank W. Smith, impressed by the use of the Renault tank against rioters, mused publicly about its advantages in crowd control:

> The suggestion of getting some tanks was made some time ago, but the riot Thursday was the first real demonstration we have seen. . . . They could be run by any of our chauffeurs, who would be protected within the steel turrets. No horses would come back slashed.

Not to be outdone in repressive measures, Prosecutor James L. Lind suggested to Law Director W. S. Fitzgerald that Socialists be forbidden to sell pamphlets and magazines, the source of some of their revenue. Lind, however, cautiously admitted that "their sales literature included several periodicals of liberal but not Socialistic nature and that close distinctions would have to be made." Just what subtle distinctions might have to be made in curtailing First Amendment rights became apparent on May 6 when *The Cleveland Press* reported a crowd gathered around two men arguing about "Reds" in Public Square. One of Cleveland's Finest pushed his way through to the two men and said, "Cut this Red talk out, or I'll call the emergency patrol for you." The incident dissolved when it was explained that the topic of dispute had been baseball, specifically the Cincinnati Reds.

The three Cleveland daily newspapers competed lustily for the shrillest note of jingo super-patriotism. The *News*, probably the most sensationalistic of the trio, struck a fortissimo note of bellicose nativism:

> Thanks to the enthusiastic activity of policemen, former soldiers and other volunteers, some hundreds of these enemies of America were made to feel American sentiment in the concrete form of jail cells, scalp wounds and bodily injury of divers sorts. . . . It is hoped . . . this community will proceed promptly toward deportation of the alien rioters and suitable imprisonment of the few native or naturalized citizens who aided and abetted them.

A second editorial in the same May 2 edition struck an even more muscular pose:

> It is probable that [the Cleveland Police force's] instant and determined action saved Cleveland the disgrace of some serious outbreak of red-flag incendiarism. . . . A policeman's night stick, descending with right good will on a Socialist's cranium is a form of argument that even an admirer of Marx, Trotzky, Debs et al. should be able to understand and remember.

The *Press* weighed in on May 2 with a moderately more sedate opinion. Under the head, "GUTTERS RUN RED WITH THE FLAGS OF BOLSHEVISM," its editorial noted with satisfaction the consequences of May Day's Socialist folly:

> The Cleveland Bolsheviki followed their leaders through the streets—looking for trouble. They found it . . . This is not Russia. This is America.

The Plain Dealer, although taking a more temperate rhetorical line, attempted to use the incident as a way to influence public policy toward immigrants and the apparatus of the government's police powers. Beginning on May 5, a special week-long series of articles by staff writer Paul Bellamy (the author's grandfather) highlighted with alarm the overwhelming percentage of unnaturalized aliens arrested as rioters (108 out of 116) and called for vigorous and systematic efforts at Americanization of Cleveland's apparently unmelting ethnic groups. On the whole, it was a thoughtful and responsible series, emphasizing in particular the need and opportunity for employers of aliens to aid in the Americanization process. But those familiar with Bellamy's background must have been amused by his alarmed characterization of the radical rioters and their dangerous ideas:

> For after the shots and blows had subsided . . . one fact loomed ominously above all the rest—the disturbers were predominantly eastern European importations, just as their ideas were imported European ideas.

One assumes that Bellamy was making a private distinction between Socialism and the violent Marxist-Leninist brand of Communism espoused by some, but not all, of the jailed marchers. For Paul Bellamy, a future editor of *The Plain Dealer*, was the 35-year-old son of Edward Bellamy, the author of *Looking Backward,* easily the most famous and influential novel espousing Socialism ever written by an American. Meanwhile, a hard-line statist Red Scare rationale was endorsed by *The Plain Dealer's* J. L. Wright, who worried in print on May 3 that unless wartime measures like the Espionage Act were altered to deal with domestic "Reds," "the strong arm of the federal government, so effective in keeping down the rise of bolshevism during actual warfare, will be paralyzed."

And that was the end of it, except for the mourners of the dead, the aliens deported to Europe, and all the rest with broken heads.

MACHINE GUNS, TROOPS READY TO GUARD CITY

Mobilized Just Outside City for Action if Needed; Ruthenberg to Be Prosecuted for Inciting Disturbance; 2d Victim Dies.

Government authorities, incensed over the Socialist demonstration and display of red flags which precipitated Thursday's riots, took steps Friday to deport every foreign-born person who participated on the side of the Bolsheviki element.

At the same time, it became known that federal

Cleveland News.

The jailed rioters served their terms and most of them returned to lives of obscurity. Charles Ruthenberg went on to become General Secretary of the American Communist Party and spent much time in and out of courtroom and jails until his unexpected death from appendicitis complications in 1927. He is the only American besides John Reed buried in the Kremlin Wall. The Socialist Party disappeared as a political force in Cleveland. And Joseph Ivanyi, the radical killed in the Buckeye Road melee, was buried at Highland Park Cemetery on Monday, May 5. Although Cleveland Police forbade his funeral procession to march by scenes prominent in the May Day rioting—as intended by his mourners—his graveside service at Highland Park Cemetery was, or so Cleveland newspapers reported, a veritable "Bolsheviki rally." Floral tributes in evidence included I. W. W. motifs and a predominance of red flowers. Revolutionary songs were sung with bravado at the grave site. The Cleveland Police may have had the last laugh. After patrolmen had searched mourners for weapons and dispersed at least 500 marchers who wished to follow the funeral procession, the *Cleveland News* gloated:

> It had been arranged by the police that the driver of one of the funeral automobiles was to observe proceedings and carry back to the police any disloyal utterances of speakers.

Whether any "disloyal utterances" were relayed back to the police is unknown, but the police probably weren't laughing a month later when a powerful bomb was detonated at Mayor Harry L. Davis's residence on East 97th. No one was hurt in the explosion, but it served notice that Cleveland radicals did not forgive or forget the events of May 1.

Which is more than you can say for present-day Clevelanders. The 1919 May Day Riots have never attracted serious historical attention here and are virtually unknown to contemporary Clevelanders. That's something to think about the next time you wander by the northwest quadrant of the square. One only hopes that present and future residents of the Forest City will deal better with the issues of free speech, free assembly, and tolerance for "strangers in the land" than the men and women of 1919.

Chapter 13

HIGH NOON AT BEDFORD

The Violent Saga of George "Jiggs" Losteiner, Cleveland's Baddest Man

The worst desperado in Cleveland history? Several names come to mind. Clevelanders of the 1880s would have cited "Blinky" Morgan. Ultimately involved in a lucrative 1887 downtown fur robbery, badman Blinky subsequently masterminded the daring rescue of a fellow gang member from armed detectives at a Ravenna, Ohio, railroad station. One of the detectives, alas, was murdered, and after losing a gun battle with Michigan lawmen, Blinky paid for the Ravenna homicide at the end of an Ohio hangman's rope.

Then there was John Leonard Whitfield, the "Cleveland Sheik," whose exploits are chronicled elsewhere in these pages. Whitfield did not lack for the requisite nerve, and his month-long flight from justice attracted a nationwide audience in 1923. But with only one homicide to his credit—albeit an unknown number of bigamy charges, numerous car thefts, and zillions of stolen sparkplugs— we must, regrettably, disallow the admittedly flashy Whitfield as a serious contender for the title of Cleveland's all-time Public Enemy #1.

More modern Clevelanders might plump for either "Shondor" Birns or Danny Greene. Before both of them were separately smithereened by powerful car bombs in the 1970s, they carved out impressive, indeed competitive, careers of personal violence, loan-sharking, numbers running, and murder. But even these modern monsters pale before the exploits of Cleveland's all-time most dangerous man: George "Jiggs" Losteiner. He was the baddest man of Roaring-Twenties Cleveland, and it speaks poorly for the civic pride of our Forest City that this truly satanic criminal is virtually forgotten today. He was violent, depraved, trigger-happy, and a lifelong "career criminal" before the term was even conceived. He was *bad*—so bad, one is tempted to think, that only James Cagney could have ever brought him to life on the screen.

Like the proverbial bad seed, "Jiggs" went bad from the beginning and just kept on going. Arrested on January 12, 1901, for purse-snatching, 15-year-old Jiggs earned his first $50 fine and 30 days in the Warrensville Workhouse. Six months later came his first "disorderly conduct" rap and another semester at the Workhouse. His first grand larceny charge didn't come along until 1905, but he quickly made up for lost time. His next decade passed in a blizzard of criminal charges and incarcerations, including convictions on larceny, highway robbery, parole violations, burglary, armed robbery, concealed weapons, and divers other felonies and misdemeanors. At the end of this brutal process the finished Jiggs was formed—or deformed. One *Plain Dealer* writer described him in his prime:

> A powerfully built man . . . who is said to have ruled more through the force of terror than through any personal qualities. To the police he has been known as a man who would be "quick on the trigger," ruthless to both friend and foe when cornered.

Things really began to heat up for Jiggs in 1918. On August 3, he and another vicious felon, John Grogan (grand larceny, burglary, car theft, rape)—both wearing bogus Cleveland Police uniforms—robbed the Walker Manufacturing Company payroll. Ambushing Norman Walker with a $22,834 payroll near Taft Avenue and East 131st, they relieved him of his money at gunpoint and fled east in a red Hudson. Run to earth by pursuers at Richmond and Mayfield, they engaged in a fierce gun battle that left policeman Perry Smith shot through the left eye and with six bullets in his arm and leg, while fellow office Edgar H. Smith took slugs in his left leg and right arm. Although the money was recovered in the melee, both Grogan and Losteiner escaped.

Losteiner and Grogan's lingering fears from the Walker job soon culminated in a more terrible crime. On the evening of December 19, 1918, East Cleveland policemen Patrick Gaffney and Patrick Hendricks approached the garage of William Butler's home at 14905 Elm Avenue. Butler had recently rented the garage to two

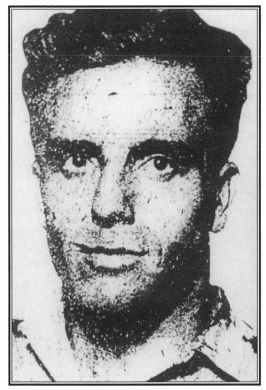

Cleveland Press Collection, Cleveland State University.
Elvor Porter.

men, but had become suspicious and notified police because his tenants used their car only at night. As Hendricks chatted with Butler at the front of the house and Gaffney walked towards the garage, Grogan and Losteiner suddenly appeared in the driveway. Firing once without effect at Hendricks, Losteiner put his pistol up against Patrolmen Gaffney's side and fired once. Gaffney fell, yelling the obligatory "They got me!" while Hendricks traded several shots with Grogan and Losteiner. Although everyone involved was apparently wounded, Grogan in the back and Losteiner with two slugs in his legs, the gunmen escaped. Six days later, on Christmas Day, Gaffney died of complications of his lung wound in East Cleveland Hospital. He left a widow and four kids. Murder warrants were issued for Grogan and Losteiner, and rewards of $650 and $250 were offered, respectively, for the two killers.

Cleveland police had no idea of the whereabouts of either gunman. An hour after the shootout with Hendricks and Gaffney, two wounded men had shown up at a hospital on Carnegie Avenue at East 89th. Threatening Dr. J. F. Doubrava with death, they forced him to treat their gunshot wounds. Grogan insisted on keeping the bullet Dr. Doubrava removed but Losteiner, unwisely, left the .38 slug pulled from his leg with the doctor. The gunmen then disappeared into the winter night.

But not for long. As if to show no grass grew under their feet, a gang led by Grogan and Losteiner hit the safe at the General Baking Company office on East 35th in the wee hours of January 12, 1919, a scant three weeks after the killing of Gaffney. Using a gang of six or seven men, they tied up two employees and plied the sturdy safe with successive nitroglycerin charges until it finally blew open. Curiously, they arrived at the heist in a taxi and had it wait for the hour or so it took to complete their business. The take was $4,000 in cash and $500 in Liberty bonds, and the same gang was undoubtedly responsible for other armed robberies that year and the next.

The same gang, that is, except for Grogan. Wanted for the Gaffney murder and divers thefts, John Grogan was arrested in Martins Ferry on February 19, 1919, after a tip-off by a railroad detective brought a flying squad of Cleveland Police to arrest Grogan in his bed. Returned to Cleveland, he pleaded guilty to manslaughter and was awarded a life term in the Ohio Penitentiary. A crucial piece of the evidence that put him there was the .38 slug extracted by Dr. Doubrava from the leg of Jiggs Losteiner, which prosecutors proved had come from Patrolman Gaffney's revolver.

Grogan's absence didn't cramp Jiggs's style much. By now, he had hooked up with another violent desperado named Albert Johnson (alias Joyce). An interesting physical and social contrast to Losteiner's unsubtle, near-simian brutishness, Johnson was quite the dapper felon, known throughout the underworld for his "nifty" wardrobe, smooth manners, and taste for polite society. It was said that unless you knew better you would never associate Johnson with the low-life criminal psychopaths with whom he spent most of his life. His sophisticated exterior, moreover, concealed the fact that at the age of only 31, he had spent almost half his life in prison. Convicted at the age of 18 of grand larceny, Johnson had served time in several states, including a stretch in San Quentin, by the time he met Losteiner. In March 1917, while leading a payroll robbery at the Rich Company, he had murdered a man named George Mowry and earned a murder indictment. Shortly afterwards, he was captured after holding up a $60,000 dice game—but the state of New York refused to return him to Ohio to face his outstanding murder rap. It was an imprudent decision: while being transferred from Sing Sing to Clinton Prison on August 26, 1919, Johnson leapt from a moving train and escaped from his guards. By December of that year, however, he was back in jail, held in Toledo on a charge of murdering Dollie Argus, an innocent bystander in a gun battle he had waged with local police. On Christmas Day, a gang of six gunmen attacked the Lucas County Jail, freeing Johnson and three other criminals. They also shot Deputy Leon Noonan, although not fatally.

It didn't take long for Johnson and Losteiner to renew their auld lang syne. On September 18, 1919, a scant three weeks after Johnson's escape, they hit the Nottingham Savings and Banking Company at 13627 St. Clair Avenue for $10,000 in bonds and cash. As with all Losteiner's jobs, it was well-planned, well-staffed, and well-supplied. His five-man force was more than a match for bank security and their high-powered Hudson easily outdistanced pursuing police.

The activities of the Losteiner-Johnson gang were by now an open scandal and a serious indictment of the laxness of the Cleveland Police force. Despite that body's boastful claims of intensive manhunts and constant surveillance, it was obvious to citizens that the Losteiner gang and similar criminal elements were operating throughout Greater Cleveland with brazen openness. Payroll and bank robberies were becoming almost daily occurrences, and civic organizations and Cleveland newspapers began to call for a thorough housecleaning—a housecleaning that would come in 1921 when the Cleveland Foundation brought in nationally known jurists and lawmen to clean up the mess.

Meanwhile, Jiggs and his goons were proving that the past had been but prelude. On June 18, 1920 at 10 a.m., they hit the First National Bank in Chagrin Falls. Driving back and forth several times in a stolen, seven-passenger blue touring car, they stopped on Franklin Street in front of the bank and four of them got out while one guarded the car. Halting by the bank's front door, they started shoving pedestrians away from the entrance, firing a few close warning shots to encourage privacy.

Pushing a passerby, J. F. Kramer of Warrensville, ahead of them,

Cleveland Press Collection, Cleveland State University.

the robbers entered the bank. Moving toward Cashier A. R. Mountjoy, the lead man fired a bullet through an adjacent door. When Mountjoy made a motion toward a nearby drawer, another gunmen put a bullet within several inches of his head. Two robbers then relieved Mountjoy of his wallet and began scooping up $2,400 in cash from the teller stations.

It was at this point that crime became tragedy. A. R. Chance, a 70-year-old electrical salesman who lived over the bank, was apparently attracted by the shooting below. He came down the stairs to the bank and asked, "What's going on here?" "Get back there, or we'll show you!" replied Jiggs Losteiner. Chance started to edge away but he wasn't fast enough for the sadistic Jiggs, ever ready to overawe the public with a show of terror. Crying, "You move too slowly, old man!" Jiggs shot him in the left leg and left him to bleed on the sidewalk outside. Chance would die a week later in Carnegie Hospital.

It was over within minutes, and the thieves piled into their getaway car and sped away, pursued in vain by several Chagrin Falls posses. And despite the fact that cashier Mountjoy positively identified a mug shot of Jiggs Losteiner as the lead gunman from a mugshot only *two days later*, Cleveland Police failed to disclose the identity of the bank robbers to the public. The hunt for the unknown Chagrin Falls culprits continued, as it were, in the dark.

During the next few months, Jiggs and his gang successfully pursued their violent craft. On June 23 they hit the Highland Park State Bank in Highland Park, Michigan; on September 22 they took $23,000 from the First State Bank of Detroit; the Ohio Savings Bank & Trust of Toledo was their target on October 1, and they probably robbed the De Pew Bank of De Pew, New York, of $16,000 in cash on October 5.

Although the whereabouts of Jiggs and his men were unknown to the police, the gang was much in evidence in Cleveland. They made several appearances downtown in October, especially Albert Johnson, who savored the Forest City's nightlife and shopping opportunities. In mid-October, for example, he enjoyed a $350 shopping spree at one of the large downtown department stores, buying a number of flashy garments, including a silk dressing gown, with a roll of $50 bills. Later that night he was spotted on East 9th and Superior by an acquaintance, who mentioned that the police were looking for him. "Yeah, and I'm looking for them, too," sneered the insouciant Johnson.

The location of Jiggs and his men, if not their infamous identities, was certainly known to their unfortunate neighbors. Sometime in early October, Albert Johnson rented an apartment at 14409 Woodworth Avenue, near St. Clair. By this time Johnson's entourage included his mother, Mildred, and his girlfriend, a young lady in her early 20s he'd picked up in California, Norma Scott (alias Hazel Grey)¬. Jiggs was at the apartment more often than not, and within days the group made itself obnoxious to its neighbors with loud, all-night parties, boisterous singing, and generally unbridled carryings-on. (Or as the *Cleveland News* archly put it, "noise and gaming and merriment.") One brave soul, a Mrs. H. M. Strauss, even attempted to complain to the police about the rowdies at 14409 Woodworth . . . but nothing was done. So the endless Johnson-Losteiner party continued, while the celebrants planned their biggest job ever: the Cleveland Trust branch in Bedford, Ohio, on Thursday, October 21.

It was a vicious crew, indeed, that piled into Jiggs Losteiner's big, black, stolen Cadillac when he picked them up at Public Square late that fine, fatal autumn morning. While there is some disagreement as to whether there were six or eight men in the car, it is a fact that Albert Johnson was at the wheel. Also in the car were Paul Rivers, Harry Wulle (alias Stone), and Orville Taylor. Rivers, an escaped convict and notorious hold-up artist, was wanted in particular for killing cashier J. W. Bonner at Thompson's restaurant on Euclid Avenue on Christmas Eve 1918. Wulle, at near 60 years old, was the old man of the gang and had a rap sheet going back to the 1890s. He had just gotten out of Leavenworth in April after six years and nine months. Despite being wanted by the Cleveland Police, he had recently been in daily attendance at the trial of his pal, Harry Holmes, acquitted in the $65,000 West Cleveland Bank heist. Orville Taylor, only 23 years old, had already served a one-year sentence for theft in the Ohio Reformatory at Mansfield.

The caper came off about 2:40 p.m. Jiggs and his men, as usual, had thoroughly researched the job and were confident that $23,000 had just been delivered to the bank to cover weekend area payrolls. Harry Wulle, moreover, had visited Bedford earlier in the week to "case the joint." The big black Cadillac cruised the street several times and then came to a halt across from the Cleveland Trust branch. All of the men except Johnson, who was left to guard the car, got out. With guns drawn—one in each hand—they entered the bank.

With closing time due at 3 p.m. there were only three customers and five employees in the bank. Shouting, "Throw up your hands and keep your feet still," the gunmen pulled down the shades and stationed themselves at the teller windows. Ordering everyone to lie on the floor, face down, Jiggs then demanded that manager George C. Flickinger open the two bank vaults. This took some time, especially as Flickinger was unfamiliar with the combination of the smaller vault, and Jiggs fumed with mounting impatience until Flickinger finally got the second vault open.

If Jiggs had been lucky that Thursday, he would have settled for the take thus far and left Bedford. Precious minutes had already been wasted over the second vault—which yielded a measly $1,000. Jiggs was greedy, however, and he now ordered manager Flickinger to open the safety deposit boxes. This was the worst moment for Flickinger. He had already accurately gauged his captor as a trigger-happy sadist, and he knew something Jiggs didn't: *He could not open the boxes because he didn't have all the keys.* Flickinger began to say a silent prayer . . . and then came the first, startling, sublime shot in the glorious Battle of Bedford.

Cleveland Press Collection, Cleveland State University.

Jiggs Losteiner in court scene.

It came from outside the bank and it hit Albert Johnson, who had been lounging at the side of the Cadillac, warning away the curious with his gun. Hit in the side, he staggered, firing wildly, into the driver's seat and attempted to start the Cadillac. Seconds later, another bullet smashed into his neck, and he began to bleed to death where he sat.

It had all happened so quickly. Two persons had watched the arrival of the bandits in front of the bank and drawn accurate conclusions. One was cashier Ruth Yates at the Bedford Restaurant across the street. Suspecting a robbery in progress, she had reached for the wall telephone, only to catch the eye of Albert Johnson outside, who motioned her away from it with a suggestive motion of his shotgun.

The other witness was Mrs. T. J. Schumacher. In town with her five-year-old-son and a neighbor's child to get haircuts, Mrs. Schumacher had noticed the dangerous-looking men going in the bank and divined the unmistakable meaning of Johnson's threatening behavior. Walking into Elvor Porter's tire shop several doors down the street, she said, "Elvor, I believe these men outside are going to rob the bank."

Porter didn't wait to hear more. Thanks to the rash of payroll and bank robberies over the past several months, citizens like Porter, Yates, and Schumacher had been sensitized to the possibility of trouble at their local bank; indeed, the Cleveland Trust Company had taken the precaution in the weeks before the Battle of Bedford of distributing riot guns to some merchants and citizens located near the bank. So Elvor Porter was ready when the word came. One look out the door at the bank front and at Johnson by the car across the street told him all he needed to know. He grabbed a nine-shot Colt revolver, dropped to the floor and aimed from the narrow doorway at Albert Johnson standing by the Cadillac. It was the very combat training Porter had learned for life during 11 months with the 135th Machine Gun Battalion of the 37th Division in France two years earlier, and it paid off again as his first bullet sped toward Albert Johnson's side.

The shot caught Jiggs and his men by surprise inside the bank. Scooping up their loot, they made for the door. As they did so Flickinger crawled on his belly to an alarm switch and hit it. As the loud electric gong outside began to sound the alarm, 17-year-old bookkeeper William Petrie grabbed a pistol from a drawer and began blasting at the fleeing robbers as they fled towards the front door.

The reception they got there must have been hell on earth to Jiggs & Company, who were used to terrorizing unarmed civilians at will. Both Elvor Porter's initial shots and the bank alarm had by now aroused Bedford's armed citizenry. As the desperate robbers poured out the bank door they were hit by a fusillade of bullets and buckshot from perhaps a dozen or more sources. After mortally wounding Johnson, Porter emptied his gun, then, after it was reloaded, joined in the now general shooting from pistols, rifles, and shotguns from up and down the street. In addition to Porter's Colt, fire was coming at the robbers from the guns of Donald B. Johnston, Salvatore Parrise, Lawrence Hay, H. W. Osborn, William Petrie, and divers other citizens who joyfully contributed fire to the melee. An employee at the Leech-Johnson Hardware Store, Johnston ran and got a riot gun from the undertaker's when he heard Porter's first shot. Edging down the side of his store toward the scene, he commenced blasting away at the embattled robbers. Parrise, a 16-year-old ditch-digger, stopped excavating a nearby street, grabbed a shotgun from another man and joined in the fray. Osborn was working at the Bedford Grocery store when a woman came running in and shouted the news. He grabbed a revolver from a desk and ran out the side door, firing as he sped toward the bank. Their spirit was infectious. J. E. Baughman, driving his truck through town, leaped down from it, grabbed a revolver from a nearby man and began shooting at the beleaguered thieves.

Brave William Petrie was the first civilian casualty. (There would be five in all, most probably wounded by friendly fire.) Emptying his gun as he pursued Losteiner's men to the bank door, Petrie reloaded and ran outside. He was soon felled, badly mauled by shotgun fire, most probably from the weapon of a Bedford vigilante who mistook Petrie for one of the robbers when he ran out of the bank.

It couldn't last long. Bunched in a defensive square near the useless Cadillac, Losteiner and his men made a stand for some minutes, while they tried in vain to start the Cadillac, and then another automobile nearby. But quick-witted E. J. Thorp, a Bedford paving contractor, had already sealed the bandits' doom. During the early seconds of the shoot-out he had shrewdly driven his truck in front of the robbers' Cadillac, blocking its escape route.

After endless minutes of being shot to pieces from all directions, Jiggs and two or three others made a break for it, à la Butch Cassidy & Sundance, leaving their $53,000 loot in bags on the street. By now both bags and the cash inside were soaked with gangster blood. Running toward an embankment by the Pennsylvania Railroad tracks near the Marble Chair Company, they resisted until they were simply too shot up and exhausted to continue. A blood-soaked Losteiner, shot through one eye, another bullet in his abdomen, and peppered with much buckshot—but still holding his rifle—finally surrendered to Elvor Porter. What Jiggs didn't know, as Porter calmly marched him back to the bank at gunpoint, was that Porter's Colt was out of bullets. As the duo arrived back at the bank, Jiggs was confronted by Mrs. Schumacher, whose anxious comment to Porter had set off the "Battle of Bedford." Only minutes earlier that afternoon, Jiggs had warned her to skedaddle with the threat, "Stand back or I will shoot you dead!" Glaring at the now gore-spattered hoodlum, she said, "You are the man who was going to kill me, aren't you?" It is recorded that when Jiggs made a "surly" reply to Mrs. Schumacher, Elvor Porter socked him in the face. Chivalry, like the vigilante spirit, was not dead in Bedford that day.

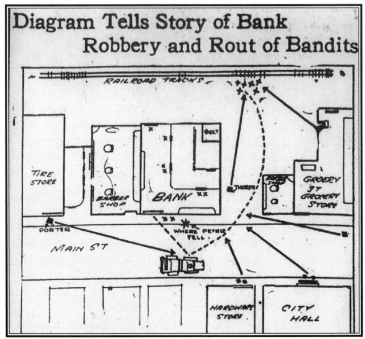

Diagram Tells Story of Bank Robbery and Rout of Bandits

Cleveland Press Collection, Cleveland State University.

Diagram of Bedford Shootout.

Albert Johnson died on the operating table at Street Alexis Hospital in Cleveland. A doctor in Bedford had attempted to clamp his damaged neck artery, but in vain. Harry Wulle, shot in the hand, surrendered tamely, and was treated and jailed. Orville Taylor, shot in the head, cheek, knee, and tongue, was unable to talk and was kept under guard at City Hospital. Paul Rivers, a man named George McCann, and at least one, possibly two, other bandits escaped. They were last seen later that evening in the vicinity of Maple Heights, unarmed and limping painfully.

Even in bloody defeat, Jiggs Losteiner held his usual center stage position. "Holy smokes, it's Jiggs Losteiner!" whispered surprised Cleveland detectives as he was wheeled into St. Alexis Hospital with three bullet wounds and more than 100 pieces of buckshot in his flesh. He tried feigning unconsciousness when Miss Martha Ridge of the Chagrin Falls bank was brought to his bedside to identify him as the man who shot A. R. Chance. But the mask dropped when she outraged Jiggs's sense of fair play, as reported in the next morning's *Plain Dealer:*

"He looks like the man." Jiggs, who was apparently in an unconscious condition, opened his eyes and looked at her. "Say, that's not fair," he grumbled, "you know you have either got to say yes or no and be done with it."

Jiggs was visited in the hospital by his gray-haired mother, Julia, who could have been a character modeled on Jimmy Cagney's mother in *White Heat.* (*"Top of the World, Ma!"*) To her he muttered:

> Keep quiet! Don't say anything to anybody, get me a good attorney at once and don't worry . . . . Kiss me again, Mother.

The tying up of loose ends from the Bedford battle was not without unintentional comedy. The Cleveland Police, continuing their shoddy work, failed to pick up Losteiner's confederates on Friday evening, when some of them frantically returned to retrieve loot from the Woodworth Road address. As Albert Johnson's mother and his moll ran down the apartment steps at 14409 Woodworth for the last time, a neighbor overheard a male voice say, "If you ever hurried in your life, hurry now!" Cleveland Police arrived there one hour after the fugitives decamped.

Fortunately for the police and public, Mildred Johnson and Norma Scott were not very smart. The day after Johnson's death, they returned to the downtown store where he had bought his sporty duds with $50 bills and asked for a refund on his silk dressing gown, gratuitously volunteering the information that the purchaser was now dead and wouldn't be wearing it. As the store clerks remembered the flashy gent with the $50 bills and had just seen the dead Johnson's photograph in the late Friday newspapers, it was just a matter of minutes before the police were summoned to arrest the two women. Taken to the station, Mrs. Johnson was further embarrassed when Police Matron Mary Stanton discovered her in possession of $3,750 in cash and $25,000 in uncut diamonds—the latter sewn into six packets in her clothing. Ms. Stanton wisely refused Mildred's offer of a $1,000 bribe not to mention the diamonds, as they had been stolen in Buffalo, New York, from a man named Maxim Lowenthal by the late Albert Johnson several weeks before. Mildred Johnson probably didn't care much for the final ignominy, which was the refusal of Cuyahoga County authorities to release her son's body until police authorities around the country had been given generous opportunities to match it with suspect photos from recent bank robberies. An oddity never explained but much remarked upon was the marked physical resemblance between Johnson's mother and girlfriend.

Newspaper reaction was predictably boisterous. "BULLY FOR BEDFORD!" shouted the *Cleveland News,* commenting that the "Bedford way is the way that leaves no room for doubt about punishment." Not to be outdone, *The Plain Dealer* thundered: "'Jiggs' Losteiner and his pals made a big mistake when they went to Bedford. . . . They have done a fine job for their town and for the state." The *Press* echoed, "BRAVE BEDFORD MAKES US ALL ITS DEBTORS."

Jiggs's subsequent trials must have been sour anti-climax for those who subscribed to the majority sentiments expressed by journalists. Tried first in December 1920 for the murder of Patrolman Gaffney, Jiggs was defended before Judge George Baer by former Assistant County Prosecutors P. J. Mulligan and Stephen M. Young, the latter at the beginning of a career that would take him, half a century later, to the U. S. Senate. The case, which was prosecuted by William J. Corrigan (best known for his later defense of Eva Kaber and Sam Sheppard), hinged on whether Gaffney's fatal pneumonia was caused by the bullet wound in his lung or was picked up in the hospital where he died, as was ingeniously argued by the defense. A dramatic feature of the trial was the presence of numerous armed guards in Judge Baer's courtroom; the word was around that Losteiner's pals planned a violent rescue, and authorities were determined to avoid a repeat of Albert Johnson's 1919 Christmas Day jailbreak. And, as in some Silver Screen melodrama, Jiggs was accompanied throughout his trial by his watching mother and three siblings. Defense counsel Mulligan pulled out all the stops of this domestic tableau in his summation, while, it is reported, the heartstruck Jiggs brushed a furtive tear from his eye:

> A child may become a criminal because of youthful surroundings. I often think—I have little children of my own—that it would be a fine thing to take all children out of the big, noisy, vicious cities and turn them out into the freedom of the country.
>
> Does it ever occur to you that maybe some of your own children might stand before a jury some day? Does it occur to you that this boy was just as precious a child once to the little lady

Citizens Who Participated in Battle

Cleveland Press Collection, Cleveland State University.

across the trial table as your own children are to you? Remember her in your deliberations; don't bring down upon her the black night of hopelessness. . . .

You may be concerned with punishment in your deliberations. Have you stopped to reflect that none of you know this man? None of you know him, nor his mother, nor his sister, nor brother. Can you imagine their feelings as they sat back of him while we lawyers were discussing technical terms and medical hypotheses. . . . While we've been arguing about technicalities, his mother has been watching his every minute.

The case went to the jury at 4 p.m. on December 15. They returned after 46 hours with a verdict of "Guilty—With Recommendation of Mercy." They had little choice; three holdouts insisted on either a life term or the disgusting alternative of a hung jury. But the jury also asked Judge Baer to include in the mandatory life sentence a rider that Jiggs spend each Christmas Day—the day Patrick Gaffney had died—in solitary confinement. In sentencing Jiggs, Judge Baer noted with satisfaction that he had met his "Waterloo at Bedford" and sentenced him to a concurrent term of 1 to 25 years for the Bedford robbery.

That the Losteiner jury had done a bad day's work in the name of compassion was borne out by later events. A "bad con" from the beginning, Losteiner quickly earned membership in the Ohio Penitentiary's infamous "First K Company," the designation for its most dangerous group of hardened criminals. On November 8, 1926, Jiggs led a prison break of 13 men in a desperate dash for freedom. About 2 p.m., as visitors were passing out and both security gates—against regulations—were open, Jiggs and his men, using knives made from bedhooks, attacked their guards and quickly seized a dozen guns. They also stabbed Guard Elmer Callahan in the face, side, arm, head and neck; not to mention six blows with a hammer to the head of Guard George Bennett.

Their freedom was short-lived. Four were wounded by gunfire as they made their break, and most of the rest, including Losteiner, were cornered after an exciting chase by police, guards, and a citizen posse in a cornfield near London, Ohio. Four years later, Jiggs resurfaced as one of the ringleaders in riots occurring in the wake of the horrific Ohio Penitentiary fire of 1930. Toothless, sick, nearly blind, and old before his time, George "Jiggs" Losteiner died at the age of 51 in the Ohio Penitentiary on July 27, 1937. He is buried in Calvary Cemetery. How far he'd come from his days as a pursued badman was reflected in his last quote for reporters: "I don't feel so good anymore. I'm packing away a lot of years."

Postscript. On August 15, 1974, the Cleveland Trust Bedford branch was robbed of $900 by a man wearing a woman's Afro wig and dark glasses. No one was hurt and the thief got away. One wonders if the envious ghost of Jiggs Losteiner was looking down on the scene of his debacle of a half-century past.

Chapter 14

"BREATH OF DEATH"

The 1929 Cleveland Clinic Disaster

Many disasters announce themselves with a bang. Most Cleveland catastrophes have done so literally. The 1944 East Ohio Gas fire began with an explosion that could be heard in Shaker Square and seen in Chagrin Falls. The 1932 Ellington Apartments inferno and the 1916 Waterworks tragedy likewise came with impressive blasts. And the 1908 S. S. Kresge fire started with probably the greatest fireworks display in Cleveland history.

Not so with the Cleveland Clinic disaster. It came, initially invisible and unknown, through the walls and pipe conduits of the Clinic building. It then announced itself indirectly to its victims as powdery flecks and puffs of smoke from heating vents and radiators. And many of its 123 dead may already have died when the first blast came at about 11:25 a.m., May 15, 1929.

Even then, as now, the Cleveland Clinic was one of the greatest success stories in Cleveland history. Founded in 1921, it was the joint medical dream of Doctors George W. Crile, Frank E. Bunts, and William E. Lowther. The three had served together in Cleveland's Lakeside Medical Unit in France during World War I, and had been much inspired by the model of team medical practice and technique the unit had perfected to treat the mass medical casualties of the Western Front. Joining with Dr. John Phillips and drawing on the model of the Mayo Clinic, the four doctors had, in only eight years, created a medical powerhouse that was known throughout the world. Already it was the pride of Cleveland, and celebrities, rulers of state, and thousands of more mundane folk came yearly to find comfort and cure at the hands of its skilled staff.

Although miniscule, compared to its present size, the 1929 Clinic was an impressive physical plant. Located just west of East

93rd on the south side of Euclid Avenue, the grounds included a 184-bed hospital and a research building used for special laboratories, such as X-rays. The main building, on the south side on Euclid Avenue at 93rd, was a four-story structure of reinforced concrete and brick. Used for both administration and diagnosis, its dozens of offices were employed by doctors for consultation and outpatient procedures.

It was to the main building—considered "fireproof" when built in 1920—that tragedy came on the morning of May 15, 1929. The bulk of the building's activities occurred in dozens of consulting rooms on the upper three floors. An interior court arched from the second floor up to a 30-foot-by-38-foot skylight at the roof. Two elevators and two staircases provided access to the three floors above, with offices off the mezzanine-style balconies that flanked the interior court.

Like most buildings of the era, the Main Clinic building's vital physical functions were centered and controlled from its basement. About a third of the area of the 75-foot-by-124-foot building, the basement included unused steam boilers (rendered unnecessary by the Clinic's new central heating plant), heating pipes, and storage rooms for files, supplies, and drugs. Fatally, it also contained a storage room for Clinic patients' X-rays.

Clinic chief Dr. George Crile would insist, in the wake of the disaster, that there was "no precedent" for the Clinic tragedy. That wasn't quite true, whether he knew it or not. In September 1923, gases generated from burning X-ray film and driven through a ventilating system had overwhelmed victims at a Syracuse hospital. And in Albany, in March 1928, eight persons had been killed when toxic fumes from burning X-rays had spread through another hospital.

The villain in both lethal accidents was nitrocellulose X-ray film, composed of camphor and a substance called pryoxylin (created by treating cotton with boiling nitric and sulfuric acids), with a very thin layer of gelatin added to make usable film. Usable—and very dangerous. It had already caused enough deaths and injuries by 1924 to warrant its replacement with a new acetate-based film marketed by Eastman Kodak that year.

Given its lethal contents, the Clinic's basement X-ray storage room was dangerous enough. The room contained about 70,000 X-ray sheets—at least 4,200 pounds of film, each pound capable of

Cleveland Public Library Photograph Collection.
Victim being taken out of Cleveland Clinic window, May 15, 1929.

producing between 3 and 6 cubic feet of toxic gases. Several factors—most in violation of American Hospital Association guidelines—made the situation more dangerous. Unlike those in many other medical facilities, Clinic X-rays were not stored in metal containers. Although some were stored in metal filing cabinets, many films were filed in open wooden racks and all films were filed in flammable paper or manila folder jackets. Unlike many other large medical facilities, the Clinic had no fire sprinkling system in the storage room, nor in any other area of the building. And, going against an increasingly common practice in American hospitals, X-ray films were not stored in an area isolated from patient areas. Worst of all—almost unbelievably—the main Clinic building's ventilation system was also located in the X-ray storage room.

Like most terrible accidents, the Clinic tragedy was the cumulative product of mundane and individually innocuous circumstances. About January 1929, Miss Enid Critcher asked Clinic chief custodian Walter Adams to do something about the poor lighting in the X-ray storage room. Although the room was lit by four 100-watt drop fixtures, Critcher found it difficult to see in some areas of the room when she filed X-ray films. Adams responded by putting a "Y" double outlet at the end of one of the drop fixtures. Such an outlet could service either two 100-watt bulbs or one bulb and an electrical plug outlet. Adams would later deny that he even *knew* that an eight-foot extension cord was hooked up to a female end of that "Y" fixture. Or, as Miss Critcher testified, that it was connected to a 100-watt bulb "trouble light," which was strung over a "big spike" and hung down near the film cabinets. "I wouldn't do anything like that or I wouldn't allow it if I knew of it," Adams later insisted.

There was no inkling of the woe to come when a man with the improbably Dickensian name of Buffery Boggs arrived at the main Clinic building about 9 a.m. on May 15. A steamfitter's helper employed by the W. R. Rhoton Company, Boggs was there to repair a leaking steam pipe in the basement X-ray storage room. Water from the leak had already damaged some films, and the damaged ones had been removed from racks and placed away from the faulty pipe *on top of the storage cabinets* to prevent further damage.

Boggs got to work right away. Stripping away 14 inches of half-inch magnesia insulation, he quickly located the source of the leak. The pipe was too hot for patching work, though, so he went to the central power plant and requested that they shut the heat off. He then left the building. Before he departed, however, he took note of the improvised lighting that custodian Adams denied: "Just a common everyday light bulb dropped down on an extension cord from the ceiling."

Did Boggs smoke a cigarette or two while he was stripping that steampipe? Investigators of the Clinic disaster, especially a panel of lawyers hired by the Clinic to take sworn statements in its own probe, focused on the possibility that film combustion had been triggered by a cigarette left by Boggs in the X-ray room. All witnesses examined were queried as to their smoking habits, their observation of any smoking by anyone in the vicinity of the film room, and in particular, the smoking habits of one Buffery Boggs. Boggs admitted to a moderate smoking habit, but the official City investigation of the tragedy noted that during his testimony Boggs "appeared to be an incessant cigarette smoker." In retrospect, this would seem a gratuitous slur, as no physical evidence was ever produced to indicate that Boggs smoked in the X-ray film room on May 15.

Boggs returned to his task shortly after 11 a.m. As he walked through the door to the X-ray storage room he heard a "hissing sound." Although he didn't smell any odor, he noticed that "the room was warm, it was darn warm." He was beginning to wonder about the hissing—the steam had been turned off for more than an hour—when he saw the smoke. It was a "thick, yellowish smoke" coming from a steam line near the north wall. Boggs ran out of the room and yelled to Clinic maintenance worker Sam Steel for a fire extinguisher, "There's a fire in that room!" Steel handed a soda-ash extinguisher to Boggs, and Boggs ran back in the film room and began to spray the spreading cloud of yellowish-brown smoke.

It didn't help. Just about the time he emptied the extinguisher, Boggs was overcome by smoke and fell to the floor. "It stopped my breath, just as you would shut off a valve," was the way the steamfitter's helper put it. Coming to, he crawled toward the open door. As he reached it, a "gigantic force" picked him up and blew him through the door and across the floor on his stomach into a machine room. Boggs recalled, "It was as if a million cushions hit you at once."

Buffery Boggs's "gigantic force" was the disaster's first explosion and it came about 11:25 a.m. There were anywhere from 250 to 330 people in the building—and most of the day's 123 dead may already have been well on the way to the grave even before the first blast came. Decomposition (flameless combustion) or "cooking" of the X-ray films in the basement storage room, caused by heat, had apparently been going on for some time. By the moment of the initial explosion at 11:25 a.m., lethal gases had thoroughly penetrated both the piping and ventilation systems of the Clinic building right up to the roof. Bromine, nitrogen dioxide, nitrous oxide, nitrogen peroxide, hydrocyanic gas, hydrogen and oxygen gases— all released from the burning film—were being forced throughout all four floors of the building as fast as the ventilation ducts and piping chases could carry them. The first blast probably came when

Cleveland Press Collection, Cleveland State University.

Fire investigator in Cleveland Clinic X-ray film basement storage room.

just enough of the free hydrogen in the walls came in contact with a convenient spark.

First hints that something was amiss in the Clinic came several minutes before the first explosion. Some employees and patients, especially women, noticed a peculiar, unpleasant odor in the air. H. W. Decker, Clinic pharmacist, was on the ground floor when he sensed the foul smell and found a group of nurses gathered by its apparent source in a radiator. Dorothy Hyde, a typist in the pharmacy, was oblivious to all but her typing—until "some fine powder, plaster or something" began falling on her work. About the same time, Mrs H. A. Brooks saw some yellow dust coming out of a hole in the wall and employee Maude Lehman became aware of a puff of smoke coming out of the wall. She had just told a staff doctor about it when the first blast shook the building, and choking clouds of dirty, yellow-brown smoke enveloped all four floors of the structure.

What went on in the Clinic building during the next 20 minutes is known only to God. Patterns of death, injury, and escape in the

Clinic tragedy would later be pieced together, but events were really a maddened, incomprehensible chaos as at least 250 persons frantically sought to escape suffocating death in a suddenly gas-filled, burning concrete and wood trap. So lethal were the gases, especially the nitrogen peroxide and carbon monoxide, that most of the victims died probably within minutes of the first explosion, if not before. Patients died without a sound on examination tables. Doctors suddenly fell to the floor, scalpels still in hand. As Battalion Fire Chief Michael Graham later recalled of a corpse he found sitting in the second floor lobby: "He looked as if he had just started to take a nap when the fumes began." Others died screaming and crawling on the floors and window sills, gasping for air.

It was a particularly gruesome death, as many eyewitnesses would testify. Although the exact chemical components and proportions of the lethal gases were never determined, it is clear that large amounts of carbon monoxide and acidic nitrogen compounds were present. The effects on the lungs of the victims was rapid and lethal. Dr. Torald Sollmann, dean of the Western Reserve School of Medicine, described them clinically:

> In some way not known, the gas gets fixed in the thin walls of the lungs. The resulting irritation makes these cells soluble and as a result the watery part of the blood stream begins to leak through them into the lungs. The lungs fill with water, drowning the patient.

Not just drowning them, however: Coroner A. J. Pearse's report noted that "those who died from the poison gas bubbled at the nose and mouth." Witnesses testified that many of the faces of corpses appeared yellow, blue, and green.

An even more graphic description came from the vacationing Dr. William G. Epstein, who had unluckily stopped off in Cleveland—"on the spur of the moment"—with his wife, Florence. He was in another Clinic building when the first blast came, and he fought his way into the building to find:

> It was too horrible to describe . . . . That gas is awful stuff. It bites into the skin like acid—worse than acid. Because acid at least is localized. This gas eats into the tissues—and eats and eats and eats! . . . . Her mouth was bleeding—her eyes and nose were bleeding. She couldn't speak.

Florence Epstein died in her husband's arms. Dr. Howard Karsner of the Western Reserve Medical School stated that he had never, in a career of 20,000 autopsies, seen conditions identical to those of Clinic gas victims.

The situation was probably worst on the second and third floors. Most of the people in the building were with doctors and nurses in the dozens of examining and diagnostic rooms on those floors, and the poison gas and explosion caught some patients in various stages of undress. Virtually all doctors and nurses behaved heroically and began trying to take patients on these floors to safety. Unfortunately, most patients were strangers to the Clinic and their ideas of safety lay in the most obvious locations: the Clinic's stairways and elevators. This only increased their peril and panic, as intense fires were already raging at blowtorch heat in the rear elevator well and stairway. Lethal gases coming up from the basement, moreover, were concentrating in the three stories of the interior court—meaning that patients were safer staying in the side rooms and awaiting rescue via the windows.

Practically no one involved in the escalating disaster knew that. Which is why most of the victims were later found stacked—sometimes a dozen or more together—in piles by the staircases and the second- and third-floor elevator doors. So frantic was the press of desperate escapees by the third floor elevator that its metal doors were later found partially pushed in by the frenzied hands of desperate victims. Their hysteria was so great that a man in a wheelchair, caught in the wild panic, was later found with his feet jammed between the half-open door and the gaping elevator shaft. Coroner Pearse thought some died of sheer fright, and one panicked man jumped to his death from a fourth floor window.

Some escaped almost immediately from the spreading gas and fire. Custodian Walter Adams was the first person out of the building, his clothes aflame. Buffery Boggs, the unfortunate discoverer of the film fire, was blown by the second explosion into a window well in the Clinic's basement. He and a companion got themselves out of it, and Boggs—after prudently moving his car—ran all the way to the East 105th St. Fire Station and shouted, "There's a terrible fire at the Clinic, a big fire!"

The first alarm, probably preceding Boggs's announcement, was pulled at Fire Box #315 at 11:30 a.m. The Eighth Fire Battalion (Hook & Ladder Company #8, Engine Companies #10 & #22, and

Ruins of 2nd Floor lobby of Cleveland Clinic.

Rescue Squad #3), under Chief Michael Graham, roared out of the 105th Street Firehouse. They could smell and see the dense yellow-brown gas several blocks before they got to the burning building and they were already donning gas masks when they got there. By now, about 11:40 a.m., fires were raging in the film room, rear elevator, and rear stairwell, with six minor fires elsewhere in the building.

Fortunately for those trapped in the Clinic, rescue efforts had already spontaneously begun. A. W. Johnson and Roy Miller were up on 40-foot ladders painting a sign just west of the Clinic when the first blast occurred. Almost immediately afterwards, Johnson saw dense clouds of "umber" smoke (after all, he was a painter) pouring out of the building. He and Miller grabbed their ladders and ran with them to the west wall of the Clinic. There, joined by a young man named Walter Jackson, they ran the ladders up to the second-floor windows, where dozens of terrified people were screaming and even hanging onto the sills to avoid gas pouring out of the windows. Jackson, Miller, and Johnson, joined by Frank Salvini and Bruce Griffith from the nearby Hupmobile dealership at 93rd and Carnegie, climbed up the ladders and began to take frantic, often injured victims down, one by one. Except for Jackson, an unexpected and veritable Porthos when the chips were down on that fatal May day; one impressed witness later testified, "I saw him walk with two people down the ladder the same as you would go downstairs."

Incredibly, Walter Jackson performed even greater feats that terrible day. As the toxic gases and heat from the building often prevented rescuers from getting close enough to maneuver their ladders to the second-floor sills, Jackson actually held a ladder up with his hands and shoulders while rescuers carried bodies down it. John Smith, an eyewitness, never forgot the sight:

> I saw him hold up a ladder, full of people, with the strength God gave no human being. When he could stand that no longer he staggered to the side of victims on the ground, tearing off his shirt to wrap around a naked person.

Walter Jackson and his companions weren't the only heroes that day. Patrolman Ernest Staab was near the Clinic when the fire started and rushed into the building. He pulled 21 bodies out before he collapsed. Like many of the day's heroes who survived, he paid a price: he was subject to fainting spells for months after the accident. (And Staab proved to be a creature of heroic habit. Before he retired in 1954 he also rescued three children from the path of a drunken driver.)

One of the heroes was an anonymous man known only as "Jimmy" to William Majury, who described him to reporters. As the two men approached the burning Clinic, "Jimmy" said, "That looks like gas; I'm going in there." Majury watched as he ran in and emerged with a body, only to return to the blazing, smoking inferno.

Some heroes came in groups. One was composed of pupils from the Wilcox Commercial School on Euclid Avenue at East 100th. Against the orders of firemen at the scene, they entered the burning Clinic and began pulling victims out.

Eight doctors and six nurses died that day, and the evidence is that they all succumbed heroically, trying desperately to save their patients. One such was Dr. John Phillips, one of the four Clinic founders. Escaping from the Clinic, he worked outside for hours, treating the victims spread out on the grass. That evening, he collapsed at his apartment and died there, despite the frantic efforts of Dr. George Crile to save him. Another hero-doctor, albeit a survivor, was Dr. Wilson J. Peart, head of the Clinic's dental wing. Treating patients on the third floor when the initial explosion occurred, he shrewdly attempted to prevent them from going out into the hall adjacent to the interior court. Although his assistant and a technician got out of the room and died, Dr. Peart managed to drag several collapsed victims back into the room and to open windows. He and fellow physician Wallace Duncan refused to leave until firemen had rescued all 18 of the other people in the room.

William Brownlow, Clinic medical artist, died in dramatic and sublime fashion. He was in his third-floor studio and already succumbing to gas when Clinic usher Susan Brantweiner ran in. As he attempted to smash a window, she crawled across the floor to him and said, "Goodbye." Brownlow muttered, "No, not goodbye," shattered the window, grabbed Brantweiner and thrust her into the air outside. Firemen eventually rescued her, but Brownlow refused to go until two other victims had been removed from the room. He died soon after. Many patients would never forget the brave Clinic nurses shouting, "Save the patients, save the patients!" as death closed in.

Heroism did not know any age, much less sex or race that awful day. Perhaps the most astonishing sight of the disaster was 81-year-old Fire Chief George Wallace carrying on like a hero of youthful years. Among the first firemen at the scene, he pulled a victim from the elevator shaft and fell twice while rescuing others. All in a day's work, though, for the doughty Wallace, who served as an active Cleveland fireman from 1869 to 1931.

A second, and far more powerful, explosion occurred several minutes after the first firemen arrived on the scene. It was probably a blessing, as it blew out many remaining Clinic windows so that firemen could now see victims at windows that had been hidden by smoke. It also blew out the roof skylight and left several holes in the roof, thus ventilating much of the toxic gas in the three-story interior court. Within minutes, firemen had snaked their new 85-foot motorized ladder to the roof. Descending through the ruined skylight, Firemen Howard McAllister and Peter Rogers were lowered into the smoke- and gas-filled interior court. Swinging from

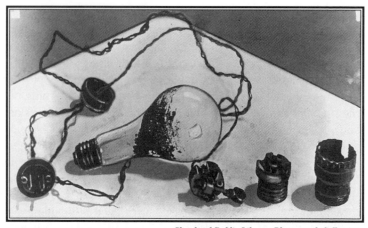

Cleveland Public Library Photograph Collection.

100-watt light bulb suspected as probable cause of Cleveland Clinic fire.

side to side, they finally got inside the fourth-floor railing and began pulling victims, packed four deep in some places, out of the stairwell and elevator areas. They sent 15 victims to the roof, some dead, and some who were revived there by pulmotors. So many bodies were taken to the County Morgue that they had to lay them out on the floor for identification by stunned relatives and Clinic staff.

It was all over by 1:15 p.m., although a third explosion occurred shortly after the second. By that hour virtually all fire units on the East Side were on the scene. All victims had been removed and all fires were under control, except for a few smoldering window frames and part of the roof area. It was not over, however, for many of the victims. The lingering or delayed effects of the gas were potently manifested in the fact that some disaster victims quoted in initial newspaper accounts of the tragedy showed up in later editions as fatalities. Some fought death for hours, some for days, and one, attorney Henry Lustig, 47, battled until June 13, almost a month after the disaster. Accompanying his father-in-law to the Clinic, Lustig had tried in vain to save him when the first blast came and had stayed in the gas-filled building to aid several women trapped there. Although the official Clinic death toll was 123, lingering casualties such as Lustig may have swelled the actual total to 128.

If careless and casual in the procedures and conditions that produced the disaster, the Clinic and its human resources were magnificent in response and recovery. Dr. Crile himself was at his best throughout the disaster, a veritable battlefield general who tirelessly marshalled resources to heal the wounded and console the grieving. After hours tending the injured, Crile established a new Clinic headquarters across the street in the old Wason mansion (former site of Laurel School) and announced: "We must carry on. The Clinic has its work to do and must go forward."

As Clinic efforts to rebuild and recover went forward, so, too, did efforts to explain this unprecedented and ghastly accident. City, county, and state probes were under way within days of the disaster, supplemented by investigations by the War Department, Western Reserve University, the Bureau of Standards, and the National Board of Fire Underwriters. The results of these various inquiries are best summarized by noting that they held no one particularly or individually liable for the tragedy and that they agreed that the Clinic disaster never should have happened, given existing knowledge about nitrocellulose film. Provoking much criticism, County Coroner A. J. Pearse's inquest was held in private, owing, Pearse said, to the reluctance of witnesses to testify in public. After lengthy sessions involving dozens of witnesses, Pearse concluded there was no need to call a Grand Jury to investigate or apportion blame for the mishap.

Probably the most thorough inquiry was the Clinic's own, undertaken by some of the best lawyers available in the city. Taking sworn statements from virtually all Clinic employees and disaster witnesses, they narrowed the disaster's origin down to three possibilities:

1) "spontaneous" combustion of the film, owing to overheating of the storage room;

2) film combustion caused by a carelessly left cigarette or match (hence the persistent inquiries about the smoking habits of Buffery Boggs);

3) film combustion caused by contact with the extension cord light dropped over the "big spike" near the film racks.

No one ever proved that Buffery Boggs or anyone else was smoking in the film room that day, although charwoman Rose Rebar testified that she often saw people smoking in the Clinic basement. And while Fire Warden J. H. Andrews had found a pack of cigarettes in the film room during his inspection *only five days before*—there was no tobacco evidence found to support the "careless smoker" theory. It is true that Boggs noted that the film room was "darn warm" on the morning of the fire, but the heat from the steam pipes hardly seemed sufficient to cause "cooking" of the X-ray films.

Which left the 100-watt bulb at the end of the spike-draped extension cord as the probable cause of the mishap. It was found in the ruins of the film storage room, and Enid Critcher testified that she had employed it for several months up to the day of the disaster. Custodian Walter Adams, for his part, adamantly insisted that it wasn't there:

> As for that light bulb extension, if it was there after the fire, ghosts must have placed it there. We took special pains that the 100-watt bulbs were not within three feet of the X-ray films.

Interestingly, Adams also denied the assertion of virtually all fire investigators that the fire door of the film room could not close on that fatal day, owing to an obstructing steam pipe:

> We closed it every night. It was left open in the daytime so the room would have the same temperature as the rest of the building.

On May 24, *The Plain Dealer* noted that one of the chief witnesses in the city probe of the Clinic disaster had made "false statements" and that "they concerned the lights in the basement room." But no one was ever legally charged with negligence or culpability in the Clinic tragedy.

The National Fire Protection Association was not so kind in its assessment. On June 12 it issued a report that blistered both the city and Clinic for sloppy practice in handling and regulating X-ray films:

> It is inconceivable that the conditions responsible for the Cleveland hospital disaster could have been permitted to exist even for a single day had the management or the inspection authorities appreciated the hazard. . . . The physical facts are well established. There was a large quantity of nitrocellulose X-ray film in the basement. It was stored in obvious violation of

Casualties being tended on ground, May 15, 1929.

proper precautions for the keeping of this material of known dangerous property.

No expense or expertise was spared in trying to arrive at a scientific understanding of the Clinic disaster. Both the War Department and Western Reserve University School of Medicine conducted elaborate tests on mice and rabbits to determine the toxicity of the probable gases involved. Mice exposed to burning of gas residue scrapings from the Clinic walls—there were copious yellow-brown stains throughout the building—died with convulsions within 1 to 2 minutes. Lesser concentrations, test reports said, merely caused "cyanosis dyspnea."

The official probes and harmless recriminations dragged on for some time. The Cleveland Clinic, however, had already put it all behind. The Cleveland powers-that-be, represented by an elite committee of Samuel Mather and 35 other similar achievers, rallied behind the Clinic, and Dr. George Crile impressively rebuilt it from the ruins of May 15, 1929. The main building was rebuilt on a different plan, to spare the sensibilities of those who might remember its appearance on that dreadful day. The massive insurance claims were paid off. And the Clinic has only waxed greater and more glorious as a Cleveland, indeed global, institution in the years since. It did, however, switch to acetate-based film and enforce some safety regulations and recommendations concerning X-ray film storage.

Why did the Clinic disaster happen? No one person was ever held accountable, so it is now a moot point. But certain notes on the

Clinic's fire inspections during the 1920s raise intriguing questions about municipal inspection procedures and enforcement. On May 4, 1925, for example, City Fire Warden J. H. Andrews inspected the film storage room and ordered the Clinic to keep its X-rays *in metal containers and to provide a fire-proof vault for same.* [Italics added.] This, obviously, was not done. Four months later, on September 15, 1929, Andrews noted that "This Company has not complied with my orders in regards to storing films [in metal cases]." There is no further record of violation or compliance. On May 10, 1929, Andrews made his last inspection and warned Clinic officials not to allow smoking in the film area. The inspection record makes no mention of a vault or metal cases at all.

Chapter 15

"WE'RE GOING TO BURN YOU..."

The Enduring Sheppard Tragedy

Mankind is not comfortable with ambiguity. Americans, especially, are notoriously impatient with it. Which is why the Marilyn Sheppard murder mystery remains for Clevelanders a most frustrating, and therefore enduring puzzle. For all the arguments argued, print printed, and years gone by, we shall never know beyond all doubt who brutally beat Sam Sheppard's beautiful, pregnant wife to death on that famous July morning of 1954. Sadly, all we can be certain of is that the tragedy ruined and scarred the lives of everyone connected with it—and continues to do so.

It all began on July 4, 1954, at 5:45 a.m. Spencer Houk, a 45-year-old butcher and mayor of Bay Village, picked up his ringing telephone to hear the voice of his neighbor and friend, 35-year-old Dr. Sam Sheppard, blurt: "For God's sake, Spen, come over here quick! I think they've killed Marilyn!"

Spencer and his wife, Esther, quickly sped—*in their car*—to the Sheppard house, only 100 yards away. Entering the Sheppards' Lake Road house through its unlocked front door, they found disarray on the first floor. Household items and the contents of Sam's medical bag were strewn about, and Sam lay slumped in a chair, naked from the waist up and dazed. He seemed to be in pain and frequently touched his neck.

Esther Houk reacted first. Going upstairs to Marilyn Sheppard's bedroom, she found Sam's 31-year-old wife lying splayed at the end of her four-poster bed. Marilyn's legs were spread, dangling under the bed's crossbar, but covered by a sheet. Her pajama top was pulled up over her breasts and she was lying in pools of her own blood. The walls, doors, and an adjacent twin bed were likewise spattered with blood. Esther staggered back downstairs to Spencer and Sam and said, "Call the police! Call an ambulance!

Cleveland Press Collection, Cleveland State University.
Sam Sheppard, 1954.

Call everything!" Spencer called an ambulance, the police, and Dr. Richard Sheppard, Sam's older brother.

Within minutes most of the important actors in the Sheppard melodrama were on the scene. Shortly after the police arrived at 6:02 a.m., Dr. Richard Sheppard walked through the door. After examining Marilyn's body and realizing she was beyond treatment he turned to Sam and said either, "Did you do this?" or "Did you have anything to do with this?" Sam said, "Hell, no!"

Or did he? Both Richard and Sam Sheppard would repeatedly deny ever having this vivid conversation, with its implied presumption—deadly to Sam at his trial—that his brother might have reason to suspect Sam's involvement in Marilyn's death. But Spencer Houk would testify under oath that he heard this brotherly dialogue, and Sam Sheppard's first jury would hear Houk swear to it.

Minutes after Richard's arrival, yet another Sheppard sibling doctor, Stephen Sheppard, arrived. After examining Sam, he decided Sam needed hospital treatment for bruises and possible neck and head injuries and had him removed to Bay View Hospital, a nearby facility owned and operated by the three Sheppard brothers and their father, Dr. Richard A. Sheppard, osteopaths all.

Stephen and the other Sheppards would later be criticized for "whisking" and "spiriting" Sam away from possible police scrutiny and "protecting" him from interrogation for critical days on specious medical grounds. But no one at the scene of the Sheppard house objected at the time Sam was taken away and, moreover, Sam was not entirely immune from police interrogation in the hours after the discovery of Marilyn's body. After talking to the Houks at the scene of the crime, he was questioned there by Patrolman Fred Drenkan of the Bay Village Police, who arrived just after 6 a.m. Going to the hospital, Sam was questioned further by Cuyahoga County Coroner Sam R. Gerber for about 30 minutes. Two hours later he was questioned by crack Cleveland Police detectives Robert Schottke and Patrick Gareau. And when Schottke returned to Sam's bedside at 3 p.m., he resumed his queries with these words: "I don't know what my partner thinks, but I think you killed your wife." Sam had just enough time to deny the accusation before an outraged Stephen Sheppard ejected Schottke from Bay View Hospital.

Whether one believes it or not, Sam's story became a famous one, and it is a fact that he never significantly changed it, despite countless retellings. It may not have made sense, it may not have been coherent, and it was not credible to many people, but it went like this . . .

Sam and Marilyn had spent the night before the murder, July 3, at home entertaining their friends, Don and Nancy Ahern. After a pleasant meal on the back porch facing the shore of their Lake Erie property, the two couples retired to the living room. Don listened to an Indians' ballgame, while Marilyn, Sam, and Nancy watched a movie on television, "Strange Holiday." Sam cuddled for awhile with Marilyn and then moved to a couch where he dozed off, despite Marilyn's efforts to rekindle his interest in the movie. He was wearing a brown corduroy jacket, white T-shirt, and tan slacks.

About midnight, the Aherns left for their nearby home. They were the last persons to see Marilyn Sheppard alive. Marilyn apparently left Sam asleep on the couch and retired to her bedroom. The Sheppards' seven-year-old son, Sam, Jr. ("Chip"), slept in a nearby room.

Sam's uncorroborated but unchanging memory was of being awakened by Marilyn's screams sometime during the night. Groggy with sleep, he stumbled up the stairs toward her bedroom. As he got to the door, he saw a "white form" or "white figure" by Marilyn's bed. He couldn't tell whether it was male or female, but he was trying to grab it when he was hit from behind on his neck and head and knocked unconscious.

Sam couldn't say how long he was out. When he came to, he was sitting up, in pain and facing the bedroom door. His wallet was on the floor and he picked it up. He could see Marilyn's body, bloody and apparently terribly injured about the head. He felt for her pulse, found none, and ran to Chip's room. Chip was asleep and unharmed but then Sam heard another noise coming from downstairs.

Sam flew down the stairs to find a figure running out the back door, down 36 steps, and toward the Sheppard beach house by Lake Erie. Sam pursued what he identified as a hefty, muscular man with "bushy hair" and grappled anew with him. Again knocked unconscious by the invincible intruder, Sam fell by the water's edge.

He regained consciousness about dawn, revived by the tide lapping at his legs. Lurching back to the house, he looked again at his wife's bloody corpse—and called Spencer Houk. That was Sam Sheppard's story then, later, and forever.

The police weren't happy with Sam's story—and no one was happy with the police. Within hours of Marilyn's death the Bay Village police, Cleveland police and the Cuyahoga County sheriff's office were stumbling over each other, ransacking the Sheppard house for evidence, and interviewing anyone who might know about Marilyn's slaying. The murder house itself became Grand Central Station as police, family members, and hordes of the merely curiously traipsed through the murder scene. And Cleveland's three daily newspapers—the *Press, News,* and *Plain Dealer*—immediately began to egg on investigative efforts and amplify police and public frustration with the unsolved case. The Sheppard murder probe already promised to become the "Roman holiday" of sensationalism later decried by Ohio Supreme Court

Cleveland Press Collection, Cleveland State University.

Sam and Marilyn Sheppard.

Justice James Finley Bell. Three aspects in particular were about to push it right over the edge.

One factor was police frustration with Sam and the Sheppard family. Stephen Sheppard, as Sam's physician, insisted that his patient was too badly injured to submit to unrestricted police interrogation during his hospital stay. This did not sit well with either Bay Village or Cleveland authorities, who fumed publicly at being shut out while Sam attended his wife's funeral and entertained a stream of family friends and reporters in his room at Bay View Hospital. Only four days after Marilyn's death, *The Plain Dealer* decried the "virtual parade" of visitors and quoted unnamed "veteran homicide officers" as being unable to "remember similar delays in other murder investigations." The stand-off between the Sheppard family members and the authorities became even more acrid when a Bay Village physician, Dr. E. Richard Hexter, examined Sam at Coroner Gerber's request and failed to agree with Stephen Sheppard's diagnosis of severe neck injury and concussion. Although Sam was available for a three-hour grilling by Sheriff Carl Rossbach by July 8 and an all-day interrogation with

Cleveland police on July 9, the half-true legend had already been created and accepted that Sam's family had "shielded" him from police inquiries in the crucial days following his wife's murder.

A second force pushing the investigation toward a state of hysteria was the public antipathy toward the Sheppard family in general, and Sam in particular. Whatever attitudes preexisted about the Sheppards, it is clear that the family became a magnet for ferocious public and private animosities that apparently had lurked before the murder—and, amazingly, have persisted down to the present day. A lot of people in Bay Village didn't like Sam and his family. Indeed, within days of the crime the Sheppards became the focus of shocking rumors and unsubstantiated slanders that have lasted 40 years (as the author discovered while conversing with aging Bay residents). It was said that Sam and Marilyn were adulterous suburban "swingers," members of a wife-swapping "key club" whose lubricious activities included disporting themselves in semi-public orgies at the Sheppards' lakefront rear beach. It was rumored that Sam, despite fathering Chip, was sterile and had murdered Marilyn in a fit of rage after discovering she was pregnant again. It was whispered that Sam was bisexual, that he was a dope addict. It was said that one of the Sheppard brothers, or even their father Richard, was criminally involved . . . the Sheppard family had run an abortion mill . . . and that Sam was protecting someone in his family . . . or maybe his friend Spencer Houk . . . or Esther Houk . . . or . . . or . . . *ad infinitium ad nauseum.* And you can probably still hear all of it said again anytime you stop by in Bay Village.

Maybe it was because the Sheppards, doctors, insisted that Sam's unrestricted interrogation be delayed. This may have been routine medical judgment but it was interpreted by outsiders as a blatant and specious attempt to shield the chief suspect. Maybe it was because they were osteopaths. Although not sharing quite the pariah status that chiropractic doctors did in 1954, the Sheppards' non-M.D. status earned them little sympathy or support from the medical establishment—well-represented in the affair by Coroner Samuel Gerber, M.D.

The third and most critical factor pushing the Sheppard case over the edge into unbridled public hysteria was the way it has handled by Cleveland's newspapers. Although all of them early voiced suspicions about Sam's story and retailed the unhappiness of police authorities with the case from the start, the *Cleveland Press*, led by editor Louis B. Seltzer, quickly took the lead in pressing for an aggressive third-degree treatment of Sam. Within the first few days, *Press* stories stressed the "lack of emotion" exhibited by Sam while telling his story. Four days after the murder, one story even dwelt on the titles of some paperback mysteries found in the Sheppard library: "Blood on My Hands," "Blood in Your Eye," and, better yet, "I Killed My Wife." Seltzer's treatment of Sam hardened further on July 16, only 12 days after the murder, with an editorial decrying the "tragic mishandling" of the case and the "unusual protection" of Sam by his lawyer and family.

Seltzer hit manhunting stride on July 20, with a front-page caricature of an ominous figure stalking a suburban street and another screaming front-page editorial: "Somebody is Getting Away With Murder."

It was not so much an editorial as a public cry of populist outrage:

> In the background of his case are friendships, relationships, hired lawyers, a husband who ought to have been subjected instantly to the same third-degree to which any other person under similar circumstances is subjected, and a whole string of special and bewildering extra-privileged courtesies that should never be extended by authorities investigating a murder—the most serious, and sickening crime of all. . . . It's time that somebody smashed into this situation and tore aside this restraining curtain of sham, politeness and hypocrisy and went at the business of solving a murder—and quit this nonsense of artificial politeness that has not been extended to any other murder case in generations.

Among the measures demanded by the *Press* was a public inquest, which coroner Sam Gerber enthusiastically commenced on Thursday, July 22. Held at Normandy High School in Bay Village and lasting three days, it was attended by several hundred vocal spectators. The inquest featured six hours of testimony by Sam Sheppard and vigorous cross-examination by Gerber. Witnesses called included the Houks, the Aherns, investigating police, and members of the Sheppard family. The inquest was memorable, but not for its testimony, most of which had already been previewed in newspaper coverage of the murder. What was significant

Cleveland Press Collection, Cleveland State University.
Sam Sheppard with his brother Stephen and Mrs. (Betty) Stephen Sheppard on the way to the inquest.

was not its content but its tone—a proceeding more appropriate to a lynch mob than a public inquiry. The crowd was hostile to Sam from the moment he arrived on Thursday morning, patted down for weapons at the door in full view of the spectators. Even the presence of Sam's counsel, criminal attorney William J. Corrigan, was held against him, one spectator jeering aloud, "What does Sheppard need a lawyer for if he's innocent?" As Gerber had stated from the outset that no witness was entitled to counsel, the denouement to the kangeroo inquest on Monday probably came as no surprise to the key actors. After repeatedly warning Corrigan to cease interjecting comments about the crowd's partisan behavior into the stenographer's record, Gerber had Corrigan physically ejected and dragged out of the room when the combative attorney insisted that the stenographer insert his remark that the atmosphere was like a "Hippodrome."

Sam was probably already doomed even before the inquest finished its run on July 26. By that time, Cleveland police were heavily involved in the murder investigation. And what they found wasn't good for Sam. Whether guilty of murder or not, it was clear he had told a pack of lies to investigators about his personal life. Worse yet, he had just repeated them during the first two days of the Normandy inquest. His sleazy untruths were about to be thrown back in his face, just as the *Press* campaign against him reached its crescendo.

It has often been said that Sam Sheppard was accused of murder and found guilty of adultery. Up to the time of the inquest, Sam had painted an idyllic picture of his marriage to authorities, admitting some past "difficulties" but rhapsodizing about his recent marital bliss and his happiness about Marilyn's second pregnancy. His portrait of Sam-the-happy-family-man exploded over the inquest weekend with the revelation that Susan Hayes, an attractive 24-year-old medical technician and former Bay View Hospital employee, had admitted an adulterous liaison with Sam extending over the past three years. Indeed, after intensive police interrogation in Los Angeles broke down her story of platonic relations, Susan admitted that she and Sam had lived together at the house of a California doctor in March 1954, while Sam was attending medical classes in Los Angeles. Cleveland newspapers titillatingly reported that Sam had even bought Miss Hayes an expensive watch; one wonders how they might have editorialized had they known he intended to deduct its cost as an "office expense."

Sam must have known what was coming. By now Marilyn's family, with the exception of her favorite aunt, had publicly distanced themselves from Sam. Three weeks after the murder, Spencer Houk, in a final conversation with his friend Sam, urged him "to confess if he had done it." And the drumbeat of the aggressive *Press*-led inquisition of Sam continued. On July 27, although no decision had been made by Bay Village officials, its headline blared, "Doctor's Indictment Near in Murder of His Wife." The next day's front-page editorial demanded "Why Don't Police Quiz Top Suspect?":

> You can bet your last dollar the Sheppard murder would be cleaned up long ago if it had involved "average people," . . . Now proved under oath to be a liar, still free to go about his business,

shielded by his family, protected by a smart lawyer who has made monkeys of the police and authorities . . . Sam Sheppard still hasn't been taken to Headquarters.

The climax of the *Press* campaign came on July 30 with front-page editorials in early editions asking "Why Isn't Sam Sheppard in Jail?"; later ones simply demanding, "Quit Stalling and Bring Him In!" That night, about 10 p.m., in the presence of a screaming mob that surrounded the house, Sam Sheppard was arrested by Bay Village police at his parents' home for the murder of his wife. Within hours Sam was subjected to round-the-clock interrogation in jail. He stoutly maintained his total innocence, despite alleged police demands that he confess to avoid the electric chair. Or as Jack Harrison Pollack memorably reconstructed Sam's third-degree treatment in his sympathetic Sheppard book, *Dr. Sam: An American Tragedy:*

> "Now look here, you dirty no good son-of-a-bitch. You killed your wife in cold blood. We know it. You know it. The whole town knows it. For Chrissake, it's been in all the papers. Wake up, you horse's ass! We're going to burn you if you don't confess."

Sam Sheppard's first murder trial lasted from October 18 to December 21, 1954. Held before Judge Edward Blythin, Sam was defended by the capable team of William J. Corrigan, Fred Garmone, Sheppard family lawyer Arthur Petersilge, and William Corrigan, Jr. But Sam's fight for acquittal was an uphill battle from beginning to end.

As in all good mysteries since Sherlock Holmes, there was the mystery of the dog that didn't bark in the night. Those who believed Sam Sheppard guilty made much of the fact that Koko, the Sheppard's Irish setter, made no outcry heard by neighbors during the murder of her mistress in the night. But Sheppard partisans claimed the dog had always been timid, a possibility plausible to dog owners familiar with the infuriating untimeliness of canine behavior.

There was lots of blood in the Sheppard case. It was all over the murder room, on both Sam and Marilyn's watches, on Sam's pants, and in various places throughout the house. Little of it could be

Chip, Ariane, and Sam.

successfully typed and linked to specific individuals or even to humans—many of the blood stains found later on the stairs and first floor may have been from Koko, who had recently been in heat. There was a bloody blotch on Sam's trousers, explained, his lawyers claimed, by his kneeling on the bed to take Marilyn's pulse. (Although not brought out at the trial, the murder house also featured the blood of Richard Eberling, now serving a life sentence for the murder of a Lakewood widow in 1984. Eberling claims he was hired to put screens in the Sheppard house several days before the murder—*in the middle of summer*—and cut his hands on broken glass).

It is often said that Sam Sheppard was convicted on circumstantial evidence. This is true enough, as there was no direct or eyewitness testimony to Marilyn's murder. But, next to his philandering, what seems to have convicted him was the *absence* of concrete circumstantial evidence to support his own story. There was no convincing evidence of an attempted burglary-gone-wrong. Sam

Sheppard could not account for the fact that his white T-shirt was missing; the state would claim that he destroyed it because it must have been covered with Marilyn's blood. (*Two* T-shirts with no bloodstains were found by investigators—but neither the defense or the prosecution was interested in them.) And Sam could not account for some implausible wrinkles in his story. Why had he called Spencer Houk—instead of his brothers or the police—when he came to the second time? Why did he lie repeatedly and under oath at the inquest about his affair with Susan Hayes? (Sam would chivalrously claim he was trying to protect her reputation but this doesn't square well with his willingness, when the heat was on, to volunteer the names of male acquaintances who may have been potential suspects in the death of his wife.) How could his son Chip have slept through such goings-on, just steps away from his bedroom? And why was Sam's corduroy coat, presumably shed in the night or during his struggles with the homicidal intruder, found neatly folded on the couch by witnesses the next morning?

Sam's worst enemy in court may have been himself. Aside from the impression made by saying "I don't know" or equivalent replies 156 times, there was the matter of his stilted, vague diction. The impreciseness of his speech was perfectly captured in his trial testimony about his struggle at the beach:

> I pursued this form through the front door, over the porch, and out the screen door—all of the doors were evidently open—down the steps to the beach house landing and then on down the steps to the beach, where I lunged or jumped and grasped him in some manner from the back, either body or leg, it was something solid. However, I am not sure. This was beyond the steps an unknown distance, but probably about ten feet. I had the feeling of twisting or choking and this terminated my consciousness.

After two months of testimony, the jury prepared to deliberate its verdict. Judge Bythin's folksy instructions to the jury on the meaning of circumstantial evidence were taken by many observers to imply a conviction of Sam Sheppard's guilt:

> Let us assume that I had on a certain day a very fine cherry tree in my yard. The family happens to be away on that day, and when I return about five o'clock in the evening I find my cherry

tree chopped down. I proceed to investigate and first make inquiry of my next-door neighbor, Mr. Smith. I ask him if he saw any stranger doing anything in my yard that day. He replies: "Yes, I saw George Washington chop it down with an ax." That would be direct evidence because Mr. Smith is relying on his own sense of sight and states what he himself saw with his own eyes. For that reason he is able to give direct evidence that George Washington chopped down that cherry tree.

Let us consider now a case of circumstantial evidence in the same connection. Assume that on inquiry of Mr. Smith, my neighbor, he, in answer to my question says that he did not see anyone chopping down my tree. I then ask him: "Did you see anyone about my place today?" He replies: "Yes, I saw George Washington walk along your driveway from the yard to the street with an ax on his shoulder."

You have to hand it to Judge Blythin. He at least didn't say, "with a surgical instrument on his shoulder." After his charge to the jury, one newspaper wit was heard to offer a wager of even money that the jury would find George Washington guilty of first-degree murder.

The jury began its deliberations on December 17 at 10 a.m. After almost 40 hours of deliberations, shortly after 4 p.m. on December 21, they returned a verdict: Murder in the Second Degree. Immediately after the verdict, over Corrigan's bitter protest, Judge Blythin sentenced Sam Sheppard to a life sentence in the Ohio Penitentiary.

It seemed like the end of the Sheppard saga. It was, in reality, only the beginning to a tragedy that has not yet run its course. Sam's mother, Ethel Sheppard, believed entirely in her son's innocence but was undone by the family ordeal and the disclosure of his adultery. Halfway through the trial, on November 19, she attempted suicide with an overdose of Tuinal. She recovered, but 17 days after Sam's conviction she locked herself in her bedroom at son Stephen Sheppard's Rocky River home and blew her brains out with her son Sam's revolver. Just 11 days later, Sam's father, Richard A. Sheppard, who had visibly declined under the relentless tragedies visited upon his family, died from hemorrhaging stomach ulcers. Marilyn's father, too, would become a probable victim of his daughter's murder when he committed suicide years later.

The rest of the Sheppard story is a relatively well-known and

Cleveland Press Collection, Cleveland State University.

undisputed chapter of American legal history. Several days after Sam's conviction, the Sheppard murder house, sealed to his family since the murder, was returned to the Sheppard family. They immediately hired a forensic expert, Paul L. Kirk of the University of California, to examine the house. Perhaps not surprisingly, his report was far more supportive of Sam's "bushy-haired" intruder story. His forensic reconstruction of the murder seriously contradicted the prosecution's theory of the crime. Based on his study of the pattern of bloodstains and Marilyn's injuries, Kirk concluded that the killer was left-handed (Sam was right-handed.) In addition, arguing from the state of her clothing, Kirk argued that Marilyn's murder had begun as a rape—a conclusion long since past proof, as her body had never been examined for rape evidence. And it was Kirk who found the third blood type—belonging most likely to Eberling (and overlooked by police)—in the murder room.

Kirk's report, like Sam Sheppard's numerous appeals, seemed all in vain. Judge Blythin rejected Kirk's report as evidence warranting a new trial in May 1955, dismissing it as "conjecture." Two months later the Eighth District Court of Appeals upheld Sam's verdict and rejected a motion for a new trial. And on May 31, 1956, the Ohio Supreme Court voted 5-2 to uphold the Court of Appeals decision.

In the meantime, Sam Sheppard had become a model prisoner, eventually assisting in the prison medical ward and even volunteering to have cancer cells injected into his body as part of a cancer research experiment.

Sam Sheppard's ultimately successful crusade for freedom has become the stuff of legal legend. After he had spent more than half a decade in prison, Sam's luck turned when attorney F. Lee Bailey became interested in his case. Pushing Sam's case up through the lower courts, Bailey drew first blood on July 15, 1964, when the U. S. District Court in Dayton ordered Sam freed on a writ of *habeas corpus* on the grounds he had not received a fair trial. In his decision, Judge Carl A. Weinman characterized the circumstances of Sam's first trial as a "mockery of justice." And on June 6, 1966, the U. S. Supreme Court upheld the decision.

Cuyahoga County officials were faced with the choice of letting Sam go free or retrying him for second-degree murder. (Sam could not be tried for first-degree murder, as his first jury had specifically acquitted him of that charge). Four days after the Supreme Court decision, Prosecutor John T. Corrigan (no relation to William J.) chose to reindict Sam.

Sam Sheppard's second trial in October–November 1966 before Judge Francis J. Talty was a relatively colorless and half-hearted affair. Judge Talty forbade any cameras in the courtroom or interviews with jurors or witnesses. Only a selected pool of 14 reporters was permitted to cover the trial, as opposed to the journalistic carnival of the first Sheppard trial.

A perusal of the record suggests that the state's heart was not in the second Sheppard prosecution. Indeed, reporter Doris O'Donnell claims that prosecutor John T. Corrigan told her at the time that he would just be going through the motions. Susan Hayes was barely mentioned and was not called as a witness, thus diluting the prosecution's motive component. And F. Lee Bailey effectively dispatched the question of means—the "surgical instrument"—in his withering cross-examination of Coroner Sam Gerber. The climax came on November 7, as Bailey bored in on Gerber:

> Bailey: You never produced [the surgical instrument] at the first trial—produce one now, if you can.
> Gerber: I can't. . . . I hunted all over the United States and couldn't find one.
> Bailey: You didn't have one in 1954 and you don't have one today.
> Gerber: That's right.

It *was* interesting, however, that Bailey never brought up the story of the bushy-haired intruder . . . .

Given the weakness of the state's case, the obvious verdict came on the night of November 17, 1966, when his second jury acquitted Sam. It seemed like his life was beginning again.

In fact, it was almost over. While in prison, Sam had become involved with a woman named Ariane Tebbenjohanns. An attractive blonde and half-sister-in-law of Joseph Goebbels, Hitler's Minister of Propaganda, Ariane had heard about the case while living in Germany and began to correspond with the imprisoned Sheppard. Two days after his release on July 15, 1964, pending final disposition of his *habeas corpus* appeal, Sam and Ariane were married. The reinstatement of Sam's medical license, after a bitter fight with the State of Ohio, seemed like the perfect finishing touch to a fairy-tale ending for Sam Sheppard.

It was too good to be true. Guilty or not, life in prison had taken its toll on Sam Sheppard. He was apparently drinking heavily during the last years of his life and persistent rumor held that he was a dope addict. His medical career ended for good in 1968, after two medical malpractice suits against him caused Youngstown Osteopathic Hospital to let him go. Almost simultaneously, Ariane Sheppard filed for divorce, citing adultery and violence as grounds. Sam, Ariane claimed, had stolen her property and even threatened her with a gun. The divorce was granted on October 7, 1969.

The end of Sam Sheppard's sufferings came on April 6, 1970. By that time he had descended to the pathetic expedient of a career as a part-time professional wrestler. He was living at the home of his manager, George Strickland, and was believed to have married his 20-year-old daughter several weeks after his divorce. (Chip Sheppard, for reasons not apparent, denies that Sam bothered to marry Colleen). Once again, as on another fateful night, Sam went to sleep, and when he woke up at 3 a.m., he was groggy and in pain. Colleen and her mother assisted him into the kitchen, where he sagged to the floor. Within a few hours he was dead of liver failure at the age of 46.

As may be clear from the above, this writer believes that Sam Sheppard killed his wife. This, of course, is not the same thing as believing either that the state *proved* he did it at his first trial or that the prosecution was a fair and unbiased one. The case against Sam was based more on a lack of evidence to support *his* weird story than any solid evidence—especially concerning motive and means—to prove the state's case. And that Sam Sheppard's chances for a fair trial were precluded by unbridled and irresponsi-

Cleveland Press Collection, Cleveland State University.

The Sheppard house at 28924 Lake Rd.

ble press coverage of Marilyn Sheppard's murder has become a truism and an enduring influence in American law.

Neither side has ever been happy with the legend of Sam Sheppard. Indeed, the case from the beginning seems to have brought out the worst in everyone connected with it. Those who thought he was guilty from the start tend still to think so, dismissing the second jury's acquittal as a compassionate gesture toward a man who, whatever his sins, had already suffered enough. And Sheppard partisans, not content with belittling the weaknesses of the state's case and the outrageous behavior of the press, have never ceased proposing alternative candidates for the role of Marilyn's murderer.

It is no secret that Spencer and Esther Houk have always been the favored heavies in alternative versions of the murder scenario. An early phase of the investigation focused on Spencer's possible infatuation or even romantic involvement with Marilyn Sheppard. But Spencer took—and apparently passed—a lie detector test in the period between the murder and Sam's arrest. It is claimed that Esther also offered to take one—unlike Sam, who refused a polygraphic examination twice. Most of the published literature about the Sheppard case, however, is pro–Sam Sheppard—and most of it has implied that both Spencer and Esther were the murderers surprised by a groggy Sam in the wee hours of July 4, 1954. The probable plot in this version is that Esther, insanely jealous of her husband's attentions to Marilyn—real or imagined—entered the

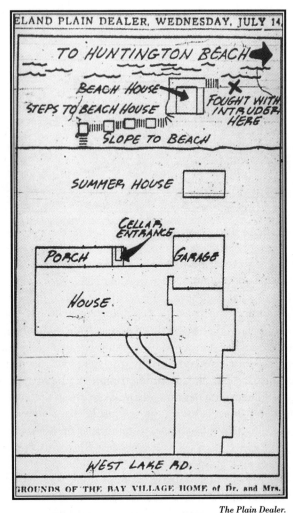

The Plain Dealer.

Diagram of Sheppard house and murder area.

unlocked Sheppard house early that morning and beat Marilyn to death with a blunt object. Spencer, awakening to find his wife gone, followed her to the Sheppard house, just in time to witness her bloody deed. But then he heard Sam coming up the stairs and knocked him out, lest he identify Marilyn's killer. Spencer and Esther then wiped the house clean of their fingerprints. Later, Spencer engaged in his final struggle with Sam at the beach, and the Houks fled the scene . . . until summoned back by an oblivious Sam at 5:45 a.m. In the more extreme variants of this hypothesis, Sam *knowingly* takes the rap for Marilyn's murder to protect the Houks from prosecution.

It is an odious story and it has been suggested or at least implied in three books on the Sheppard case. In addition, F. Lee Bailey also implied it during Sam's second trial in 1966, claiming he could name Marilyn's killer. He has never done so, but one can understand why Esther Houk's dying words to her daughter were these: "After I'm gone, if they accuse me of the Sheppard murder, promise you'll defend me." (For the record, Spencer and Esther were divorced in 1962. Spencer remarried twice and died in 1981; Esther died of cancer the next year.

All of which only serves to further obscure the theory subscribed to by many law enforcement personnel and newspaper reporters at the time of Marilyn's murder—albeit never argued in court. In *this* version Sam is the weakling youngest son of an arrogantly aggressive medical clan, unwillingly forced into a medical career by his domineering father and brother Stephen. After almost a decade in a rocky marriage, Sam decides he can no longer endure Marilyn's sexual frigidity—a lack of "sexual aggressiveness" as he so delicately termed it at his first trial—and decides to kill her so he can marry again, because his family has told him unequivocally that they will not allow a divorce. Drugging Chip into a sound sleep, Sam beats Marilyn to death and calls up his brother Stephen to help clean up the mess. Stephen arrives sometime between 3 and 4 a.m., coaches Sam about his story, they wipe up all fingerprints and stage the elements of a "burglary" before calling Spencer at 5:45 a.m. Stephen has already left for the Bay View Hospital, taking with him into oblivion Sam's bloody T-shirt and the murder weapon, a metal implement used to remove plaster casts. Sam's minor "neck injuries" are the result of a deliberate tumble down the stairs to the beach . . . if not caused by an attempt at suicide by hanging, fortunately interrupted by brother Stephen. It's a disgusting story, to be sure, but no more disgusting and incredible than the "bushy-haired" intruder tale—or blaming two dead people who can no longer defend themselves. And thus the never-ending tragedy of the Sheppard case endures, mystifying and tantalizing each new generation of Clevelanders.

CLEVELAND
Guides & Gifts

If you enjoyed this book, you'll want to know about these other fine Cleveland guidebooks and giftbooks ...

Cleveland Ethnic Eats
An insider's guide to 251 *authentic* ethnic restaurants and markets in Greater Cleveland as recommended by the experts: Cleveland's ethnic citizens themselves.
$12.95 softcover • 208 pages • 5 ¼" x 8 ¼"

Cleveland Discovery Guide
The best family recreation in Greater Cleveland collected in a handy guidebook. Written by parents, for parents; offers detailed descriptions, suggested ages, prices, & more.
$12.95 softcover • 208 pages • 5 ¼" x 8 ¼"

Cleveland Golfer's Bible
Describes in detail every golf course, driving range, and practice facility in Greater Cleveland. Includes descriptions, prices, ratings, locator maps.
$12.95 softcover • 240 pages • 5 ¼" x 8 ¼"

Cleveland Garden Handbook
Advice from local experts on how to grow a beautiful lawn and garden in Northeast Ohio. Filled with practical tips and good ideas.
$12.95 softcover • 264 pages • 5 ¼" x 8 ¼"

Color Me Cleveland
The All-Cleveland coloring book. For all ages and skill levels. Use crayons, markers, pencils.
$4.95 softcover • 32 pages • 8 ¼" x 11"

Neil Zurcher's Favorite One Tank Trips
At last! TV's "One Tank Trips" in a book. Ohio's travel expert shows where to take delightful mini-vacations close to home. Hundreds of unusual getaway ideas.
$12.95 softcover • 208 pages • 5 ¼" x 8 ¼"

Cleveland On Foot
Here are 45 self-guided walking tours through Greater Cleveland's historic neighborhoods, distinctive suburbs, glorious Metroparks, and surrounding nature preserves.
$12.95 softcover • 264 pages • 5 ¼" x 8 ¼"

Cleveland: A Portrait of the City
105 brilliant color photographs capture Greater Cleveland in all seasons. Familiar landmarks and surprising hidden details. A handsome hardcover giftbook.
$35.00 hardcover • 96 pages • 8 ¼" x 10 ¼"

Best Things in Life:
236 Favorite Things About Cleveland
A fun collection of thought-provoking quotations by Clevelanders about Cleveland.
$5.95 softcover • 144 pages • 6" x 4 ¼"

Available at Your Local Bookstore.

These and other Gray & Company books are regularly stocked at most Cleveland-area bookstores and can be special-ordered through any bookstore in the U.S.

For information, call:

Gray & Company, Publishers
11000 Cedar Avenue • Cleveland, Ohio 44106
(216) 721-2665